HEAVEN
on Earth

HEAVEN
on Earth

RELEASING THE POWER OF THE
KINGDOM THROUGH YOU

ALAN VINCENT

DESTINY IMAGE® PUBLISHERS, INC.
P.O. Box 310, Shippensburg, PA 17257-0310

"Speaking to the Purposes of God for this Generation and for the Generations to Come."

This book and all other Destiny Image, Revival Press, Mercy Place, Fresh Bread, Destiny Image Fiction, and Treasure House books are available at Christian bookstores and distributors worldwide.

For a U.S. bookstore nearest you, call 1-800-722-6774.
For more information on foreign distributors, call 717-532-3040.
Or reach us on the Internet: www.destinyimage.com

ISBN 10: 0-7684-2696-0
ISBN 13: 978-0-7684-2696-0

For Worldwide Distribution, Printed in the U.S.A.
1 2 3 4 5 6 7 8 9 10 11 / 12 11 10 09 08

THANKSGIVING

This book has been a long time in the making, and to give honor where honor is due, I have to recognize and express my gratitude to some people from my past.

In the early years of my ministry I was privileged to have the fatherly mentoring of Arthur Wallis, a great saint who is now in glory. He was not so well known in the United States but greatly honored in the United Kingdom where he was received as a fore-runner and clear biblical teacher of Kingdom truths. I thank God today for the seeds that his life and message planted in my spirit and that caused me to thirst for deeper things.

My thanks then go to a man I never met but whose book changed my life: Dr. E. Stanley Jones. While in India, at that time serving as the pastor of the Bombay Baptist Church, a man whom I did not know came to my office and, with very little ceremony, presented me with a book that he said I should read. That book was *The Unshakable Kingdom and the Unchanging Person* by Dr. E. Stanley Jones. Indeed that book changed my life; it redirected me to the Word and to the truths of the Kingdom till they became the fabric of my understanding. Thank you, Dr. Jones; like Elisha's bones you are still imparting life.

If possible I will personally give these great men my thanks when we meet up in glory!

Now to the great saints on earth. These too deserve my gratitude. This huge undertaking could never have been accomplished without the help of an amazing staff, especially Julie Larson. Natalie Hardy, our tireless coworker, has been negotiator, advisor, and editor, to say nothing of the many other hats she wears. Eileen, my wife, has passionately believed for years that the revelations God has given me must be written as my legacy for future generations. She is faithfully there, always doing whatever it takes to keep me on track.

ENDORSEMENTS

When I started reading this manuscript, I planned to quickly scan it to write my endorsement. However, I had to slow down and digest it. I found myself thinking I was reading one of the great classics by A.W. Tozer or Watchman Nee. Alan Vincent's deep revelation of the Kingdom will transform you from "passive, small, and defeated" to "hungry, passionate, and sufficiently equipped to begin to forcefully advance the Kingdom wherever God has placed you." It's more than a must-read; it's life changing.

Alice Patterson, President
Justice at the Gate
San Antonio, Texas

There is no question that the theology which is now giving primary direction to the Body of Christ is Kingdom theology. In *Heaven on Earth* Alan Vincent has done an amazing job in providing what is arguably the best textbook on Kingdom theology currently available.

C. Peter Wagner, Presiding Apostle
International Coalition of Apostles
Colorado Springs, Colorado

Alan Vincent is a pioneer, mentor, and father in the area of the Kingdom and the apostolic. His new book, *Heaven on Earth: Releasing the Power of the Kingdom Through You,* will radically transform individuals and ministries and push them into higher levels and dimensions of anointing where they will be empowered to establish the Kingdom of God by force. Apostle Alan Vincent's vast firsthand experience and knowledge on this subject has revolutionized the Hispanic community by teaching thousands of pastors, ministers, and leaders how to expand the Kingdom by force throughout their cities and nations. I strongly recommend this book and cannot wait to see it in print in every language, especially in Spanish.

Guillermo Maldonado, Apostle
El Rey Jesus Ministries
Miami, Florida

Have you been frustrated that the Church has not been having a greater impact in society? Alan Vincent strikes out into new territory with *Heaven on Earth: Releasing the Power of the Kingdom Through You.* He steps out by challenging the Church's complacency in today's world and by citing amazing examples of how the

Kingdom is currently progressing. Alan's bold treatise resonates with anyone who wants to get on with Kingdom business and do some damage to the kingdom of darkness. Alan and Eileen Vincent have a long heritage of walking out a Kingdom mentality within a variety of cultural settings. Their simple obedience and striking fruit is documented within the pages of this book. Read this, and be ready for a change in your life and those around you! They don't just talk about the dynamic power of God; they demonstrate it. As you read, you will be challenged to renew your mind's thought processes in expressing the reality of Christ in everything you do.

Bishop Harry R. Jackson Jr.
Senior Pastor, Hope Christian Church
Chairman, High Impact Leadership Coalition

What Alan Vincent teaches in this book is not mere theory. He has faithfully applied these principles in his own life, and as he has taught the Word, it has become reality in the lives of those who hear and become doers of the Word. Having walked with Alan Vincent as a spiritual son for more than 17 years, I can give firsthand testimony that the Gospel of the Kingdom that he teaches is consistent, true, and powerful. It has changed my own life and the lives of many leaders, churches, and people that I work with in Southeast Europe. I have found the Kingdom principles taught in this book to be effective and applicable in the multinational, multicultural context I work in. The laws and principles of the Kingdom work everywhere and in every culture. It transforms churches that have had an introverted attitude into churches with a passion to see all the kingdoms of this world become the Kingdom of our risen Lord Jesus Christ. I pray and hope that this book will not be published in the English language alone but in every European language, especially Slavic languages, as many leaders in Southeast Europe are longing to have solid Kingdom teaching published in their own language.

Franz Lippi, Leader of B.L.A.S.T.
Balkan Loving Apostolic Serving Team,
www.blastministries.net
Graz, Austria

CONTENTS

INTRODUCTION

For many years within evangelical Christianity, there has been no present expectation of a visible manifestation of the Kingdom of God. This was mentally postponed until after the return of Jesus at His second coming. We were taught that only then would His Kingdom become visibly established on earth.

Like most believers of my day, I grew up with this attitude. We were also taught that in the last days the devil would get stronger and stronger, and most of the Church would fall away and become very weak. This would allow satan to progressively take over the whole earth and rule over it for a short period of time.

When all seemed lost, Jesus would suddenly come in a mighty rescue operation called "The Sudden Rapture." He would first come secretly to take the true Church out of the way into Heaven so that they would escape the coming time of great trouble or tribulation upon the earth.

During that time of great tribulation, ethnic Israel would suddenly turn to the Lord, be gloriously saved, and be empowered to evangelize the world for a period of three-and-a-half years. On their own, these new Jewish believers would reap a great end-time harvest with the Church watching joyfully from Heaven.

At that point, Jesus would return visibly to earth, accompanied by the Church, and forcefully establish His Kingdom reign for a thousand years. During this time, satan would be bound and unable to deceive anyone on earth, and humankind would taste the glories of His Kingdom for a thousand years.

Then satan would be loosed again for a short time to test the hearts of the people. In those days, he would succeed in deceiving many. They would turn away from the Lord and choose again to serve satan, thus revealing the permanent evil set of their hearts.

After that would come the final act of judgment, during which time all believers would be taken safely out of the way, and God's wrath would be poured out on the earth. It would end with the eternal judgment of satan and all those who had joined him in the rebellion against the rule of Christ. God Himself would cast them all into an eternal hell symbolized by the lake of fire. The whole earth would be cleansed by fire, and a new Heaven and a new earth would be established in which His Kingdom would finally be manifested in all its eternal glory. Everything that could have defiled the perfection of that Kingdom would be permanently removed, and we who were left would worship Him and reign with Him forever and ever.

Most of this package of doctrine was taught by J.N. Darby and was popularized by the *Scofield Bible*. It has been embraced by much of the evangelical church for the past 100 years or so. For many centuries prior to that time, the doctrine of the Church had contained some similar elements, but it had a much more optimistic and victorious view of the Church in the last days.

Because of this relatively recent teaching, the Church of the 20th century was trained to think in terms of passivity, smallness, and defeat. We were taught to regard the increasing evil in the world as within God's permissive will and to expect satan to progressively take over everything. The devil was still regarded as the prince of this world; all we could look for was a way to escape this increasingly evil world through the rapture. The best that we could do was to try to save as many as possible out of this evil world before the darkness closed in completely.

I still believe some elements of this teaching, and I certainly believe there will be a visible, glorious return of our Lord Jesus Christ at the end of this age. He will come as the all-conquering King, and every eye will see Him. Those believers who are alive at His coming, Jew and Gentile alike, will be caught up in the air to meet Him in a joyful rapture as He returns with all His saints to earth. I also believe that only after this event will His Kingdom be fully established on earth in all its final, unpolluted glory. Only then will there be a new Heaven and a new earth in which only righteousness dwells.

However, I now see the course leading up to these great events very differently. My views are not really new. They are much the same as those at the cutting edge of the Church have historically believed and taught for many centuries. Our Moravian, Reformation,

Puritan, and Holiness forefathers, right up to and including the great revivals of the 18th and 19th centuries, believed in a warring but victorious end-time Church.

They looked for a glorious Church that would gain much new ground in many nations and win many victories over the devil. They expected it to be a time of great conflict, with some local battles being lost and won. However, it certainly would not be a time of general defeat but of the forceful advancement of the Kingdom against all opposition. They were expecting to conquer much ground in His name and reap a mighty end-time harvest throughout the whole world, even though it would be a time of trouble and conflict, especially as the day of the Lord's return drew near.

There would be warfare and periods of suffering, but the Church would remain powerful and victorious throughout all of this. There would be local setbacks, but on a world scale, the Church would be gaining ground all the time. The Kingdom would always be forcefully advancing and reaping a great harvest in spite of all opposition. It would continue to increase and never decrease throughout these difficult times because the zeal of the Lord of hosts Himself would be the driving force that would accomplish this (see Isa. 9:7).

At some point, not easily determined, Jesus would return with great glory and visibly appear in the clouds escorted by His heavenly hosts. He would be welcomed with great joy, in the air, by a victorious Church out of every nation. He would thus consummate His own total victory and triumph through the Church. All the kingdoms of this world would come completely under His rule, and at last they would become the one great, glorious Kingdom of our God and of His Christ.

Our primary job on earth is to work together with the Holy Spirit to forcefully advance the Kingdom of God. The Kingdom of God must first be formed within us, and then it will flow out of us. As we achieve this, we will reap that great end-time harvest, and so hasten the coming of that glorious day.

Chapter 1

THE KINGDOM COMES
TO MUMBAI

Eileen and I arrived in Mumbai, India, in March 1963. This city, formerly called Bombay, had a population of about 5 million people. It now has a population around 18 million.

Eileen and I went as missionaries. I was to work in a technical capacity with Gospel Literature Service. My task was to develop a modern, high-quality offset printing press to produce Christian literature. There were very few churches in the city at that time, and few had any real life in them. We joined the only Baptist church, which had a handful of people and was weak and ineffective. Shortly after we arrived, a Canadian missionary couple, John and Reta Hutchinson, were invited to take over the pastorate of the church. They, like us, were desperate for a move of God, and John began to preach his longing for God to come and do something among us. As a result of his preaching, a trickle of God-hungry people came to join the church, and this small group began to cry out for God to move in our city.

In April 1965, as a result of some special meetings, God suddenly came. He swept into our church, overwhelmed our evangelical reservations about expressive worship and spiritual gifts, and a small number of us were gloriously baptized in the Holy Spirit. Then everything began to change.

Several things happened to me personally because of that experience. After a few weeks, I struggled through my intellectual and doctrinal difficulties and began to speak in tongues. Even today, speaking in tongues does not make sense to me. I still cannot comprehend this strange utterance from God. But if I do what the apostle Paul tells me to do and speak frequently in tongues, I become greatly enlarged in my spirit so that God can then live within me in greater measure. As a result, He can do much greater exploits through me.

THE POWER OF THE RESURRECTION

Within a few days of being baptized in the Holy Spirit, something else happened to me. I didn't see an actual vision, but I experienced a powerful revelation of God's Word in my heart. It led to such a major change in my spiritual understanding that it literally changed my life.

Since my conversion, I had believed in the resurrection of Jesus Christ as a historical fact. I had read the words of Scripture many times, but I had concentrated on the physical miracle and not the spiritual power it released. I had not really "seen" it spiritually. That day, in an entirely new way, the Spirit showed me the power, glory, and authority of the Risen Christ. The Spirit showed me the great triumph and victory that Jesus had already accomplished through the cross, the power of His glorious resurrection, and the present authority of His throne.

Suddenly, I could see that everything that opposed Him was way beneath His feet, and He was already far above all things, ruling with complete authority. Just as importantly, I saw that I too was already raised and seated together with Him on His throne sharing in His risen power and authority.

Up until that time, I would walk up and down the streets of Mumbai, looking at all the demonic activity and power, thinking, *What a terrible, dark, demonic city this is. What hope is there for it?* I could see satan's activity everywhere, and he seemed so dominant and strong. Our church was one of the few, tiny spots of light in this vast, dark city, and it seemed very small, weak, and insignificant by comparison.

But, when this revelation of the Risen Christ came into my spirit, everything changed. Instead of seeing how strong the devil was, I began to see how strong and mighty Jesus was! I began to feel indignant that Jesus was not being glorified as He deserved in my city. It seemed very possible that the Spirit could use a few nobodies like me to throw down the powers of darkness and change our city. So, I began to work with the Holy Spirit to that end.

A few months later, after this wonderful initial breakthrough, John and Reta left India to return to Canada, and I was invited to take over as the pastor of the church. We moved into the manse, I began to preach the new things God was showing me, and the crowd continued to grow.

Preach the Kingdom

Some time later another important thing happened. I was visited by a man I had never met before who seemed to come out of nowhere. He came knocking on my office door at the church and said, "God has sent me around the world to speak to leaders." He was carrying a bag of books, and he handed me a specific book saying that I must read it. He went on to say, "This is a message from God to you: You must see the Kingdom, you must believe in the Kingdom, you must preach the Kingdom, and you must forcefully advance the Kingdom. Then, you will see the glory of God come to your city."

He handed me the book, written by a man who had given his whole life as a missionary to India. His name was Dr. E. Stanley Jones. It was called *The Unshakable Kingdom and the Unchanging Person*. Then, suddenly, this visitor was out the door and was gone. Several times since I have wondered, "Who was that man who showed up on my doorstep?" He didn't give me his name, and I never thought to ask him. He looked like an ordinary human being and had an American accent, yet he came carrying a strange presence. He came from nowhere and disappeared into nowhere, but he left me with these words burning in my heart. To this day, I honestly wonder if I had an angelic visitor without realizing it.

This visit and this book changed me. I began to see the Kingdom, I began to understand the Kingdom, and I began to preach the Kingdom. Other people came to join us, and together we began to forcefully advance the Kingdom of God in our city. But, it didn't all happen overnight.

A SUCCESSFUL CHURCH IS NOT ENOUGH

Through preaching this message, the first thing that happened was that our church grew and turned into a living, powerful, and effective church. Miracles began to take place in the church. One Sunday a demon-possessed madman came running into our morning service. As he ran down the aisle toward me, I rebuked the demons in him in the name of Jesus, and he fell down. The demons came out, and the man was gloriously delivered, saved, and transformed. Another time a Hindu man came in coughing up blood. He was in the last stages of tuberculosis in both lungs and was gloriously healed. These things were happening in what had been, until then, a respectable, traditional Baptist church. It was no longer traditional or "respectable," but it was a lot more biblical! Sometimes, in order to become a Kingdom church, we will have to choose between what is biblical and what is respectable in the eyes of others. In these cases, we must ask ourselves, do we want a biblical church, or do we want a respectable one? Which is more important?

It would have been so easy to stop there with what had become a living church that was regarded as a great success. I could have traveled to other cities to tell the stories and explain how God had blessed us, and, no doubt, I could have become an "expert" on church growth. But God then showed me something else. He was not content with a living church in a demonized city. He wanted the city! He began to show me that taking a city was not too difficult for God.

THE KINGDOM REALLY COMES TO MUMBAI

Several years later, with the church now bursting at the seams, Eileen and I were led to leave that church in good hands and begin planting new churches in a different area of the city. It was the area where Catholics lived. It was well known that many criminals, violent gangs, and drunks came from this area where more than a million people lived. God said, "Go and start there!"

With two other people, we planted a church from scratch. Over the next few months, about 40 people from the most horrendous backgrounds were saved and added to the church. They were delivered from demons and began to change. It was not a sudden, overnight transformation, but God was beginning to work.

Each one of those 40 people was a miracle of deliverance and transformation, and that was enough to stir up serious demonic opposition against us. The demonic powers ruling over that region came against us, and we were attacked in every way. The Catholic Church came fiercely against us, warning people not to go near us and saying we were a dangerous sect. The civil authorities were stirred up by one or two people, and they tried to get us thrown out of the country. Many of our new converts were targeted; as a result, they backslid, and our numbers went down from about 40 to 8 people. Eileen and I were physically attacked by demons. One demon actually tried to choke the life out of me one night. We went through some very bizarre experiences, but somehow we were given the grace to stick to it and not give up.

One Wednesday night, just the two of us were doggedly having a warring praise night. It didn't at all fit my mood. All our circumstances said that we were being defeated, and I was not feeling too well physically. I was depressed and wanted to quit. Nothing was attractive about this time; nothing was enjoyable. We were just held by a dogged commitment to obey God and do what He had given us to do.

Nothing in our circumstances declared Jesus to be Lord, but the Word said He was Lord, and our spirits knew that He was the triumphant victor at the cross. We forced ourselves to sing and shout these truths against the wall of opposition we were facing, although it seemed a totally futile and stupid thing to do.

There were not hundreds of people doing this, just two people: Eileen and me. We are told several times in the Bible that two are enough. It is better to be 20. It is wonderful to be 200. Since those days I have led a crowd in Kenya, Africa, of about 8,000 people all roaring together like lions against the demonic powers in that land. These things are exhilarating and powerful, but they are not absolutely necessary. Jesus said that two are enough! (See Matthew 18:20.)

At that time, we knew nothing about spiritual warfare. No one had any revelation on this subject. There were no books, no tapes, no conferences, because no one was doing anything like this, at least as far as we knew. But the Holy Spirit knows all about spiritual warfare, so we just did what He told us to do, and we were successful.

On that particular Wednesday night, the two of us were having a determined shout and positively proclaiming the lordship of Christ to these demonic powers in our little meeting room in Mumbai. During this time, something cracked in the spirit realm, and I felt something happen. This was in April 1972. I can even tell you the date; it was the 19th. The next Sunday things began to happen. Some of the backslidden people came back to the church, the atmosphere changed, and it all became very different.

A FAITHFUL WITNESS

A short time later, while I was a thousand miles away visiting our children in boarding school in South India, Eileen went into labor for the birth of our fourth child, David. She went into labor earlier than we expected, and I wasn't even there. It seemed like a disaster, but it was the plan of God.

We had originally made plans to go to a nice mission hospital about 100 miles away around the time of her delivery, have a few days rest with some lovely Christian friends, and wait for our little baby to be born into this wonderful atmosphere of Christian love. We had to change our plans because no one was able to give us an accurate prediction of when our baby would be born. So we booked Eileen into a nearby Catholic hospital instead, just to be on the safe side.

As Eileen lay there in labor, she began to witness to the nuns who were helping her. One of them had just read David Wilkerson's book *The Cross and the Switchblade* and was hungry to experience the power of God. Eileen talked to them for hours. As a result, she put a seed into them, and they became hungry for God. This was just a small act of obedience. Eileen was being faithful in such a small thing. But who knows what God will do through one small act of obedience! Those words of hers triggered something in these God-hungry nuns that was destined to change Mumbai.

A SMALL SEED BECOMES A GREAT TREE

These nuns invited me to do some Bible studies to prepare them for the Feast of Pentecost, which was about six weeks away. Other God-hungry nuns came and joined the group. (It was not a large crowd; there were only 10 to 15 of them.) They were expecting the Holy Spirit to come according to the church calendar on the Thursday before Whit Sunday, and He graciously obliged. That Thursday the Spirit of God came and fell upon all who were present.

The majority of them were already lovers of Jesus, but that night the rest were truly born again; all of them were baptized in the Holy Spirit, and God began a great movement. Four years later, at least 100,000 people had been born again and filled with the Holy Spirit with a mighty display of God's power. Great miracles took place, many people were healed, and many demons were cast out.

The Kingdom began to be manifested just as we had read in the Bible in the days of Peter and Paul. These new believers quickly began moving out as powerful witnesses across the city of Mumbai and then across the nation.

In those four years, many new churches were started. Today as I write, over 30 years later, this powerful move still continues. Between 3,000 and 5,000 churches are now estimated to have sprung out of this movement in Mumbai alone. Hundreds are being saved every month. Catholics are still responding, and now many Hindus and some Muslims are also being touched. Hundreds of mighty leaders have been raised up to go all over India and other countries of the world to preach the Gospel of the

Kingdom. It is impossible to measure quantitatively what has flowed out from those small beginnings. Only God knows, and only God needs to know.

I am saying all of this because I want you to see that even if only a few people get a revelation of the Kingdom and are truly empowered with the Holy Spirit, it is enough for God to do a great work. The purpose of this book is not just to pass along information. I am praying that God will start a fire in you and that you will see the Kingdom at least as clearly as I do. Then, as a result, you will be compelled to go out and work to see this glorious Kingdom established wherever He may send you. It is by revelation of the Spirit, but it is also founded on a solid base of Scripture and requires sustained hard work.

God began to show me in a new way what some Scriptures really said and meant. I realized how much of my former teaching had to be undone in order to receive the new and more accurate truth that God was giving me. I want you to be open to hear what the Spirit of God is saying to you. As you go through this book, you are going to repeatedly hear the message that you don't need a huge crowd of people to change your city. If there are two of you, there is enough Kingdom power in the two of you, when it is properly released, to change the place where you live.

I am not teaching you theory. I am teaching you what I myself have experienced and what others are presently experiencing in a number of places around the world. Wherever I have gone since those days, I have always believed that our cities can be taken for our Lord Jesus! Several of those cities are now being changed by the power of God through people who can see the Kingdom.

Since 1991 God has located us in San Antonio, Texas. That city is definitely changing, but I don't have time to tell you all the stories. Texas is changing. The United States is slowly being influenced by these Kingdom people. I am not talking in forlorn hope but in spiritual fact. It is already done in the spirit realm, and it's beginning to be manifested visibly in a number of places.

Chapter 2

WHAT ON EARTH IS
THIS KINGDOM?

THE KINGDOM IN THE BEGINNING

The Kingdom began on earth when God created Adam and Eve and set them as rulers over all that He had made. They were given authority, but it was a delegated authority that only worked as long as they stayed in the Kingdom under the rule and government of God. As long as they remained perfectly submitted to Him, the eternal life of God could flow into them without restriction, thus filling their humanity with the power of that life. By the power of that life, they were enabled to rule over themselves, and all that God had made, successfully.

While that situation continued, everything remained in perfect order. It was all very good and beautiful because all of it was within the Kingdom. There was no corruption, evil, hatred, sin, sickness, disease, or death. Such things were entirely unknown in the Kingdom. It was paradise in every sense of the word.

Satan was outside this Kingdom and was unable to penetrate it. Even to this day satan has never been able to enter the Kingdom of God and never will be able to do so. Anything inside the Kingdom is out of his domain, and he cannot touch it.

Satan longed to somehow get control of what God had made. He longed to put his corrupting fingers all over God's perfect creation and then steal it for himself.

THE KINGDOM LOST

Satan perceived that mankind was the weak link. As God had given the rule of the earth to them, satan's scheme was to gain control of Adam and Eve so that through them he could get control of all that God had created and become the usurping prince of this world.

To accomplish this, he had to tempt the man and the woman to step outside the Kingdom. That meant he had to persuade them to come out from under the government of God and become independent or self-governing. While they remained inside the Kingdom, they were protected, and the devil could not touch them. If Adam and Eve could be persuaded to step outside of the Kingdom and its protection, they would become vulnerable, easily attacked and conquered.

Satan did not directly invite Adam and Eve to become sinners. That would have been too obvious. Instead, he insinuated that while they remained under God's controlling rule, they could never reach their full potential. Satan cunningly persuaded them to step out from under God's rule by implying that, through their own effort, they could develop their inner potential to become like God.

Satan came to the woman as a serpent and enticed her to step out, with her husband, into independence and self-governance instead of continuing to live in joyful, submitted obedience to God's will. With subtle lies, satan convinced them that they could quickly become like gods by utilizing the resources of their own self-sufficiency.

First Eve and then Adam fell for this lie and stepped out of the Kingdom into independence. They had no intention of becoming sinners, but expected to continue in the same moral perfection that they had previously enjoyed. They expected to emancipate themselves to become fully like God in their own strength. What a tragic decision, and what an enormous price has been paid in the ensuing suffering and misery that has been the lot of Adam and Eve and all their descendants!

When they made this tragic decision, God's first cry was, "Adam, where are you?" It was a cry of pain over the separation and broken relationship that now existed between God and man. Adam and Eve felt for the first time the defiling contamination of sin and could no longer stand pure, naked, and unashamed before Him. They went and hid from a holy God instead of running joyfully into His presence as they had so often done before.

God now had an important decision to make. He could swiftly bring the rebellion of satan to an immediate end by destroying his fledgling kingdom and casting him and his angels into a pit of eternal judgment. Then, He could cleanse the earth and start all over again. However, because of His perfect righteousness, He would also be compelled at the same time to mete out the same judgment to an equally guilty man and woman who were partners and accomplices with satan in this terrible rebellion.

But God so loved Adam and Eve, even in their sin, that He chose to save them and their descendants instead, even though it would cost Him dearly to do so. He decided to redeem Adam's race rather than to cast it away in judgment. He purposed to be reconciled to all who were willing to receive His Kingdom rule and to reestablish the glory of His Kingdom upon the earth through their joyful obedience to His will. At some point, satan would finally be judged, and then the opportunity for mankind to be saved would be over.

God Delays Satan's Judgment

In order to give mankind the opportunity to repent and return to God's benevolent dictatorship within the Kingdom voluntarily, God delayed satan's judgment and allowed the dispensation of human rule over all the earth to continue. Thus, the door of salvation remains open to all until the day of final judgment.

This also means that for righteousness' sake, God has to limit Himself to work on earth through the agency of men and women. Mankind thus has become the door through which either the rule of satan or the rule of God is established upon the earth. During this dispensation, the earth has literally become a battleground of the two kingdoms.

In order to keep the door of salvation open, God permits satan to rampage all over the earth with his deceptions, convincing many that they have the right to live their own independent lives and that this is much better for them than being under the "oppressive rule" of God. Satan constantly encourages individuals to exercise their own independent "free will"; to live according to their own desires; and to follow the fashions, pressures, and lusts of this world just as they see fit (see Eph. 2:1-3). In this way, satan has brought multitudes into bondage, and they have become the prisoners of sin and death.

God occasionally has found a man or woman who did not go with the crowd but sought after Him and tried to live according to His will. With such people, God has been able temporarily to throw back the tide of wickedness, and for a time that man or woman was able to be a light in the world to his or her generation. Such people have been able to turn many back to righteousness, at least outwardly, and bring in a semblance of the Kingdom for a time, but none have lasted. Because the people's hearts have generally still been inclined toward evil, the change has never lasted for long after that person's death.

THE KINGDOM REGAINED

The Scriptures say several times that God looked for a man but never found one who could fulfill the necessary conditions in order to become the kinsman-redeemer that Adam, Eve, and all their descendants so desperately needed. (See Isaiah 41:28; 59:16; 63:5; and Jeremiah 5:1.) So, as we are told in Isaiah 59 and First Corinthians 15:45-49, God Himself decided to become that Man: God incarnate, Jesus Christ. As the last Adam, He would take on human flesh and the whole debt of sin upon Himself; and through His death, He would pay that debt on behalf of the whole of Adam's race. Christ Himself would bear the full wrath of God against sin on behalf of all men and women in order to save them from bondage to satan and to sin.

By His blood, He would also redeem the whole earth from satan's rule and earn the right to destroy completely the kingdom of darkness and all the works of the evil one upon the earth. By His resurrection and endless life, God would permanently establish this Man as King, and through Him the full glory of His Kingdom would finally and permanently be established upon the earth.

JESUS, THE NEW BEGINNING OF THE KINGDOM OF GOD

So, in the fullness of time, God Himself came in the person of Jesus Christ to be that Man. He took up residence on earth in the same humanity in which Adam had lived in his innocence before he stepped into independence. In order to cut off the hereditary line of sin through Adam, Jesus was directly conceived by the Holy Spirit in the womb of Mary without the seed of a man. To fulfill all righteousness, Jesus the man had to live within the limitations of that humanity and could not for one moment draw on the power of His own deity, even though He was at the same time fully God.

From the first moment of His conscious ability to choose, to the last moment of His earthly life, Jesus made unswerving decisions regarding how He would live. He would live in total dependence and total obedience to His Father and make Himself fully available to the Holy Spirit. That is, He chose to live His entire human life within the Kingdom of God; never, for one moment, did He step out of it into independence; never did He leave its security or its power. As a result, His human life was untouchable by the evil one.

The great difference between the life that Adam lived and the life that Jesus lived was simply the decision that each of them made regarding the rule of God over their lives. Jesus chose to live in obedience and dependence upon God the Father, and so throughout His whole human life He stayed within the Kingdom. Adam chose to live in independence; when he stepped out of the Kingdom into self-sufficiency, he immediately lost the Kingdom's protection and power and became a sinner and prisoner of satan instead.

JESUS ALSO CAME TO DEMONSTRATE THE KINGDOM

Apart from coming as the Lamb of God to take away the sins of the world, another great purpose of the life of Jesus on earth was to give a living demonstration of the Kingdom of God. From the beginning of His public ministry, Jesus preached the Kingdom of God. That is, He invited lost men and women to repent, to leave their independent, self-governing lives, to come back into the Kingdom of God, and to live like Him. This would mean they would have to stop living to please themselves and instead live as Jesus was. They would have to live a life of total obedience and dependence upon God the Father. Once that primary decision of repentance was made, it was possible to grant them unconditional forgiveness of all their sins and deliver them completely from satan's power through the cross.

Chapter 3

THE KINGDOM IN THE NEW TESTAMENT

STARTING IN THE RIGHT PLACE

Let me first share a valuable tool for correctly interpreting Scripture that I received from someone years ago. Repeatedly this has helped me to stay in the truth of what the Scriptures really say. This principle, which I call "starting in the right place," teaches the following:

1. **The seed and essential core of every major doctrine is always found in the words of Jesus Himself.**

Jesus Himself is the Word of God, and while on earth He alone had the full revelation from the Father and the Spirit. He alone had the ability and the authority to add to, redefine, and clarify all the words of the Old Testament.

Hebrews 1:1-2 says, "In times past God spoke to us through the prophets but in these last days He has spoken to us through His Son" (see Heb. 1:1-2).

Hebrews 2:3-4 says the Gospel "was first spoken by the Lord and then confirmed by those who heard Him, God also bearing witness by signs, wonders, and various miracles..." (see Heb. 2:3-4).

Several times in the Sermon on the Mount, beginning in Matthew 5, Jesus takes the words of Moses and corrects, expands, or redefines them—taking them to a higher level in the Kingdom where the heart is examined as well as the outward action. He taught on prayer (see Matt. 6:5-13), giving (see Matt. 6:1-4), fasting (see Matt. 6:16-18), anger (see Matt. 5:22), lust (see Matt. 5:28), adultery (see Matt. 5:27-28), forgiveness (see Matt. 6:14-15), and murder (see Matt. 5:21-22). In Matthew 19:3-10, He corrects Moses' teaching on marriage and divorce, and there are many other such examples.

2. **These doctrines of Jesus are then expanded in the writings and revelation of the Holy Spirit through the apostolic writers of the New Testament.**

Jesus promised that once the Spirit came He would lead those first apostles into all truth and reveal to them everything the Father had shown Him. Jesus had, in some measure, tried to teach these things to them, but until their spirits were illuminated by the Holy Spirit, they were unable to understand.

But on "that Day" (the day when the Holy Spirit came), as Jesus had promised, everything changed. Immediately, when the

Spirit was given at Pentecost, this new amazing understanding of the Scriptures poured forth from their spirits and was recorded through the various inspired writers of the New Testament.

3. **Finally, equipped with this new revelation from Jesus and the insights of the inspired New Testament writers, and with our own spirits now illuminated by that same Holy Spirit of revelation, we can go to both the Old Testament and New Testament Scriptures and begin to understand them properly in a much deeper way.**

In the Old Testament, these truths had their beginnings and were put into their right historical setting. They were filled out and enriched by story, example, and allegorical illustration. We are told that they are types (allegories) and were actually written for our example, warning, and instruction, and that they apply particularly to those "upon whom the end of the ages have come" (1 Cor. 10:11).

The full meaning of these Old Testament Scriptures is brought out by the revelation of the Holy Spirit. Through revelation of the Holy Spirit, we discover that every page of the Old Testament is testifying by example, admonition, type, and shadow of the Lord Jesus Christ and of His glorious Kingdom.

This is what the first disciples discovered on the road to Emmaus and then in the Upper Room when Jesus opened up the Law of Moses, the Prophets, and the Psalms to them. Jesus showed them on every page of these writings all the things concerning Himself. As a result, their hearts burned within them, the veil was taken away, and they could see (see Luke 24:27; 44-46).

Only by using the principle of *starting in the right place* can we come to full understanding of the actual writings of the Old

Testament. Although opposite to the chronological order in which the Scriptures were written, it is the true revelatory order by which we come to understand the truth. Therefore, we must always allow the superior revelation of Jesus and the New Testament writers to define, explain, and correct the meaning of the Old Testament Scriptures. So let's first learn all that Jesus had to say about the Kingdom.

WHAT DID JESUS SAY ABOUT THE KINGDOM?

First of all, notice the priority that all the writers and preachers in the New Testament gave to the subject of the Kingdom of God. After His death and resurrection, they did not just preach Jesus as a Savior from sin, but they always preached Jesus *and* the Kingdom of God.

Let's begin in Matthew 3:1-2, where John the Baptist begins his ministry. The first words out of his mouth are "Repent, for the kingdom of heaven is at hand" (Matt. 3:1-2). He began his ministry with the proclamation of the Kingdom and claimed He was the fulfillment of Isaiah's prophecy in Isaiah 40:3. He had come as "a voice crying in the wilderness to prepare the way of the Lord" (see Matt. 3:3; Isa. 40:3). He concluded in Matthew 3:11: "I indeed baptize you with water unto repentance, but He who is coming after me is mightier than I, whose sandals I am not worthy to carry. He will baptize you with the Holy Spirit and fire" (Matt. 3:11).

Notice that here, and throughout the New Testament, there is very little preaching that just invites people to receive forgiveness of their sins. Repentance is the first step into the doorway into the Kingdom. According to Scripture, being "born again" is the means of entering the Kingdom of God. It is not just a decision to believe in Jesus, have our sins forgiven, and go to Heaven when we die.

In the New Testament, the forgiveness of sins is not the main issue at all. It is proclaimed as a consequence or by-product of something much more fundamental that must come first. That primary thing, according to Scripture, is to believe the good news of the Kingdom of God and then by repenting to actually enter the Kingdom! To those who have come into the Kingdom, forgiveness of sins can then be subsequently granted to them. But repenting and entering the Kingdom must come first.

There are two things that come out in these first few words about the Kingdom, spoken by John the Baptist. The first is a call to repentance; the second is a call to receive the baptism of the Holy Spirit and fire. No one in the Bible ever preached the Kingdom of God without immediately bringing up the issue of repentance. The first question we need to consider is: what is the heart and essence of true repentance?

TRUE REPENTANCE

Repentance has little to do with sorrow for sins; repentance really means a total change of mind that radically changes the way we actually live. It is a change of mind that leads to action. This action produces a complete change of life. We stop pleasing ourselves and doing our own thing. Instead, we turn right around and go in the opposite direction, living only to obey God and please Him, just as Jesus did. If we don't deal with the basic issue of repentance, it is impossible for God to deal with our sins. God cannot forgive the sins of someone who continues to live their own life in self-sufficiency and independence and who will not surrender their life to the total lordship of Jesus Christ.

This is the message God has proclaimed to mankind. It is the message God sent John the Baptist to preach. "The kingdom of heaven is coming," he said, "Repent!" (See Matthew 3:2.) Once you have repented, it is possible for God to receive you into His Kingdom and forgive all your sins.

RECEIVE THE HOLY SPIRIT

The next matter immediately mentioned is the need to receive the Holy Spirit. Once you have repented, you need to be empowered with Someone! Not something, but Someone. This Someone is the Holy Spirit. He will come and take over your life completely and will use you as a human instrument to forcefully advance the Kingdom.

To truly repent, you have to see how wrong it is to live a life where you are in control, making all the decisions about your own life. What is wrong with humanity is that everybody has taken charge of their own lives instead of letting God rule. That is the basic problem. Sin is the awful, evil fruit of this basic problem. The real root of all sin is selfish independence.

Many people want to improve themselves but are not prepared to give up control of their lives to let God really do it. This is what many people try to do spiritually when they "come to Jesus." They may ask Him to help them to improve their lives. They may say, "Jesus, please come into my life and help me to be a better person," but they never really give control of their lives to Him. They go to Jesus and treat Him as someone who may be able to give some help, but they still regard their lives as their own and seek to change themselves by the power of their own moral strength.

Every religion works this way. A religion may contain good moral principles, but it puts the responsibility upon individuals to improve their lives by their own self-effort. This doesn't work because no one has the power. Whether a person is a Muslim, a Hindu, a Buddhist, a Jew, or a nominal Christian, it does not make any difference. Nobody is able to live up to the standards of behavior that their religion sets for them. I know from experience that I, as a secular, self-righteous atheist, could not even live up to the standards that I set for myself. Similarly, the zealous Pharisee Saul could not keep the just requirements of the Jewish law however hard he tried (see Rom. 7:15-24).

Many religious people remain firmly in charge of their own lives, and then when there is a problem or a need, they cry out to some god for help and say, "Please help me. Please meet my need." Many people even cry out to the true God for help in a time of trouble, or ask for help to change their unsatisfactory ways. People go to psychiatrists, doctors, gurus, and even pastors to try to get help to take better control of their lives and become the better person they want to be. But they try to do it in their own strength. God's only response to such people is "Repent and seek first the Kingdom of God, then everything else you may need will be yours as well" (see Matt. 6:33).

That is what God is saying, "You yourself are the problem, and you cannot be improved to come up to My standard. If you struggle in the flesh to improve yourself, then the devil will always be able to overcome you. I have not come to try to make you a better person, but I have come to replace you with Myself."

Unfortunately, the basis of much Gospel preaching and much Christian counseling in the church today is to help people to try to improve themselves. You are taught the "the seven steps to improve yourself and become the success you want to be" or something similar. Then you may even be taught to strive "with God's help" to do it.

But God has no intention of doing it that way. He only has one plan for you and your unreformable, independent self-life, which is what the Bible constantly calls "the flesh." His plan is to totally kill your flesh life and wipe you out completely as an independent, self-willed person. Then God can come and live His own life in you. Paul describes this life in Galatians 2:20. He writes, "I have been crucified with Christ; it is no longer I who live, but Christ lives in me; and the life which I now live in the flesh I live by faith in the Son of God, who loved me and gave Himself for me" (Gal. 2:20).

THE HEART OF REPENTANCE

Repentance is that kind of change of mind. The biblical word *repentance* means a change of mind so radical and so complete that it leads to a permanent change of lifestyle. It is like the owner of a car saying to God, "I will never drive this car successfully. Please take over completely. From now on I'm happy to just be a passenger and let You drive my car any way You choose."

Until that happens, a person has not truly repented. Feeling sorry for sin is not repentance. Crying out that you want help to change yourself is not repentance. These may be good steps along the way, but until that fundamental decision to hand everything over to the rule of God has been made, there is no real repentance, and you have not really come into the Kingdom of God. This is the root and heart of the Kingdom.

Only people who have already entered the Kingdom of God themselves can bring forth the Kingdom in a city. Only Kingdom people can bring forth Kingdom families, Kingdom communities, or Kingdom churches. If the Kingdom has not come to you, then how can you possibly bring it to your city? That is the major problem God has. Satan is not the real problem. God's main challenge is to get God's people to stop doing their own thing and to unconditionally do His will. Once that objective is accomplished, dealing with the devil and his kingdom of darkness is a relatively simple matter.

As we consider this very simple introduction, we need to understand what it really means to preach the Gospel. As we move through the New Testament, we will see the Gospel that Jesus and the apostles preached was not primarily a Gospel of forgiveness of sins. It always was the Gospel of the Kingdom of God.

Jesus defined the Kingdom perfectly when He taught us to pray in Matthew 6:9-13 and again in Luke 11:2-4. He said that when we pray, we should ask for the Kingdom to come, even before we seek to get our legitimate needs met! He then defined the Kingdom as "God's will being done on earth just as it is being done in Heaven" (see Matt. 6:10; Luke 11:2)—which, of course, is perfectly!

When the principle of submitting to God's total rule is accepted, the source of sin, which is an independent self-life, can be cut off completely. Then there will be no more fruit of sin because there is no more root of self-will. It is then easy for God to forgive all our sins and make us righteous before Him because we are now in the Kingdom.

Once the issue of true repentance has been settled, you will see that living in the Kingdom for us is really no different from living the way Jesus lived all His years on earth. The humanity of Jesus was totally surrendered to the will of the Father and totally available to the possession and control of the Holy Spirit. Through Jesus, God reestablished the Kingdom of God on earth. In Him the reclamation of this world began. If we present our bodies in the same way that Jesus did, then the Spirit can possess us just as He possessed Him and work through our humanity just as He worked through His to forcefully advance the Kingdom on earth.

JESUS PREACHED THE GOSPEL OF THE KINGDOM OF GOD

Jesus began His preaching of the Kingdom after John the Baptist was imprisoned. In Mark 1:14, we read that "after John was put in prison, Jesus came into Galilee, preaching the gospel of the Kingdom of God" (Mark 1:14). Verse 15 tells us again that it was the Gospel of the Kingdom of God. He said, "The time is fulfilled, and the kingdom of God is at hand. Repent, and believe in the gospel" (Mark 1:15).

What you need to see is that there is an important addition spoken by Jesus here. It's the same message, a call to repentance, plus something else. You must come to the place where you actually believe that it is good to have no rights of your own and that it is much better for you to be ruled by God wholly. It is very easy to tell if the Kingdom has really come to you. Ask yourself some simple questions, and please be honest with the answers.

- Who really makes the daily decisions in your life? Is it you or God?

- How do you use your time? Does God have absolute say, or do you still spend your time as you choose?

- Why are you living where you are now living geographically? Did you put yourself there or did Jesus appoint (or place) you there?

- What about your present career? Did Jesus choose it for you, or did you decide for yourself? What about the actual place where you are now working? Did Jesus put you there, or did you choose that for yourself?

- What about your money? Not just the tithes or other offerings you may give to God, but what about the rest? You might say, "But that's my money, I can do whatever I like with it." No, you can't! Not if you are in the Kingdom. It's all His money, and He must have the rule over it.

- Did God truly place you in your present church situation, and do you keep good relationships with those He has joined you to? Do you know that you cannot leave until you get His direction and their blessing and release? Or are you an independent, unrelated person going wherever you choose and doing whatever you like? A person who has really seen and entered the Kingdom joyfully lets Jesus have the control of everything. It's a totally transformed life.

As soon as Eileen and I were converted, we quickly learned to live this way. We have always lived geographically where Jesus located us. We have always moved when and where He told us to go. We have always moved immediately when He told us to do so. It did not matter whether we liked the place or not; neither did we respond to what other people were saying as they tried to persuade us either to stay or to go. We were in the Kingdom, under His rule, and we just did whatever He said.

If someone will do that, Jesus promises that he or she will always be fruitful. In John 15:16, Jesus says, "You did not choose Me, but I chose you and appointed [placed or located] you that you should go and bear fruit, and that your fruit should remain, that whatever you ask the Father in My name He may give you" (John 15:16). Jesus highlights the deliberate nature of God here; in this passage we see the clear relationship between being chosen and appointed (geographically and relationally) by Him and being fruitful in the place of obedience.

Some people become very useful to God, and as a result they become very fruitful. However, they do not become fruitful because they are fantastic, wonderful, or especially gifted; they become fruitful because of their obedience. It is amazing what God can do with obedient nobodies. It is also amazing how little God can do with very talented and gifted people who will not obey Him and instead choose to do their own thing.

Jesus said He came to preach the Gospel of the Kingdom. He did not just come to preach forgiveness of sins. Forgiveness of sins is an important issue, but it is not the central issue. Jesus asks, "Will you let Me come and totally rule over your life?" That is the real issue. If you say yes, then you repent from self-government, move to God-government under Jesus' rule, and come into the Kingdom of God. He can then come and have complete rule over all your life as a perfect, loving, benevolent king who only has our best interests at heart. He can freely forgive all your sins and make something wonderful of your life. Then the Kingdom has really come, and you had better believe it's good!

IT REALLY IS GOOD NEWS

I went through several phases to get to where I am today. As soon as I was saved, I knew I had to let God have rule over me because it was biblical, but I wasn't too sure if it was always going to be the most enjoyable way to live. It was clear to me from the first day that once you had really met God, you had to obey Him. This was the "good news" of the Kingdom that Jesus preached. You must decide that it is the best way to live even if your reason and your circumstances raise various doubts. So I just made a decision to live a life of obedience because I knew it was right and not because I was feeling particularly good about it.

But then I got to another stage. After having lived this way for a number of years, I came to love it! I came to realize that the worst thing that could happen to me even in this life was for me to do my own thing against the will of God. Even if I was to do this accidentally, I would suffer great loss in the present as well as in the future. I became really fearful of getting my own way, and have earnestly sought only to do His will ever since. That is still my primary concern: I don't want to waste even one day living my life my way and so miss God's plan and purpose for that day.

Now let's study what Jesus had to say about the Kingdom so we can learn how to enter into it fully and, as a result, live the way He lived on earth.

Chapter 4

THE KINGDOM IN MATTHEW

Matthew's Gospel really focuses on the Kingdom. It was written primarily to the Jews to convince them that Jesus was their long-expected Messiah, the son of David, their King.

Matthew refers to the Kingdom about 60 times. More than 40 times he calls it the "Kingdom of Heaven," and Matthew is the only person to use this term. Mark, Luke, and John never use it once. Surprisingly, John hardly mentions the Kingdom by name. This is probably because the principles of the Kingdom were well established and understood through the first three Gospels, which had been circulating for at least 30 years before John wrote the fourth Gospel.

THE KINGDOM IS POWER

In Matthew 4, Jesus is just beginning His public ministry. We are told in Matthew 4:23 that Jesus came preaching "the gospel of the Kingdom." Not the Gospel of forgiveness of sins, but the Gospel of the Kingdom. Matthew and Luke both emphasize that preaching the Gospel of the Kingdom is always accompanied by healing the sick and casting out demons. It is the ability to do these things that proves that the Gospel of the Kingdom has come near.

Every church in the New Testament was founded on the power of signs, wonders, miracles, and the casting out of demons. The Bible is very plain about this, stating very bluntly that if God cannot do signs and wonders through us, if He cannot cast out demons through us, then we are not preaching the Gospel of the Kingdom. If we let the true message of the Kingdom sink into our hearts, and if we deal with our chronic unbelief, we will be able to move in this power.

It took me several years to realize this. I discovered that the problem was not the lack of God's power or any unwillingness on God's part to do His works. The problem was simply my unbelief. When I stopped living in unbelief and began to believe and obey like a little child, then miracles, healings, and deliverance from demons began to happen through me.

Our Western Christianity is loaded with terrible unbelief, and we need to hate it as much as God hates it. If you come to hate it, then you will not want to live that way any longer. It is normal in the Kingdom for signs and wonders to be taking place. You shouldn't have a week go by without something miraculous happening, and preferably, it should happen every day. So get your thinking reoriented to the Scriptures.

Jesus said, "But if I cast out demons by the Spirit of God, surely the kingdom of God has come upon you" (Matt. 12:28). He also said to His disciples, "Preach, saying, 'The kingdom of heaven is at hand.' Heal the sick, cleanse the lepers, raise the dead, cast out demons. Freely you have received, freely give" (Matt. 10:7-8). Where these things are happening, we can freely tell people that the Kingdom of God has come. If we can't do those things, then the Kingdom of God has not come, regardless of what we say. There is no better answer and argument for unbelief than a flow of the signs, wonders, and miracles of the Kingdom.

JESUS SAT DOWN

"When Jesus saw the crowd, He went up on the mountain; and after He sat down, His disciples came to Him" (see Matt. 5:1). The word "sat down" is the Greek word *kathizo*. It was used in Jesus' final commandment to His disciples in Luke 24:49. Literally translated this verse should read: "Sit down in the city Jerusalem until you are clothed up with power from on high." Jesus meant something much more than just passively waiting.

This word comes more than 50 times in the New Testament and is frequently connected with the three "seats" of power and authority, namely: *thronos*, representing political authority; *bema*, representing judicial authority; and *kathedra*, representing religious authority. Unfortunately, at this present time, in almost every city on earth, these "seats" are occupied by demonic powers. They need to be repossessed so the Kingdom of God can truly come on earth. At the end of chapter 1 in the letter to the

Ephesians we are told that after His resurrection Jesus Himself sat down on His throne far above all these authorities (see Eph. 1:17-23). Furthermore, we are then told that He has now "raised us up...[to] sit together" with Him (Eph. 2:6), with the result that these powers are now way beneath our feet and we have power to rule over them in Him.

As things began to move in Mumbai, God showed me these things and He urged me to literally believe them. He told me to sit down confidently and comfortably with Him on His throne as somebody who has the right to sit there and rule in His name over the demon powers that were coming against us. He taught us to come against these demonic powers in His name, and we saw them cast down—with many thousands of people being liberated as a result. By His risen life He now empowers all of us who will fulfill the conditions to exercise rule over all these authorities on His behalf.

Once seated on that throne, you have a purpose, which is to exercise the rule, government, and authority of the Kingdom from that throne. If you go through the Gospels, you will find that when Jesus taught, before He began to speak, Scripture frequently mentions that He "*kathizo-ed*" or sat down (see Mark 9:35; Luke 5:3; John 8:2). He spoke from the throne. As a result, His words had authority. His words were not like the words of the scribes and the Pharisees.

Years ago when I first saw this truth, I heard God say to me, "You must also learn to speak like that." If you are an evangelist, learn to sit on that throne in your spirit before you begin to preach. If you are a pastor, sit on that throne in your spirit before you begin teaching. If you are a Sunday school teacher, sit down on that throne in your spirit before you begin teaching the children. If you do this, it will totally change the way you minister the Word of God. I know that the words that are written in this book are going to change many people's lives and situations because I sat down or "*kathizo*-ed" before I began. I know that sounds arrogant, but it's true. It is not what I say to you, but what God's Spirit will say to your spirit as you read these written words. It is His Word, and it is His work. I am completely confident of this because I know the power of God.

LAYING THE RIGHT FOUNDATIONS

Notice how Jesus begins His teaching in Matthew chapter 5. This is the beginning of a long teaching about the Kingdom that goes through to the end of chapter 7, usually called the "Sermon on the Mount." It was His first major teaching. He was setting out the foundational teaching of the Kingdom.

In Matthew 18, Jesus started to teach on how we deal with demonic principalities and powers and how we can speak to them and overcome them with words of authority. The problem with many people is that they want to begin moving in the power of Matthew 18, binding and loosing principalities and powers in the spirit realm, before they have absorbed the teaching of Matthew chapters 5–17.

In the same way in the Ephesians letter, from Ephesians 6:10 onwards, Paul teaches on spiritual warfare, but before we get to this passage, there are five other long chapters that come first. Many people rush into Ephesians 6:10, but they have not been first grounded in the truths of the first five chapters. So instead of seeing victory, they experience defeat.

It is the same in the Book of Hebrews. At the end of Hebrews 12, we are told about the power of the Kingdom. It has the power to shake and destroy every other kingdom but will itself remain unshaken! However, there are 12 chapters before we come to these words. We have to see, understand, and become established in these preparatory stages first in order to become the powerful, victorious, devil-destroying, Kingdom people that God wants us to be.

In the world, our secular governments are not as foolish as we sometimes are in the Church. Secular governments do not send out raw, untrained, enthusiastic volunteers to fight on the front lines of a battle. If they did, they would not be successful, and there would be heavy casualties. But in the Church we are often that foolish. As enthusiastic novices, we think we can go to war for God against principalities and powers before we have been properly trained. We need to make sure that our foundations are properly laid based on the earlier chapters before we go on to the chapters dealing with strategic spiritual warfare.

Begin in Matthew 5:1-9 with what are called the "Beatitudes." These are the things that we have to be. These are the "Be" attitudes that first must be established in us. Please check out the list and see if they are in you. If you are a pastor or other leader, check the list and make sure that they are truly in you, your leadership team, and your people before you go to war. If you don't take the time to make sure these things are established in you and in your people, then you will not destroy the demonic powers in your city; instead, they will come and rip you and your church apart.

I have functioned as an apostolic father with responsibility for many churches in various places around the world, and I have watched this tragically happen a few times because of immaturity and ignorance. When leadership teams are ripped apart, I can usually point to these verses and see that they were not practically fulfilled in the members who made up that team before they went to war. They may have had great enthusiasm, great gifts, and great abilities, but that does not scare the devil. If the foundations are not there, he can easily overcome them. So let's look at the list.

BLESSED ARE THE POOR IN SPIRIT

When we begin at Matthew 5:3, we read, "Blessed are the poor in spirit, for theirs is the kingdom of heaven." We need to understand what this means. Here, Jesus is teaching us the first principle of the Kingdom: we are not to trust in ourselves and our own resources; we are to trust in God and be totally dependent on Him. Poor people are not usually independent. They are not usually proud. They are usually willing and grateful to receive gifts and help from other people because they know they are unable to provide for themselves.

We need to recognize that *without the fullness of God totally possessing us, we are spiritually very poor.* We have no resources of our own; provision must come entirely from God. So look at yourself and ask: just how poor in spirit am I? How aware am I of my need for God and the fact that I have no resources of my own? Do I dare not attempt to do anything without Him?

If you can produce this attitude in yourself and in your leadership team, you have the beginnings of a city-taking team. Even Jesus had no independent self-reliance whatsoever. He said, "The Son can do nothing of Himself" (John 5:19; see also John 8:28). He lived in 100 percent dependence on the Father and the Holy

Spirit. That was the way that He lived. And that is what made Him so powerful.

On the one hand, we find Jesus saying in John 15:5, "Without Me you can do nothing." Do you really believe that? I mean *really* believe it? On the other hand, Jesus says, "If you abide in Me, and My words abide in you, you will ask what you desire, and it shall be done for you" (John 15:7). Jesus is saying that if we habitually dwell, or abide, in Him and allow His words to abide in us, we can do all things, and nothing will be impossible to us. These two things, doing nothing apart from Him and doing everything with Him, are the foundation of continuous fruitfulness.

If I look out across the Christian Church, particularly in the United States (my own country, which I love very much), the tone of the nation is, "We can do it. We will make it happen." So much of current teaching involves coaching people in "how you can make it happen; how you can be successful." Many ministries fail because they are not truly poor in spirit but are too self-sufficient. If you are poor in spirit, then you will not experience this type of failure.

If you were poor naturally with no resources of your own, but had a very rich benefactor who was prepared to give you everything you needed, then it would be foolish not to live in deep, grateful dependence on him. Can you see that? I want you to get this deep in your spirit. This must not be just a scriptural text on a wall. It must become a lifestyle that deeply affects our hearts. It must become our attitude and our way of life. *In Him everything is possible, but without Him we can do nothing* (see John 15:5-7; Matt. 17:20).

BLESSED ARE THOSE WHO MOURN

In Matthew 5:4, we read, "Blessed are those who mourn, for they shall be comforted." What does this mean? I will quickly give you a summary of what I have learned. You will find many examples of people in Scripture, particularly intercessors, who were mourning in travail over the situation they found in their nation or city. That is what we are also called to do. When I walk through the streets of almost any city in America or Europe, I want to cry. It doesn't matter which nation it is; I just want to cry. I think of its historic roots and how far it has fallen.

I think of nations like the Czech Republic and Germany, from which came John Huss, the Moravians, Count Zinzendorf, Martin Luther, and many others who shook the world with their spiritual power. Germany had a continuous hundred-year Moravian prayer meeting that changed the world, but when I walk the streets of the cities of the Ruhr valley, the industrial heartland of this great nation, I meet strange young people who have no knowledge of the true God.

Some years ago, I was told by some Christian leaders in the Ruhr valley area of Germany, where approximately 10 million people live, that there were at that time about 12 spirit-filled churches, and none of them were more than 200 strong. In the same area, there were thousands of satanists actively worshiping satan. Near Essen there was one satanic community with over 1,500 members. It's heartbreaking to meet young people in the streets. They know far more about the occult than they do about the simple facts of Scripture.

I feel the same way about Great Britain. It has experienced so much of God's favor in the past. It has brought forth some great Christian leaders, sparked some great revival movements, and sent missionaries all over the world. Now as I walk the streets of London and other cities, I want to cry, I want to mourn, and I desperately want God to do something.

If you walk in the downtown area of any major city in the United States, especially at night, whose presence do you feel? Who seems to have control over that area? Is it satan or Jesus? Doesn't that make you want to cry and make you long for God to come and do something?

When you feel like that about your city and your nation and begin to really cry out to God, then Jesus promises you are going to be comforted, and something powerful is going to happen.

Jesus read aloud most of the first two verses of Isaiah 61 as He began His ministry, and He deliberately stopped in mid-sentence. He concluded the Isaiah passage where it says that He had come "to proclaim the acceptable year of the Lord." Then He stopped and said, "Today this Scripture is fulfilled in your ears" (see Isa. 61:1-2a). He did not complete the sentence from Isaiah because it was not the time for the rest of that sentence to be completed.

That verse in Isaiah continues, "...and the day of vengeance of our God." This part was not quoted by Jesus because it was not time for it to be fulfilled. But there is a time coming when the world will see this "day of vengeance of our God."

Read the rest of Isaiah 61:2-9, and you will see what the day of vengeance of our God is. It is not God's vengeance against lost sinners, but it is God's vengeance against satan and his works in the earth. God spoke to me at the beginning of this new millennium that the time had now come for this Scripture to be fulfilled. He said, "You will see this begin to happen in the first few years of the new millennium." He also said to me, "The Church has never seen Me really angry before." My hair stood up on end, and I tingled as I wondered what it would be like to see the full anger of God loosed against the works of satan.

When that happens, we are told in Isaiah 61:3, it will affect those who mourn. Suddenly their mourning will be turned to laughter! Their spirit of heaviness will be changed for the garments of praise (see Isa. 61:3). Instead of weeping over your cities, those of you who are intercessors are going to be dancing for joy over what God is doing in them. You watch! If I am speaking by the Spirit of God, then you are going to say, "Alan, you didn't tell us the half of it!"

It is great to mourn because you will never really pray for your city until you feel grief for that city. You will never see transformation until you mourn over your city. When you, by the Spirit of God, shed tears of mourning for your city, then God will use those tears to bring transformation to that city. You cannot come to faith for the city until you have mourned for her. If you don't love your city, you won't mourn over it. If you love it, you will cry out for it. Oh, blessed are those who mourn, for they will be comforted (see Matt. 5:4)! Your sorrow will be turned into joy (see Isa. 61:3). Your heaviness will be changed into praise because you will see God fulfill your wildest longings and go beyond your greatest expectations (see Isa. 61:3). It doesn't matter how bad the city is. The city just needs someone to mourn and cry out to see transformation.

BLESSED ARE THE MEEK

In Matthew 5:5 we read, "Blessed are the meek [or the humble], for they shall inherit the earth." Let's try to explain biblical meekness or humility. Biblical meekness is not self-effacing weakness. Its root meaning is denial of self so that you no longer care about yourself or how you look in the eyes of others; your only concern becomes the honor and reputation of your God. In contrast, the root of pride is the exaltation of self and the pursuing of self-interests.

Let's first go to Numbers 12 where Moses is being confronted by his brother Aaron and his sister Miriam. First, remember that Moses wrote the first five books of the Bible. So here we have Moses writing about Moses. This is what Moses says about himself:

> *Then Miriam and Aaron spoke against Moses because of the Ethiopian woman whom he had married; for he had married an Ethiopian woman. So they said, "Has the Lord indeed spoken only through Moses? Has He not spoken through us also?" And the Lord heard it. (Now the man Moses was very humble, more than all men who were on the face of the earth.)* (Numbers 12:1-3).

Now, who wrote those words about Moses? Moses did! This will give some insight into the assumptions we make about biblical humility.

Let me give you another example.

In Acts 20, Luke records Paul's final words with the Ephesian elders; Paul begins this farewell and exhortation by describing the nature of his own service among them: "You know, from the first day that I came to Asia, in what manner I always lived among you, serving the Lord with all humility, with many tears and trials which happened to me by the plotting of the Jews" (Acts 20:17-19). Paul is writing about himself as a man who served the Lord with all humility.

Jesus said the same thing about Himself, *"Take My yoke upon you, and learn from Me, for I am **gentle and humble** in heart; and you will find rest for your souls"* (Matt. 11:29 NIV).

When you begin to see this, you will recognize that many of our concepts regarding humility are not biblical at all. We think the meek or humble man would never talk about himself like that and would be very self-deprecating. We also think that if he was meek, he could not at the same time be a strong leader. *But the root of real biblical meekness is disinterest in self and a burning passion for God.* True meekness says, "It doesn't matter what happens to me; it only matters what happens to God. I am not concerned about my reputation; I am only concerned about His reputation." That is biblical humility. It is the denial of self in order to magnify the person and purposes of God. This kind of humility can be very strong. It can be ruthless, absolutely determined, and very decided that it will not give up. This kind of humility will be violent to see God glorified in the earth!

What Paul recorded in Philippians 2:20-21 could be an accurate assessment of many leaders today: very few have the right spirit. Paul basically said, "Apart from me, only Timothy has the same spirit. He is humble like Moses and like me. Even more important, he is humble like Jesus."

Timothy didn't care about himself, he did not seek his own, and he had a genuine concern for the welfare of others. Paul said that all the other leaders he was dealing with didn't have this spirit. They sought their own, rather than the things of Christ, and they had no genuine concern for the welfare of God's sheep (see Phil. 2:20-21). How many leaders today talk about "me and my ministry…"? They are concerned about *their* church, *their* ministry, *their* success, and what is in it for *them*, but they are not filled with passion for the whole Kingdom of God and the issues and problems of the whole city. Such self-centered churches and leaders will never inherit the Kingdom of God.

If you want the Kingdom to come to your city, you must stop playing personal, political games regarding who will be the most important person on the team, or which church will be the most important church in the city. All of this stops the Kingdom from coming. The meek will inherit the whole earth.

The next three beatitudes are easy to understand but harder to obey. These declare:

Blessed are those who hunger and thirst for righteousness, for they shall be filled (Matthew 5:6).

Blessed are the merciful, for they shall obtain mercy (Matthew 5:7).

Blessed are the pure in heart, for they shall see God (Matthew 5:8).

To know the blessings of His mighty Kingdom upon our lives, these must be obeyed unconditionally. However because they are pretty straightforward, I am not going to spend more time explaining them in this book.

BLESSED ARE THE PEACEMAKERS

This next one, however, probably does require some explanation. It states: *"Blessed are the peacemakers, for they shall be called sons of God"* (Matt. 5:9).

The problem is that the English word *peace* does not adequately explain the Greek word for "peace," which is *irene*, nor does it adequately explain the two Hebrew words for peace: *shiloh* and *shalom*, which have a similar meanings to *irene*.

Irene does not mean "peace" in the sense of an atmosphere of tranquility or simply the end of a war. It is primarily a word of relationship and means the mending of a relationship that was formerly broken and hostile so that the two parties who formerly hated each other are perfectly reconciled and have actually come together relationally to be inseparably joined in love. The verb *ireneo* has the meaning of binding together that which has been separated or broken and further underlines this. Both of these words are usually closely connected with reconcile or reconciliation, which is the result of successfully making peace.

At the time the Bible was written, the same word *irene* was used in the medical profession as a term to describe the healing of a fractured bone. When a bone is mended and fully fused back together again after being broken, it usually becomes harder, thicker, and stronger at the point of fracture than at any other part of the bone. As a result, it is most unlikely to break again in the same place. When this process was completed in Bible times, it would be said, "The bone has now come to peace," using exactly the same Greek word *irene*.

Once we understand this, we can better comprehend what Jesus means (and what a number of other Scriptures are actually saying) when peace and peacemaking are mentioned. These Scriptures are talking about mending broken relationships so they become unbreakably healed. We can also understand why the Scriptures prophesied concerning Jesus' body that "He would keep all His bones and not one of them would be broken" (see John 19:31-33; Ps. 34: 20). God will not have any broken bones in the body of Christ.

A biblical peacemaker is someone who goes out of his or her way to mend strained or broken relationships, even at the cost of laying down his or her own life. As previously mentioned, the word "reconciled" or "reconciliation" is closely connected to the word "peace" in most of the New Testament Scriptures (see Col. 1:20; Eph. 2:11-18).

John Wycliffe, in the first translation of the Bible into English, created a new English word by putting together three separate English words "at-one-ment." He was trying to convey the full meaning of the Greek word *katallage*, which is the word translated as "reconciliation."

We are told in Colossians 1:20 that God "made peace through the blood of His cross." On the cross, a totally innocent God took the initiative and laid His human life down to make peace with a totally guilty man, who at the time was an enemy of God not wanting reconciliation. God did this so that once again He could be one with mankind and have a real relationship with them. This is God the peacemaker.

In Ephesians 2:11-18 we are told that through the cross God has perfectly reconciled Jew and Gentile together into one new man, "thus making peace" (Eph. 2:15). We are told that Jesus came and preached "peace" to those who were far off and "peace" to those who were near so that they could become perfectly one (see Eph. 2:17). There are many other examples of this in the New Testament.

It is possible to be a child of God and still be an immature troublemaker and cause division. However, to be a grown-up, mature son of God, you must be a peacemaker: "Blessed are the peacemakers for they shall be called [the grown-up, mature] sons of God" (Matt. 5:9). These are those who enter the Kingdom and come into their sonship inheritance here on earth.

LIVING KINGDOM LIFE

The whole Sermon on the Mount deals with the way we should live in the Kingdom. In the Kingdom, it is not enough to look good on the outside. We must truly be living right on the inside. In the Kingdom, it is a matter of heart attitude and not just outward behavior.

Under Moses' law, if you did not kill anyone, however mad you were on the inside, you were not a murderer. If you kept it all hidden on the inside, you were blameless before the law. However, in the Kingdom, if you are angry with someone on the inside, you are spiritually a murderer already. How many people have thought of someone else, "Oh, I would like to strangle him!" Well, in the Kingdom you can't think like that. In a leadership team, you cannot have these attitudes toward one another. If it is in your heart, then it is not acceptable in the Kingdom.

Sometimes these things are hereditary, and we need to be cut off from our hereditary past. When I look back along my family line, the one thing I can remember about my grandfather was his awful temper. He was a godly man and a faithful deacon in the Baptist church, but he would lose his temper terribly over small, frustrating things. I was sometimes terrified of this angry grandfather. My father was just the same, and all my boyhood I feared the temper tantrums of my father. Then I found it in myself, and then I saw it manifesting in the lives of some of my children. I began to realize that this was a hereditary, devilish stronghold in the life of my family. I was helpless to do anything about it. I could not control it, however much I tried. I had to go to God poor in spirit and get Him to do what I could not do. I knew I could not live that way in the Kingdom. It had to be dealt with.

According to Mosaic law, if a man lusted after a woman in his heart but never did anything on the outside, he was not guilty of anything. But in the Kingdom, if you just think lustful thoughts, you are already a fornicator or an adulterer in your heart.

Soon after I was converted, I found I needed to get honest with God about these things and get them out of my heart. When I was a young man, I polluted my mind. When I got saved, the physical habits stopped, but the battle in my mind continued.

THEN THE SPIRIT CAME

When I was freshly baptized in the Holy Spirit, certain Scriptures suddenly began to leap out at me, such as:

*We have the **mind** of Christ* (1 Corinthians 2:16).

*Let this **mind** be in you which was also in Christ Jesus* (Philippians 2:5).

*...and be renewed in the spirit of your **mind**, and that you put on the new man which was created according to God, in true righteousness and holiness (Ephesians 4:23-24).*

*Set your **mind** on the things above, not on things on earth (Colossians 3:2).*

*Do not be conformed to this world, but be transformed by the renewing of your **mind** (Romans 12:2).*

*This is the covenant that I will make with them after those days, says the Lord: I will put My laws into their hearts, and in their **minds** I will write them (Hebrews 10:16).*

I realized that I was not living the way the Bible said I was supposed to be living. So I shared this with a close brother I was working with in Mumbai. I said to him, "I'm often battling with unclean thoughts." He said, "So am I. That's pretty normal, unfortunately."

I said, "It's not normal according to the Scriptures, so I'm going to ask God to take it away and give me the mind of Christ as He has promised!" We came together one morning, and we got on our knees before God.

I said, "God, I'm claiming my inheritance in Christ. Come and clean up my mind. If I've opened myself up in the past to demons in the area of uncleanness and lust, I repent of this. Please forgive me and deliver me. I command them to leave me now in the mighty name of Jesus!"

Immediately those foul things left me. They were no longer inside of me. The next morning I was a different man. The temptations still continued for a while, but at a totally different level, and I was easily able to resist them.

Let me try to explain this. Imagine that you have opened the door of your house to some very pushy salesman. He has come right inside the house and is trying to sell you something you do not want. Imagine he's right inside your house, you can't get away from him, and he's putting tremendous pressure on you to buy. You begin to melt, and you end up buying it. That was what I was formerly experiencing concerning lustful thoughts. This demon was right inside me and could sell me what I didn't want.

That particular morning, it was like God grabbed this pushy, demonic salesman that was inside me and threw him out of the house and shut the door. However, this salesman didn't immediately go away completely. For a while, he stayed around outside the house hoping I would let him in again. It was as if he started ringing the doorbell, or he went to the windows of my house and knocked on them, or he came back to the door of my house and said, "Please let me in! Let me in!"

However, having him on the outside was so different from having him on the inside. Although he was a great nuisance, it wasn't like having him on the inside. I now had the power to resist him. I could say "No!" and keep the door shut.

Now I had a choice. I could have opened the door and let him in again, but that would have been foolish, and I had no intention of doing that. Now I had the power to keep the door closed and say, "No!" I wanted nothing more to do with him, and I could tell him this from the safety of my locked house: "Go away, I won't open this door! I will have nothing more to do with you. Go away!" After a while, when he saw he wasn't getting anywhere, he finally gave up, went away completely, and never came back. Now for years I have been totally free with a wonderful, new, pure mind.

So my deliverance had two phases. There was the crisis—when he was thrown outside the house. Then there was the process—when I learned to resist and deny every temptation until I became permanently free!

At the end of about three months, this spirit of lust gave up completely. He stopped trying to get back in, went away, and didn't bother me anymore. That was 1965. Since that time, I have lived with a pure mind with no defeat in this area. But I have been very careful what I do with this new, pure mind that God has given me. I almost never watch television because it is so polluted. I hardly ever watch secular movies because there is always some dirty content in them, and I don't want those dirty images to pollute my lovely, new mind. I have lived in victory for so long now that it is sometimes hard for me to remember what it was like to be in such bondage.

We must deal with these things now before we go into any kind of spiritual warfare. Demons respond to our attacks on them by looking for any place of weakness in us where they can counter-attack. If you are living under any kind of law (whether it's Moses' law, Christian evangelical law, Pentecostal traditional law, or even holiness law), and you are struggling to live up to some imposed standard in your own strength, if there is any stronghold of satan still left working inside you, satan will find opportunity through that area to bring you into defeat.

But if you are truly living in the spirit in the Kingdom, the battle is not even going on inside of you anymore. It is on the outside where it is possible to resist the devil, and he will flee from you, and you will experience victory every time. There is such a power in the risen Christ that we don't have to yield to temptation and live in failure anymore.

GOOD THINGS DONE THE WRONG WAY

Jesus then continues in Matthew chapter 6 by confronting a number of good things that many do in the wrong way. Because of our religious background we have often been trained to do these good things in a wrong religious way.

Jesus concentrates on three particular things: (1) the way we give financially; (2) the way we pray; and (3) the way we fast. Jesus is teaching religious Jews who have learned these practices in wrong, religious ways. Before He can teach the right way, He must undo the old, wrong ways of doing them. I don't have time in this book to deal with the right Kingdom ways of giving and fasting, although they are very important aspects of the Kingdom, but I do want to say a little about prayer, as it is the absolute foundation of Kingdom life.

One of the benefits of never having been in religion is that you are not taught the wrong way. When Jesus taught the religious Jews about prayer in Matthew 6:5-13, He had to begin with the things we should *not* be doing in prayer before He could get to the way we *should* be praying. He basically said that:

1. We must not "play act" (be hypocrites) and put on a show of empty words.

2. We must not pray in front of other people just to impress them.

3. We must not use vain repetition and think that we will be heard simply because of our frequent asking.

He then summarized the heart of an effective prayer life in Matthew 6:6. The first thing you need to do is establish your own secret place where you can go alone, shut your door, and have your own time with God, really getting to know Him as your Father. If you will take the time to do this, then you will find He is already there eagerly waiting for you. And God will reward you openly. That is the foundation of all Kingdom life and Kingdom prayer power.

It doesn't matter how busy you are. It doesn't matter how many responsibilities you have. It is not enough just to come to a prayer meeting. It is not enough just to lead out in public prayer. The power of everything else you do will be decided by the private prayer time you have alone with God every day.

Every one of the men and women whom God has used as warriors and leaders to transform cities, deliver nations, conquer invading enemy armies, subdue hostile nations, and forcefully advance the Kingdom have had a lifestyle of personal intimacy in prayer. They spent quality time alone with God and knew Him as a friend and as a father. Five stand out particularly:

1. **Abraham** — He met God face to face and was called God's friend (see 2 Chron. 20:7; James 2:23).

2. **Moses** — He had a private prayer tent where he met with God face-to-face long before the tabernacle was built (see Exod. 33:11).

3. **Joshua** — You couldn't get Joshua out of the presence of God in that private tent where he went along with Moses (see Exod. 33:11). He loved God's presence.

4. **David** — All the Psalms, and the intimate language that David used, demonstrate David's deep prayer relationship with God. Once David became king over all Israel, he raised up a simple tent called David's tabernacle where worship, praise, and prayer went on continuously (see 2 Sam. 6–7). He, and those of like spirit, had face-to-face fellowship with God before the ark without any curtain separating them from His presence. David, it seems, never went to Moses' tabernacle although it was still standing on Mount Gibeon about six miles away. He had no interest in it because God's presence was not there.

5. **Jesus Himself** is the supreme example. In John 1:14, we read that He "tabernacled" or "lived in a tent" among us. His human body was that "holy tent" in which the Spirit and the Father permanently dwelt. It was the beginning of the new temple that He said He would raise up after three days (see John 2:19-22). It was made up of many living stones like Peter. This is the only building that God really delights to dwell in. Luke's Gospel particularly records Jesus' intimate prayer life, while John's Gospel records His deep relationship with His Father.

All the apostles of the early Church had this kind of lifestyle and gave themselves "continually to prayer and to the ministry of the word" (Acts 6:4). Each of these men became a mighty warrior in the Spirit and was used by God to save and shape the nations. The powerhouse of each one of these men, including Jesus, was their personal prayer life. We cannot live effectively any other way. It is not enough just to come occasionally to a corporate prayer meeting. If those who gather in corporate prayer don't have their own personal lives of effective prayer, they won't experience anything near the same power as these men of God did.

Listen to Matthew 6:6 again, "But you, when you pray, go into your room and when you have shut your door, pray to your Father who is [already] in the secret place, and your Father who sees in secret will reward you openly" (Matt. 6:6).

Wherever possible you must find a room of your own where you can meet God. It doesn't have to be a physical room. What is important is that there is a set place where you can go every day and get alone with God. Even if your wife or husband is a wonderful, spiritual prayer partner, you still need your own private time with God. This is absolutely foundational.

It is the same with fasting and with giving. We have to unlearn the old religious ways and learn a new Kingdom way of doing these things so the full benefits can flow into our lives and ministries.

In Matthew 7:21 Jesus says, "Not everyone who says to Me, 'Lord, Lord,' will enter the kingdom of heaven, but he who does the will of My Father in heaven." Then He describes those who listen to His teaching but don't do what He says. He teaches exactly the same thing in Luke 6:46-49. Jesus divides the people who hear Him speak into two categories: the wise and the foolish.

Jesus defines a wise man as someone who hears the words of God and then is careful to do them. The foolish man hears the same words but doesn't do them. Jesus divides the whole world in this manner. Which side are you on?

We cannot advance the Kingdom unless we produce Kingdom communities that are characterized by those who hear and then do the Word of God. As leaders, we cannot produce such communities if we ourselves are not already a personal demonstration of the Kingdom. We truly have to become like Jesus and demonstrate our obedience to the Word of God in everything we do.

Chapter 5

THE POWER OF THE KINGDOM

In all the synoptic Gospels, we read of a great flow of miracles as Jesus began to demonstrate the power of the Kingdom. Great multitudes from Decapolis, Jerusalem, Judea, all of Syria, and beyond the Jordan were healed of sicknesses, and many tormented by demons were delivered (see Matt. 4:23-25).

In all three of these Gospels, there is a strong connection between the prayer life of Jesus and the power life of Jesus. In John's Gospel, Jesus taught that we, through prayer, must come into the same relationship with the Father that He Himself enjoyed. We must live by the Father and obey Him just as Jesus did. Then we will be able to demonstrate the same power of the Kingdom and do the same mighty works that He did (see John 14:8-12).

Once the Spirit had fallen on the disciples on the day of Pentecost, they moved out in a mighty display of the Kingdom through signs, wonders, and miracles. The first breakthrough came in Samaria through Philip. By the power of mighty signs, wonders, and miracles through Peter and Paul, it then broke into the Gentile world and began to touch many nations. This is just as true today. Where the Kingdom is powerfully advancing in various parts of the world—and a great harvest is being reaped at this present time—it is always accompanied by a powerful manifestation of signs, wonders, and miracles.

ADVANCING THE KINGDOM IS A MATTER OF VIOLENCE

In Matthew 11:1-11, Jesus testifies about John the Baptist. John the Baptist could proclaim the Kingdom, but he could not demonstrate it. He could talk about the Kingdom and preach powerfully that the Kingdom was coming, but he could not make it come into visible manifestation. John was a forerunner to prepare the way of the Lord, but he never actually entered the Kingdom or established the Kingdom while on earth. Jesus tells us in verse 11, "Assuredly, I say to you, among those born of women there has not risen one greater than John the Baptist; but he who is least in the kingdom of heaven is greater than he" (Matt. 11:11).

Jesus continued, "And from the days of John the Baptist until now the kingdom of heaven suffers violence, and the violent take it by force" (Matt. 11:12). This verse is translated in various ways in our different English translations, and some translations are misleading. In the Greek, the verb for "suffers" is in the passive voice, so the only proper translation should read:

The Kingdom of God has violence done to it. In other words, whenever the Kingdom of God begins to be manifested, it is immediately and violently attacked by the devil (particularly in its early stages) because the manifestation of the Kingdom is the thing that satan most fears.

Ever since the cross settled the matter, the devil has been sitting illegally on God's property. There is not a single person or one square inch of the earth that Jesus did not legally buy back with His own blood at the cross. Jesus can now rightfully and legally claim ownership, and He already has been given the right to rule over all things. However, in order to reestablish the Kingdom of God on earth, the kingdom of darkness must be attacked and dispossessed. So any talk or action to establish the Kingdom of God is automatically a declaration of war against the devil and his continuing illegal occupation of all that belongs to Christ.

The moment anyone starts talking about the Kingdom of God and seeking to establish it, alarm bells go off in hell. "What's the problem?" the duty demons ask. "There are Christians talking about God's Kingdom!" is the reply. "Oh, no! Oh, no!" is the response of hell. This terrifies them because they know we are going to take their territory from them, but the demons of the kingdom of darkness will not sit there in passive acquiescence. The enemy will fight intensely to keep what does not belong to him for as long as he possibly can.

We need to recognize that Kingdom talk is war talk. You will be violently attacked if you dare to preach the Kingdom of God and seek to advance it. The only way to deal with that kind of devilish attack upon you is not to back off, but to respond by becoming even more violent toward the devil. That is what Jesus was saying, and that is what He and the early Church always did.

Jesus was saying that until John the Baptist there was no one on earth manifesting the Kingdom of God. But from the moment Jesus was anointed by the Spirit, He began to reestablish the Kingdom of God on earth. From that moment, all the demonic powers came against Him. So He responded by drawing on the infinite resources of His Father in Heaven and became even more violent toward them on earth.

You must understand that this is the only way to advance the Kingdom. You cannot advance the Kingdom peacefully. In the Spirit, you must become a violent man (or woman). To successfully advance the Kingdom, you must become a spiritual warrior like Jesus. He was the first violent man, and everyone who comes into the Kingdom must become violent like Him. The devil is basically a bully. He will attack and fight anyone to try to get them to back off. You must respond to every demonic attack by standing your ground and saying something like this, "I know who I am in Christ; I am a man (or woman) of God. I am God's son by grace with access to the same infinite, heavenly resources as Jesus. I am an ambassador of King Jesus whom I joyfully serve. You are just a demon from the pit of hell, and I come against you in His mighty name! You get out of here, because I am staying here to establish His Kingdom. I don't intend to move, and there isn't room for both of us."

Before you can do that kind of thing successfully, you must be sure of your own righteousness. You must have put on the whole armor of God. You must be sure of your own impregnability. You must be sure of your own authority. You must have faith to believe that what you say is true. You can never say, "Oh, devil, please leave. Just go. I don't want to fight with you. Please, just give us a peaceful take-over." You can't do that. There is only one way to advance the Kingdom, and that is violently.

Look at what the apostle Paul wrote to Timothy as he was finishing his ministry. "Timothy, I have had 35 years of wonderful, peaceful ministry. The Lord blessed me, and the devil stepped politely out of the way everywhere I went and never gave me any trouble." Is that what he wrote? No! Not at all!

He basically said, "Timothy, I have fought a good fight, and you must continue the same good fight!" (See Second Timothy 4:7.) A good fight is one you win! It's never described in Scripture as just a fight. It's always a good fight, and it's always a fight of faith. It takes faith to win this fight. Jesus made it very clear that the coming of the Kingdom was a declaration of war and that those who come into the Kingdom must become violent like Jesus. They must join with Him in advancing the Kingdom by force.

If you don't like that kind of Christianity, then forget about the Kingdom. Just have a local, friendly Christian club. You can have a nice time together just loving one another, and one day Jesus will come and take you all away. Until then just stay away from the devil, and he may just possibly leave you in peace if you are not troubling him—but I doubt it. He most probably will attack you even more because you don't resist him.

Anyway, that is not the Kingdom, and you really have no choice. It is amazing how many Christians do not want to be people of war. But biblically there is no other kind of Christianity.

THE SUPERIORITY OF THE KINGDOM

In Matthew 12, Jesus is teaching a principle. Literally translated it reads, "But I say to you, *that something* [not someone] *greater than the temple is here*" (Matt. 12:6). He is not emphasizing Himself as a person (someone) but as the initiator, forerunner, and founder of "something," which is the Kingdom.

Jesus knew that He had three-and-a-half years to demonstrate and establish the Kingdom before He returned to the Father. If His disciples did not get His message before He departed, then there would be no continuation of the Kingdom. He expected the Kingdom to become greater, mightier, and more powerful after His departure than anything that was seen during His earthly life. Jesus not only came to die for our sins, but He also came to demonstrate this "something," which He called the Kingdom.

In this passage, He wanted them to stop looking at Him as a person and instead see the Kingdom that He had initiated as a separate entity, having its own identity and ongoing force. That was the "something" that He had established by His submission and obedience to the Father. Jesus was the beginning of that "something." In just over three years, He was going to leave earth and go back to be with the Father, but the Kingdom of God on earth was not going to depart with Him. On the contrary, it was just beginning. Daniel prophesied long ago that the Kingdom would begin as a stone (Jesus) thrown into the governmental systems of this world. But it would grow and grow to become a great mountain that would eventually fill the whole earth because many other obedient, violent men and women would be empowered by the same Spirit to forcefully advance the Kingdom (see Dan. 2:34-35; 44-45; 7:9-14,18,22).

During Jesus' time, the temple was a collection of impressive buildings built over a period of 46 years, supposedly "to the glory of God," but actually developed by Herod the Great for reasons of political expediency and to improve his relationship with the Jewish people. The presence of God and the Kingdom were not there in those buildings. The Kingdom only came into that temple twice, once at the beginning of Jesus' ministry, and again for one day at the end of Jesus' ministry when He came to cleanse the temple, throw out the moneychangers, and put things right. The Kingdom came into the temple in the person of Jesus for one day and then was gone (see Matt. 21:12-27).

In this passage, Jesus was indicating that while God is not against buildings, which can be a great blessing provided they are properly used, He is against buildings that contain spiritual corruption and do not house the Kingdom of God. He is against buildings that are themselves worshiped instead of God. The Kingdom must come and be practiced in the buildings through extravagant worship, the teaching of God's Word, prayer for all nations, and a ministry of healing the sick and casting out demons. If those things are not happening, the buildings are useless.

If you have to choose between the Kingdom and buildings, you must choose the Kingdom. If you can have the Kingdom and also have great buildings that are serving the purposes of the Kingdom, then you are in the best position. Just remember that the Kingdom is greater and more important than any building.

Let's look at two more verses. First read Matthew 12:40-41:

> *For just as Jonah was three days and three nights in the belly of the sea monster, so will the Son of Man be three days and three nights in the heart of the earth. The men of Nineveh*

will stand up with this generation at the judgment, and will condemn it because they repented at the preaching of Jonah; and behold, something greater than Jonah is here (Matthew 12:40-41 NASB).

Jesus was teaching here that the evangelistic power of the Kingdom is far greater than the power of any single evangelist working on his or her own. If Reinhard Bonnke were to come to your city, I am sure he would have a profound impact, but the coming of the Kingdom would be even greater. When Jonah came to Ninevah, the people repented of their sins from the top political leaders right down to the lowest citizen. Everybody was affected. The city was changed for almost 150 years because of the preaching of one man. However, what we are being told by Jesus is that the Kingdom is even more powerful than that great, evangelistic thrust of Jonah's day. If you want to see cities changed from the top to the bottom with multitudes coming to Jesus, the Kingdom will do far more than any great evangelist can.

Now please look at Matthew 12:42:

The Queen of the South will rise up with this generation at the judgment and will condemn it, because she came from the ends of the earth to hear the wisdom of Solomon; and behold, something greater than Solomon is here (Matthew 12:42 NASB).

Solomon, in his day, was considered the wisest man on the earth. In his early years, he established a kingdom with great power, glory, prosperity, and wisdom. The Queen of Sheba came all the way from Ethiopia in North Africa to see if what she had heard was true. She discovered that it was much better than she had heard.

Listen! The leaders of nation after nation are looking for answers to problems they cannot solve. There are so many political problems in the world with no answers. No one has the power, wisdom, or understanding to solve these problems, but "something greater than Solomon is here." If the Kingdom really came with power to your city and to your nation, all your political, social, and economic problems would be solved. Like the Queen of Sheba, people would come running from the ends of the earth to see what you did to change everything. In the Kingdom, there is power to solve every political, social, and economic problem.

If you think the beginning of Solomon's kingdom was fantastic, then you wait until the Kingdom of God really comes. We haven't seen anything yet. We will see such righteousness, holiness, and wisdom come. It will solve every problem. It will bring the glorious peace, justice, and compassion of the Kingdom to our needy world and create great economic prosperity. You will see the Kingdom in all these practical ways. When the Kingdom begins to break out, people will come running from all over the world to the places where these glorious answers are being manifested to find out what you did. The answer must always be "the Kingdom of our Lord Jesus Christ has come." It solves and answers every need.

There are many promises in Scripture about this. Before Jesus returns to consummate this age and bring it to completion, He is going to rebuild ruined cities. He is going to restore the desolation of many generations. Instead of our cities being hellholes of devilish activity, the Kingdom is going to come, and they will be filled with the glory of our God. I believe that until this happens some important Scriptures are left unfulfilled, but they will all have to be fulfilled before Jesus comes. Amen!

Chapter 6

The Parables of the Kingdom

In Matthew 13 we find a number of the parables about the Kingdom. Every one of them is very important and very powerful. Many are repeated in Mark chapter 4 and again in Luke chapter 8. These are three very important passages concerning the Kingdom, and to get the full truth we must study them together.

In Matthew 13 Jesus divided His listeners into two categories of people. He also talked several times about the "mysteries" of the Kingdom. The word *mystery* is a commonly used word in the New Testament, and it means a spiritual truth that God has deliberately chosen to hide from some people and selectively reveal to other people. No amount of natural intelligence or academic study of the text can penetrate these mysteries of God. They can only be revealed to us by the Spirit of God showing them to our spirit as and when He chooses through the instrument of His Word.

God makes choices. He chooses to reveal the mysteries to some, and Jesus calls these people the *you* category. God also chooses to hide them from others, and Jesus calls these people the *them* category. Certain heart attitudes are needed in order to be classified in the *you* category, and we find them listed in Matthew 13.

Starting in verse 9, Jesus says, "He who has ears, let him hear." That statement, or something very similar, comes 13 times in the Gospels. Jesus is not talking about physical ears but about having spiritual ears or a teachable, hungry heart attitude when the Word of God is being presented. In some people there is a desire, a great longing to know the truth, and that desire opens their spiritual ears.

Jesus makes it very clear that everyone really chooses for themselves the category to which they will belong. If you want to be in the you category, then you have to fulfill certain conditions. If you fulfill those conditions, then you are in. If you don't fulfill those conditions, then God will not reveal His mysteries to you. You will end up in the *them* category and never understand the mysteries of God's Kingdom.

In verse 10, we read, "And the disciples came and said to Him, 'Why do You speak to them in parables?'" (Matt. 13:10). We are told in Mark's version that Jesus only taught in parables, a deliberate policy of His.

Jesus primarily taught by telling stories, and these stories had a deeper spiritual meaning that only some could see. Even the miracles recorded in Scripture had a deeper meaning than just the miracle itself. They are there to teach us, by allegory, the hidden truths of God's Kingdom.

John's Gospel says that if all the things that Jesus did were written down, the world could not contain the books (see John 21:25). But John, led by the Spirit, took eight miracles and built his Gospel around those eight miracles. That is the key to understanding the Gospel of John. Each miracle is a wonderful miracle, but that is not the only reason it is written down. Each miracle also teaches a spiritual principle of the Kingdom that we need to understand. Gradually the Spirit of God will teach us how to understand these parables.

Matthew 13, Mark 4, and Luke 8 all teach many of the same things, but each Gospel adds extra, important detail. The first parable in each passage is the parable of a sower who went out to sow in four different kinds of soil. Jesus said to His disciples in Mark 4:13, "Do you not understand this parable? How then will you understand all the parables?" (Mark 4:13). In other words, if you do not understand the spiritual principles taught in the parable of the sower, other parabolic teachings of Jesus will be difficult for you to grasp. That is frightening. I have met people with theological degrees who still cannot really understand one word that Jesus said.

When the disciples asked Jesus why He spoke to them (primarily the scribes and Pharisees) in parables:

> *He answered and said to them, "Because it has been given to **you** to know the mysteries of the kingdom of heaven, but to **them** it has not been given. For whoever has, to him more will be given, and he will have abundance; but whoever does not have, even what he has will be taken away from him" (Matthew 13:11-12).*

91

Become Teachable Like a Child

The number one requirement for God to reveal the mysteries of the Kingdom is *intellectual humility*. No matter how much intelligence or education we have, we must come to God like a teachable child. Paradoxically, this child-like attitude causes us to become very wise and to grow up quickly to spiritual maturity. On the one hand, Paul spoke many times to the Corinthian church, especially in the first three chapters of his first letter, about their arrogance of mind. As a result of their intellectual arrogance, they had remained spiritual babes, and he could not teach them anything of depth.

On the other hand, the Thessalonian church received his teaching hungrily for what it really was, the Word of God. It was able to do its work in them because they believed (see 2 Thess. 2:13). As a result, they rapidly became mature in faith and were soon doing miraculous works like Paul and like Jesus.

Now Corinth was a much more important city. It was the major commercial capital for two great regions called Macedonia and Achaia. It was the natural center of the whole region. It was also a numerically large church, but it was of little use to God because of the intellectual arrogance of the Corinthians. God simply could not teach them or use them, and they remained spiritual babes.

Paul spent almost three years in Corinth. Apart from Ephesus, it was the longest time he spent anywhere. But it did not have the effect it should have had because of their arrogance of mind. He spent only three weeks in Thessalonica, but this had far more effect because of their teachable, hungry attitude. Thessalonica was a smaller, less significant town, but because of their response to the Word of God, they became a powerful, regional church that reached the whole region of Macedonia and Achaia with their faith (see 1 Thess. 1:8). This is why Jesus frequently said that if you want to come into the Kingdom, you must become like a little child. The first requirement is intellectual humility: to be humble and teachable like a little child.

REVERENCE FOR THE WORD OF GOD

The second requirement is the *value that you place on hearing the Word of God*. Turn to Mark 4:24 where Jesus says, "Consider carefully what you hear." He continues, "With the measure you use, it will be measured back to you—and even more. Whoever has will be given more; whoever does not have, even what he has will be taken from him" (Mark 4:24-25 NIV). If you value the Word of God, it will come to you in the power of the value that you place upon it. If the Word of God is awesome to you, then awesome power will flow through you because of your attitude toward the Word of God.

Essentially, you decide by your attitude how powerfully the Word of God is going to work in and through your life. Some people see mighty miracles; others can't even cure a cold. It is their attitude toward the Word that causes the difference. If you prove that you value His Word, then God will give you much more of His Word. But if you don't value the Word, even what you have will be taken away from you. You will become poorer and poorer because of your disrespect toward the Word of God.

Obedience and Faith Toward the Word of God

The third requirement is *the degree to which you choose to obey the Word.* You must prove your attitude to the Word of God by your obedience. You must become a doer of the Word and not a hearer only. It says in Hebrews chapter 5 that the believers never became exercised in the Word of God, and as a result they remained babes and became dull of hearing (see Heb. 5:11-14). It says in Hebrews chapter 4 that they heard the Word, but it didn't profit them or help them because "those who heard it did not combine it with faith" (Heb. 4:2 NIV).

To hear the Word of God without faith, and with no inclination or intention of obeying, is very dangerous. You are actually doing yourself harm. It is better not to hear the Word than to hear it and not obey it. There is only one way to prove that the Bible is the Word of God with power and that is to step out and do it! Don't wait to be intellectually convinced. Just do it! Then you will become experientially convinced, which is much better because it will work, and you will really know it is truth. In John 7:17, Jesus said that anyone who "wills to do His will" shall know whether His teaching comes from God, or whether He was speaking on His own authority. Just step out and do it, and you'll soon know.

Within a few weeks of my conversion in 1958, I began to read the Bible for the first time. I first tried to read it intellectually like any other book and found myself doubting many things and not getting much out of it. Then God spoke to me very strongly; He told me that I was using the wrong instrument and that I needed to change. I needed to use my spirit and not my mind. Then His Spirit could communicate directly with my spirit and show me wonderful things hidden in His Word.

I was to stop trying to understand everything intellectually and just make a decision to believe every statement as literally true, like a little child, even though it didn't necessarily make any sense to me. He then said that in the future I was to live by three principles concerning His Word: (1) I was to make a decision to believe every statement as literally true; (2) I was to obey every commandment; and (3) I was to claim every promise.

I now have almost 50 years of experiential evidence that God's Word, the Bible, is absolutely trustworthy. Every promise of God that I have ever claimed has been proven to be true. Our unconditional obedience to His Word has led my wife and me into some seemingly impossible situations, but God has never failed. Eileen has said more than once, "You cannot prove God to be the God of the impossible, until you find yourself in an impossible situation."

These things will qualify you for the *you* category, and then God will gradually reveal to you the mysteries of the Kingdom. Also, because you deeply value what you have received, He will give you more. You will read the Bible, and God will explain many things to you by revelation. You will wonder why these skeptical doctors in theology cannot understand what has become so obvious to you. Like me, you will begin to think, "What's wrong with these guys? Why can't they see what I can see?"

I feel this is a fundamental principle to grasp. If we have the right attitude of childlike humility and trust, if we hunger for and place great value on the Word, if we literally claim every promise and obey everything the Word tells us to do, then we will be members of the you category. The mysteries of the Kingdom will be revealed to us. However, to those who do not do these simple things, the mysteries of the Kingdom will remain hidden. Even so, there are still further conditions to fulfill to qualify us for the full revelation of the Kingdom.

THE KEY PARABLE OF THE KINGDOM: THE PARABLE OF THE SOWER

This parable is found in all three synoptic Gospels (see Matt. 13:3-9; Mark 4:3-9; Luke 8:4-8). Jesus said that if we can't understand this parable, then we will not be able to understand any of the other parables (see Mark 4:13). It is one parable that Jesus Himself carefully explained.

The fact that I lived in India for many years has helped me to understand the Bible better, as many of the agricultural stories that Jesus told come to life before your eyes. I saw oxen plowing fields and treading out the grain on threshing floors just as Jesus described. I saw men and women drawing water from wells and men scattering seed by hand, etc. These were still very much a part of everyday life when I lived in India in the 1960s and '70s.

THE PARABLE EXPLAINED

In this parable, a sower goes out to sow good seed in four different kinds of soil. These soil conditions represent four heart conditions as follows:

1. The Hardened Heart

I've seen this happen many times in India. Imagine there is a village well in the corner of a farmer's field that everybody uses. One day the farmer plows the field with yoked oxen and a wooden plow, but several days may pass before he gets around to sowing the field with seed. All the villagers continue to come to the well every morning and every evening to get water, and they quickly trample a hardened path to the well across the field. When the farmer comes a few days later to sow the field by scattering the seed by hand, this path is already trampled into a hard, non-absorbent surface. On this path, the seed just lies on the surface, and the birds quickly come, take the seed, and eat it before it has any chance to germinate.

This soil condition represents those who already have a rigid mindset of traditions of religion and doctrine and therefore immediately reject any truth that does not conform to those traditions. They will not change their ways or their beliefs, no matter what God says or does. Jesus several times charged the scribes and Pharisees with rejecting the very Word of God for their traditions, and as a result they could not receive any new word about the Kingdom from Him.

2. *The Shallow Heart*

This heart condition is represented by a thin covering of soil lying over a rocky substrate. The seed goes into the soil and lies just below the surface. It germinates very quickly because the soil warms more rapidly in the sun, and, because of the shallow depth, the shoots will appear sooner than those of a seed more deeply sown. But the roots cannot penetrate the rocky substrate and have no depth, so the plants quickly shrivel up and die in the heat of the sun. Jesus explained that this represents people who respond quickly and emotionally when the Gospel of the Kingdom is preached without really counting the cost first. When trouble and persecution arise because of the way, they fall away, deny their conversion, and quickly go back to their old ways.

3. The Divided Heart

With this heart condition, the soil is good, but two very different kinds of seed are growing in it at the same time. The good seeds of the Kingdom were planted first, germinated first, and appeared to be growing strong plants that would produce a good crop at harvest time. Unfortunately, some bad seed had been subsequently planted and was growing as well. This latter seed grew more vigorously and overtook the good seed, twisted itself around these good plants, and choked them to death before they could come to harvest. Jesus said that these bad plants, which choke the good plants, are the cares of this world, the deceitfulness of riches, and the desire for other things. Jesus made it very plain in many passages that we cannot serve God and mammon. We cannot love God and at the same time love the riches, desires, fame, and rewards of this world.

We are not being called to live a life of poverty, but to a life where the material things of the world (like riches, fame, and position) do not have our heart. If we genuinely seek first the Kingdom of God and His righteousness, then everything we legitimately need will be ours as well, without us even having to worry about it (see Matt. 6:33).

4. The Good and Honest Heart

This final heart condition is represented by good, fertile soil with no bad seed. It is called a good and honest heart.

According to Jesus' teaching, it is possible to experience a measure of harvest (from 30 to 60-fold) by observing three steps. However, to experience the full 100-fold harvest, two extra steps are necessary.

The first three steps occur when someone: (1) spiritually hears the Word; (2) spiritually understands the Word; and (3) receives it as a Word to be obeyed.

This will produce a measure of harvest up to 60-fold.

If, in addition, this heart is not just a passive receiver, but becomes actively engaged in a definite pursuit of the Word, then that attitude will contribute significantly to the quality and size of the harvest. To get the full 100-fold return we must do two other things: (4) hold the Word fast; and (5) doggedly persevere in it.

Regardless of delay, lack of visible evidence, counterattacks of the enemy, or the conflict of adverse circumstances, we persevere until there is a full manifestation of the Word. This dogged perseverance of faith alone will produce the full harvest of the Word in all its 100-fold richness in our lives and circumstances.

Chapter 7

THE KEYS OF THE KINGDOM

In Matthew 16:19 Jesus gave the keys of the Kingdom to Peter following his declaration, "You are the Christ, the Son of the Living God" (Matt. 16:16). Jesus responded by saying, "Blessed are you, Simon Bar-Jonah, for flesh and blood has not revealed this to you, but My Father who is in heaven" (Matt. 16:17). Peter had become the beneficiary of divine revelation. Because of this, Jesus was able to move and begin to build a Church that would overcome every obstacle and hindrance that stood in the way. Jesus was saying to Peter that as the beneficiary of God's revelation, He could now give him the keys of the Kingdom and show him how to lock and unlock spiritual situations. That is a big subject, which I will spend more time on when we deal with the "gates" that obstruct the advance of the Kingdom in the sequel to this book.

That promise is connected with another promise which immediately follows it: "Whatever you bind on earth, will be bound in heaven, and whatever you loose on earth will be loosed in heaven" (Matt. 16:19). In the Greek, there is an unusual construction here. It has a past-perfect tense verb connected to a future tense verb. This is grammatically strange, but it makes perfect sense in the Kingdom. It is better translated as follows: "Whatever you bind on earth will be, because it already has been bound in heaven, and whatever you loose on earth will be, because it already has been bound in heaven."

You will find this past-perfect/future combination in several places where Jesus is talking about faith. In Mark 11:24, Jesus tells the disciples that when they pray for anything, they must first believe that they *have already received it*, and then they *will receive it*. He also says that there are occasions when we don't just continue to pray about things, but we speak to them with a word of authority, and then they will move. Such things are demons, sicknesses, demonic strongholds, demonic weather patterns, mountains of opposition, trees of religious tradition that need to be rooted up and cast way. These are all treated in this way by Jesus. He wants us to learn to speak to them in the same faith-filled way that He always did.

COMING TO REAL FAITH

Faith is not the main subject of this book. (For more on the subject of faith, please see my book *The Good Fight of Faith*.) However, faith and the Kingdom are so inseparably joined; we have to say a little about real faith at this point.

What we are being told in such Scriptures is the following: To come to real faith, we have to know that the object of our faith has already become an accomplished fact in the spirit realm. We must know that it is already a "done deal" even though nothing can be seen yet or experienced with our natural senses. It must be perceived as a completed fact in the spirit realm before there will be a visible (future) manifestation in this physical, time-space world. Then, at the right time, it will certainly become manifested physically right before our eyes.

Let me use my physical healing as an example of this. As I write this book in the year 2007, I am a physically fit 77-year-old man. However, in the 1960s I was struggling with a very debilitating physical condition that was getting progressively worse and for which there was no medical cure.

I was experiencing increasingly frequent serious hemorrhages from a blood vessel at the back of my nose. It would suddenly rupture and begin to bleed and was very difficult to stop. I would sometimes lose pints of blood at a time and needed emergency hospital treatment including blood transfusions. I nearly died several times from loss of blood during my first few years in India as it got progressively worse. Through these experiences, God taught me the ways of faith. During the seventh year of my time in India, through the writings of Smith Wigglesworth, I received the revelation that I already had been healed. I came to really know in my spirit that it already was a done deal in the spirit realm although there was no visible manifestation.

God told me it was done, but He also said the symptoms would continue for a time to teach me the ways of faith. In the spirit realm, my healing already was an accomplished fact, so I couldn't go on asking to be healed. I could only thank God for what was already done, even though I could not yet see any sign of it physically.

My physical condition continued to deteriorate for another five years. God was teaching me how to live in the eternal realm of the spirit by faith. Altogether, I struggled with this disability for about 12 years. They were very difficult years, but I learned some very important lessons.

Some of my Hindu friends were very concerned about me. They said, "We have some tremendous healers who use Ayurvedic medicine. Why don't you go and see one of those? We love you, and we don't want to see you die. Your Jesus does not seem to be doing anything for you." They meant well, but I could not yield to them. I told these well-meaning friends, "Thank you for your loving concern, but I have already been healed by Jesus although it is not yet visibly manifested. In any case, I would rather die believing in Jesus, than be healed by the devil." Within a few days of that statement, I was visibly healed, and everybody could see the manifestation of what I had been believing for over five years.

I have been able to use the principles and lessons that I learned in those days to believe God for much bigger things, such as a city. In basically the same way, I was able to believe God for Mumbai to become a transformed city in the spirit realm more than 30 years ago. I am not praying that it will happen, but am thanking God that He has already made the decision to transform that city, and it is already happening. This is a very important principle when it comes to the Kingdom. One of the greatest keys of the Kingdom is the key of faith. You have to learn to shut and open according to the word that God has already spoken to you, and you have to know it is done in the spirit realm even before it becomes visible in the natural.

In 1976 I returned to London, England, the city where I was born; I was brokenhearted over what I saw, and I began to weep. God empowered me to come to faith to fight for London in 1980 when I met some fanatical Muslims in the streets of London. They were Iranians sent to convert London to Islam. In the area of Spittalfield, almost all the churches were closed, and new mosques were appearing everywhere. I was walking the streets with a converted Hindu friend of mine, and we were both feeling the deep distress of seeing these things happening before our eyes. Then we met these two Iranian Muslim evangelists. They boasted, "We are pouring millions and millions of dollars into the conversion of London to Islam. By the year 2000, London will become an Islamic city, and from London we will conquer Europe." I said, "Oh, no you won't!" I remember spiritually and symbolically drawing a line in the sand and taking a stand of faith to fight for London until it was healed from its backsliding and once again bowed the knee to Jesus and welcomed His Kingdom rule.

That was when I was first driven desperately to get hold of God for London. Within a few years, I had come to faith for that city also. London is changing. Although it is not fully manifested yet, it is already a done deal in the spirit realm, and it will surely come to pass in our time-space world.

In 1991, much to our surprise, my wife and I moved to San Antonio, Texas, because we received a very specific word from God. My main concern in obeying that word was that I was leaving London before the transformation had visibly taken place.

God assured me that some of my sons, spiritual and natural, had already taken on the burden, and they would complete the job.

In the past few years, God has brought a number of us to faith for the city of San Antonio. Now you watch! There is going to be a mighty breakthrough of God in the city of San Antonio. God has given us the keys of the Kingdom. We can open and shut things because of these keys of faith. We're learning how to do these things in the spirit realm, but we can only do them as, when, and where God tells us.

He also wants to bring revelation to you and give you the keys of the Kingdom for your city. When you have received them and have learned to use them properly, you will be able to decree the spiritual, political, economic, and social future of your city. These are big issues we are talking about. Are you getting excited about the Kingdom, and are you willing to pay the price to receive the keys of the Kingdom for your city?

THE PRAYER OF AGREEMENT

In Matthew 18, Jesus teaches us some other important things. Once again, in the first few verses of this chapter, He says that we have to become like little children to be great in the Kingdom (see Matt. 18:3-5). Then we have to deal with any differences, offenses, and broken relationships that are between us (see Matt. 18:15-17). Then in verse 18, we come to this promise already spoken about in Matthew 16. Listen to what Jesus says here in an expanded, literal translation: "I tell you the truth (I really mean this), whatever you bind on earth will be bound because it already has been bound in heaven, and whatever you loose on earth will be loosed because it already has been loosed in heaven" (see Matt. 18:18). Then He continues, "Again, I say to you that if two of you agree on earth concerning anything that they ask, it will be done for them by My Father in heaven" (Matt. 18:19). It doesn't say that if you can get 2,000 people praying for your city, then you may see some changes. It only needs two.

However, notice something about the two: "If two of you *agree* on earth concerning anything that they ask...." The word *agree* is translated from the Greek word *sumphoneo* (soom-fo-neh'-o) from which we get our English word *symphony*. It literally means to make exactly the same sound together. It is like two violins in the same orchestra perfectly tuned to play exactly the same sound together. That is what this word means. If two of you can get together in perfect spiritual symphony and make the same sound together, then you can have whatever you ask for. That should not be too hard to accomplish.

The obvious and most natural expression of this is a husband and wife praying together, but it can often be just two people who find a special empathy in prayer. To have this kind of prayer life, you must have this kind of "symphonic" unity. If you can pray like this as a couple, you can put a wall of protection around your family. When you get a leadership team in a church in real symphony together, they can put a protective wall around the members of that church so the devil cannot easily attack them. Being in agreement not only forms an impregnable defense, but it also becomes a very powerful weapon in the Kingdom. That is why Jesus also said the opposite to us in Matthew 12:25: "Every kingdom divided against itself is brought to desolation, and every city or house divided against itself will not stand." If there is true symphonic unity, it is unassailable. It cannot be successfully attacked because it is the Kingdom.

Can you see what would happen if we took these words seriously, first in our family, then our local church, and finally in the churches of any given city? A city divided against itself cannot stand. Do you know any city in the world where all the Christians in it are in symphony? Can you imagine what would happen if they came into real symphony? They could ask anything they wanted, and it would be done for them. They could bind anything, and it would be bound, and they could loose anything, and it would be loosed. There is tremendous power in real symphonic unity, and there is tremendous weakness in division.

THE BENEFITS OF FORGIVENESS

Immediately following that story, Peter says to Jesus, "Lord, how many times shall I forgive my brother when he sins against me? Up to seven times?" Peter thinks that is being very generous, but Jesus says, "No, not seven times, but seventy times seven in one day!" (See Matthew 18:21-22.) This is 490 times in one day, which is about once every three minutes all day long!

Imagine a proud housewife who has just cleaned the beautiful new tiles of her kitchen floor; it is shining beautifully. Her husband, who is working out in the garden, comes in to wash his hands at the kitchen sink and forgets to take his boots off. He looks back with horror at the dirty mess he has caused and says, "Oh, dear! I'm so sorry!" He washes his hands and goes back into the yard. She forgives him, cleans up the mess, and gets everything shiny and clean again.

Now imagine him doing that same thing every three minutes for the whole day. How many times would she be willing to forgive him, even if he said he was sorry? Would she not feel more

108

like strangling him after the third or fourth time? But Jesus says you have to go on forgiving; there cannot be a limit.

Jesus goes on to tell a story about a great king. I always like to do the mathematics of these Bible stories. It is amazing how much more truth is often revealed. If you calculate what Jesus is saying in this passage, you will find that these wonderful mathematical truths powerfully bring home what He is saying.

In this story, there was a servant who owed the king 10,000 talents. A talent was not a coin that you put in your pocket! A talent was a bar of gold weighing about 30 kilograms or 66 pounds, so 10,000 talents would weigh about 300,000 kilos or about 660,000 pounds. That is approximately 300 metric tons of gold! Its value today would be over $6 billion U.S. dollars. That is a lot of money!

This is the point that Jesus is making. In order to forgive other people's offenses freely, we have to comprehend fully the magnitude of the sins that God has forgiven us and the magnitude of the inheritance He has also freely given us. It is like being completely forgiven a debt of over $6 billion. He has just canceled the debt and now says, "You owe Me nothing." Then in addition to that, He has made us joint heirs with Christ of all His vast riches and resources. We are now rich in Him beyond measure.

Yet most Christians walk around with only a $100 sense of forgiveness. They feel they weren't that bad, and God didn't need to forgive them of that much. Jesus spoke in Luke chapter 7 concerning the woman who had been a prostitute and was forgiven everything. She could not stop pouring out her love and gratitude to Jesus. Jesus spoke of this woman to Simon, the Pharisee who had invited Him to his house, "Therefore I say to you, her sins, which are many, are forgiven, for she loved much. But to whom little is forgiven, the same loves little" (Luke 7:47). Most Christians have a $100 sense of their forgiveness, and so they do not love Him very much. They feel, "I wasn't that bad, and it's not that big a deal."

God is saying that it is not a $100 debt but a $6 *billion* debt that He has forgiven you of. Because He freely forgave you so much, your love and gratitude to God should be overflowing all the time. Furthermore, He then made you His very own son and gave you exactly the same inheritance as His own beloved Son, Jesus. That is what He has done. It's absolutely fantastic. As a free gift, instead of being hopelessly in debt, I am now gloriously rich through my inheritance in Christ. That ought to make me very grateful to God and very generous to others!

When you comprehend these two things, there are two effects. The first effect is deep gratitude and love to God for forgiving so much and then by grace giving so much in terms of inheritance. When you really see this, it overwhelms you and fills you with love, gratitude, and worship. The second effect is that it changes your attitude toward other people when they sin against you. If you have been forgiven so much, you ought to be just as willing as God to forgive those who sin against you—the large offenses as well as the small.

Now let's go on to the next point in the story beginning in Matthew 18:28. This just forgiven servant is owed some money by another servant. The amount the other servant owes him is 100 denarii. One hundred denarii does not represent billions of dollars, but it is not a small amount either. One denarius was the daily wage for a skilled workman. How much would a skilled electrician earn in one day in the United States today? Let's say

$150. So we are talking about a 100 days' wages, or about a third of a year's wages, so that would be approximately $15,000 in present-day American terms.

That is not a small amount, and this is the point that Jesus is making. Suppose I arrived in your town for some ministry, and I said to your pastor, "Oh, I forgot to bring any money with me. Could you please lend me $20 to buy a few things I need? I will send you the money when I get home." He says, "Sure," and gives me the money. But let's imagine that when I return home, I forget to send him the money. Now that's a bad thing to do, but the pastor, no doubt, can forgive that. He says, "Oh, Alan just forgot. It's not the end of the world. I can forgive him that much," and he easily forgets all about it.

But in this parable we are not talking about $20. No! It is $15,000. So imagine I said to the pastor, "Hey, we are just about to buy a new building, and we need a little more money to close the deal. Could you give my ministry a temporary loan for about one month? We just need $15,000. I promise you will have it back within two months." He says, "Sure, I can do that," and he writes me a check for $15,000. Two months go by, and I don't send him the money. Four months go by, still no check. What's happening to the pastor? He's getting offended with me. "That Alan Vincent! He promised to send the money back in two months, and it's not come." It is now really bothering him, and he cannot just forget it as he could when it was only $20. It is easy to forgive $20 offenses, but it is much harder to forgive $15,000 offenses.

That is the point that Jesus is making here. Jesus says you still have to forgive, and do it again and again if necessary. Otherwise, God cannot forgive you your much greater offenses.

Imagine that someone has agreed to meet you at 9:00 A.M., but they don't get there until 10:00 A.M., or they forget all about it and waste your time. That's a $20 offense. It's irritating, but it's not too hard to forgive.

But imagine a daughter who is sexually abused by her own father. That is a terrible offense. How do you measure such an offense? Or imagine that you are a pastor and have a trusted leader, a covenant brother who said he would serve you in the ministry for the rest of his life, suddenly walk out on you, take half of the church with him, and start his own church. How can you just forgive him for that? You must because you've been forgiven more than $6 billion.

Can you hear what Jesus is saying? Like most people in ministry, I have had some terrible things done to me, and the most painful experiences are when these things are done by other Christians. However, I learned years ago that I must deal with those offenses, and by a determined act of my will, I must decide to forgive the offender as freely as God has forgiven me. If I don't do that, then I will destroy myself with bitterness, resentment, and hurt. Jesus said if you don't do this, the tormenter (the devil) will come, and he will torment you until you have paid to the last penny (see Matt. 18:34).

Every time Jesus or any New Testament writer speaks on prayer, they always conclude with a commandment to forgive one another unconditionally. (See Matthew 6:14-15; Matthew 18:21-35; Mark 11:25-26; and Colossians 3:12-13, for a few examples.) If we won't do this, all our prayers will be negated. This is an important Kingdom principle that many in the church choose to ignore, and they pay a very heavy price for doing so.

In my hometown of San Antonio, the southern part is mainly Hispanic. At one time, the City Reachers ministry, which

Eileen leads, had several hundred intercessors who gave an hour per day or per week to pray night and day over the city of San Antonio. In the early days of this ministry, God told Eileen that they were to target the pastors of this southern part of the city and pray that their hearts would change, become reconciled, and start to desire unity.

After four months, things suddenly began to happen. Pastors began to come together in groups to pray. They had never been able to do that before because of the offenses between them.

A few months after that, someone called Eileen at the City Reachers office saying, "I represent a group of Christian businessmen who own their own businesses. We take four weeks off every year as a group, and we go one week at a time to different places that God shows us. We stay in a hotel and pray together every morning. In the afternoon we prayer-walk the streets looking to see what God will do. We like to go to small businesses and speak to the owners and say, "Can we pray for your business?" We try to bring anyone we can to salvation. If anyone is sick, then we pray for healing. We also pray for God to prosper these businesses—or for anything else that God may indicate."

This representative said, "We feel very strongly that God is telling us to come to San Antonio. We would like to come under the covering of your prayer ministry. Would you cover us in prayer as we go out and do our street evangelism and visitation?" Eileen said, "Sure."

They asked her, "Where do you think is the best place to go?" She said, "There are many small businesses in the southern part of the city which is mainly Hispanic. That's the place to go." She was not thinking about the way the pastors had been praying; somehow that never entered her mind at the time.

So the Christian businessmen came, and in the first four days they had many people make decisions for Christ. They saw miracles and wonderful conversions. They were absolutely amazed and asked, "What have you been doing? We've never walked into an atmosphere like this before."

Then they went to the affluent, middle-class, northwestern part of the city, and in those three days, they saw little impact and did not lead one person to Christ. It was the unity of the pastors and their prayer—the united prayer of spiritual leadership—that made the difference between the two parts of the city. We learned a tremendous lesson from that.

I suggest that you get before God and ask, "Lord, is there anyone I am not forgiving that I should be forgiving?" Maybe you need to see somebody right away. Go visit them, telephone them, or write to them. Get that thing resolved. Until you do, it will make you powerless in your attempt to advance the Kingdom. If we come together in unity, in real symphony, we can ask whatever we will and, it will be done for us. We can bind whatever we need to bind, we can loose whatever we need to loose, and it will happen. Then the Kingdom will be forcefully advancing.

Now go back and just think about what has been taught—and then think about your own situation. Let's agree, first of all, that you want to be in that you category, in which case you may want to pray:

> God, I want to qualify, so that all the mysteries of the Kingdom can be revealed to me and to those who work with me. Together we want to be like little children, humble, obedient, and submissive. Oh God, we want to value Your Word. We

want to give it great value so that it becomes very powerful in us and through us. We are hungry to see how You will change our cities. We really believe that You can do it. We really believe the problem is not the devil and his power, but it's an unbelieving and divided church. Oh Lord, please change the hearts of the people that really know You, the real believers. May the mysteries of the Kingdom be revealed to them.

May we come together in symphony, in agreement, to ask for powerful things to be done in the cities we represent. Lord, we want Your Kingdom to come. Thank You, God, that it does not have to be thousands, but it can be as few as two. If we are in true symphony, we can make it happen. Bring us to absolute symphony as husbands and wives together and as prayer partners. May we make the same sound. May our prayers be in absolute unity. As leadership teams in the same church, may we be in symphony according to Your Word. May there be no divisions among us so that You can give us the keys of the Kingdom and so that we can open and shut doors according to Your Word.

Lord, I pray for the pastors in our city. I pray for the churches that already exist. May we repent for our wrong attitudes, our offenses, and our wrong behavior. Let reconciliation come. May there be seeking and giving of forgiveness. We want to hear that this brother has come together with that brother, that churches that have split have joined back together again, and that forgiveness has flowed.

We are beginning to obey Your Word, and the power of Your Kingdom is coming. May this be our testimony. In Jesus' mighty name! Amen!

Chapter 8

THE KINGDOM IN MARK AND LUKE

Because the truths of the Kingdom are so intertwined through-out the Gospels, we have already looked at a number of Scriptures in these Gospels while we were studying Matthew. However, there are a few additional things we need to note.

THE KINGDOM IN MARK'S GOSPEL

Mark mentions the Kingdom of God 15 times. The occasions when Mark mentions the Kingdom are almost all the same as the ones mentioned by Matthew except that Mark always uses the term "Kingdom of God" while Matthew uses both "Kingdom of Heaven" and "Kingdom of God" (see Mark 4:11; Matt. 13:11; Mark 9:1; Matt. 19:23, etc.).

Mark takes some of the same incidents, adds extra details, and spends more time on some of the underlying principles. For example:

1. *The Primary Activity of the Kingdom Is Catching Men*

Mark 1:14-17 records how Jesus began His ministry. He began by preaching the "Good News" of the Kingdom. He first called all men to "repent, and believe the gospel" (Mark 1:15). Here Jesus explains what the bottom line of the Kingdom really is. Jesus is only able to come as a Savior to those who first of all accept His Kingdom and receive His total rule over them in that Kingdom.

Jesus came to reestablish on earth the original purpose for which Adam was created, which was to live his whole life under the benevolence of God's absolute rule. Only then could he become God's effective delegated ruler over all the earth and over everything that God had made upon the earth.

If the disciples came under the Father's absolute authority, Jesus' first promise to them was that they would definitely become fishers of men (see Mark 1:17). Here the primary activity of the Kingdom of God on earth is declared to be catching men and women and gathering them into His Kingdom. This was to be accomplished by preaching the Gospel of the Kingdom and demonstrating its power by signs, wonders, and miracles being done in His mighty name, including the casting out of demons and the healing of sicknesses.

2. *True Greatness in the Kingdom*

This teaching comes in all the Gospels, but it is more strongly taught in Mark's Gospel. Once Jesus had settled forever the issue of His indisputable headship role by His glorious appearance and the verbal witness of the Father on the Mount of Transfiguration, neither Peter nor any of the other disciples ever challenged His headship again.

Instead, the debate shifted as to which of them, after Jesus, would be the greatest in the Kingdom of God. Who would be at His right and left hand in the Kingdom? (See Matthew 20:20-28 and Mark 10:35-45.) There was hot competition between the Bar Jonah family, represented by Peter and Andrew, and the Bar Zebedee family, represented by James, John, and their mother. At least six times in the Gospels we find the disciples disputing, debating, or discussing which of them was going to be the greatest. Their attitudes were highly competitive, and Jesus could see they would never hold together as a team unless something radically changed. It was obvious that Peter and John didn't really like each other, and there were relational tensions between several of the other team members also. Peter and John are never found doing anything together until after the day of Pentecost.

Beginning in Matthew 18 and ending in Luke 22, as the disciples met for the Last Supper, this subject came up repeatedly. Jesus always responded in the same way. On most occasions he set a little child in their midst and said that if they wanted to be great in the Kingdom, they must become like this little child (see Matt. 18:1-5; Mark 9:33-37; Luke 9:46-48; Luke 22:24-27).

He taught them that the Kingdom was not at all like the world. To become great in the Kingdom you had to become the servant of everybody, and you had to become like the youngest rather than the eldest (see Mark 9:33-36). Nevertheless, in Mark 10:35-45, James and John Bar Zebedee, with their mother, were still trying to secure the two best places in the Kingdom for themselves. So, Jesus repeated the same teaching with the same warning. But the disciples seemed unable to receive the message and did not change.

The heated debate continued right through the Last Supper where they were still arguing over this matter (see Luke 22:24-30). After Jesus once again corrects the disciples regarding the nature of true greatness, He turns to Peter and says, "Simon, Simon! Indeed, Satan has asked for you, that he may sift you as wheat. But I have prayed for you, that your faith should not fail; and when you have returned to Me, strengthen your brethren" (Luke 22:31).

It was only after Peter ran away in fear and denied the Lord that he was humbled to nothing. Only the prayers of Jesus kept him from falling away completely. God thus turned him around to become a humbled, broken team member who was glad to be still accepted by Jesus and the rest of the team on any terms. He was then able to strengthen his brethren instead of competing with them (see Luke 22:24-34).

It wasn't until the 120 disciples had spent ten days under the convicting power of the Holy Spirit in the Upper Room after Jesus had ascended to His Father that things really changed, and their various relationships and offenses were truly mended. As well as being gloriously anointed by the Holy Spirit, the men and women who came out of the Upper Room were totally different from those who went in:

- They went in self-seeking and came out broken and humble.

- They went in divided and came out united.

- They went in full of fear and came out as bold as lions.

- They went in full of unbelief and came out full of faith.

- They went in without spiritual understanding and came out full of amazing scriptural revelation.

- They went in unable to pray and came out as mighty intercessors.

- They went in powerless and came out full of all the power of the Kingdom.

- They went in without the Spirit and came out full of the Holy Spirit, moving in all the gifts of the Spirit.

When the disciples came out of the Upper Room, they were finally able to forcefully advance the Kingdom against all opposition.

THE KINGDOM IN LUKE'S GOSPEL

Luke uses the phrase "the Kingdom of God" 32 times and, like Mark and John, he never uses the term "Kingdom of Heaven."

Luke repeats many of the incidents mentioned by Mark or Matthew, but he alone spends much more time on two things: the sending out of the 12 in Luke 9 and the sending out of the 70 in Luke 10. Only Luke mentions the sending out of the 70.

The 12 were named as apostles and sent only to the lost sheep of the house of Israel (see Matt. 10:5-7). The 70 were also sent out apostolically but were not called apostles. They went with a delegated authority from Jesus to move in the power of the Kingdom and to preach the Kingdom in every place where He himself would come (see Luke 10:1). They were to declare,

"The Kingdom of God has come near you." They were commanded to heal the sick, cast out demons, and by these acts declare that the Kingdom of God had come. To these 70, Jesus promised a great harvest and to them He gave authority (*exousia*) over all the power (*dunamis*) of the enemy (see Luke 10:2,19). Jesus also promised them that nothing by any means would be able to harm them (see Luke 10:17-24).

In the Gospel of Luke, as in the Book of Acts, *the main agent for advancing the Kingdom is the Holy Spirit*. For this reason, we all need to be constantly filled with the Holy Spirit and become His sword so that through us He can destroy the works of the evil one just as Jesus did.

The main emphasis is on warfare, and the primary manifestation of the Kingdom in Luke's Gospel is its power, demonstrated by signs, wonders, miracles, and the casting out of demons.

Secondly, the prayer life of Jesus is emphasized. Luke shows clearly that the driving force of the Kingdom is prayer. He first pointed to Jesus as the great example of a man of prayer. Luke then showed how Jesus prayed until at last His disciples began to want to become like Him in His prayer life. Then Jesus carefully taught them how to pray.

LUKE 11—THE PRAYER LIFE OF THE KINGDOM

In Luke 11:1, when one of Jesus' disciples asked Him to teach them how to pray, He began by teaching them the basic steps to powerful praying. In the first few verses He describes the kind of prayer life that will meet all our personal needs (see Luke 11:1-4). This outline is today widely known as "The Lord's Prayer." It is clearly an outline and not intended to be used as a religious prayer of vain repetition, for that would have directly contradicted what Jesus had just taught.

However, Jesus didn't stop with just teaching them to pray so as to get their own personal needs met. He was anxious to take them further into a life of prayer and teach them how to get the needs of others met by calling on their great friend, the Triune God, on behalf of their friends in need.

He taught them to seek the Spirit persistently so that they had the power to cast out demons and eventually bind the strongman. Luke shows Jesus at prayer many times and directly connects His prayer life with His authority and power to heal and to cast out demons.

In Luke 3:21, by His prayer, Heaven was opened, and the Spirit came down.

- In Luke 5:16, by His prayer, the power of the Lord was present to heal.

- In Luke 6:12-13, by His prayer, He knew who to choose as the 12 apostles.

- In Luke 6:7-19, by His prayer, power flowed out from Him to heal and deliver a whole multitude. He healed and delivered every one of them.

- In Luke 9:18-20, by His prayer, the disciple's eyes were opened by revelation to see who He really was.

- In Luke 9:28-29, by His prayer, He was transfigured before Peter, James, and John, and they had an unforgettable mountaintop experience.

- In Luke 11:1-22, by His prayer, He produced a great longing in His disciples to be able to pray like Him. He then carefully taught them six steps to powerful praying.

- In Luke 18:1-8, by His prayer, He taught them the power of persistent prayer and how faith must be found on the earth. He longed for His Father's house to become a house of prayer for all nations (see Luke 19:46; Isa. 56:7).

- In Luke 22:31-32, by His prayer, He kept Peter's faith from failing in his hour of trial. He prayed for Peter's conversion so he would not compete with his brethren, but would strengthen them instead.

- In Luke 22:41-46, by His prayer in Gethsemane, He fought and won the battle of His victorious death, and by faith He had obtained His resurrection before He went to the cross (see Heb. 5:7).

- In Luke 23:34, by His prayer on the cross, He obtained forgiveness for those who crucified Him. One of the thieves and the centurion in charge of His execution were converted on the spot (see Luke 23:42-43; Mark 15:34-39).

- In Luke 23:46, by His prayer of faith on the cross, He obtained the Church and the nations as His inheritance plus many other wonderful things (see Ps. 22:1-31).

There are many such examples in Scripture. Now if we live the same way with the same intimate prayer relationship with the Father, the power of the Kingdom will also flow through us.

In Luke 11:20-22, Jesus says that something (not someone) stronger than the demonic strongman has come, which is of course the Kingdom. All those truly in this Kingdom have the power to attack this demonic strongman, take away the armor on which he has relied, and rob him of all his goods (i.e., set at liberty multitudes of the captives satan thought he already had bound forever).

Once again, Jesus is not talking about some supercharged "James Bond" kind of Christian. He is talking about the corporate power of the Kingdom through the Church. The Church, moving in the power of the Kingdom, can bind the strongman, throw him down and rob him of all his possessions, but the individual Christian, however brave, will not be able to accomplish that alone.

Jesus declared that this "Stronger Man" was the agency of the Holy Spirit working through His humanity to manifest the Kingdom. If this was true of Jesus while on earth, how much more must it be true of Jesus in His resurrection power now living and continuing to do His works through His new Body the Church?

WINNING THE LEGAL BATTLE

In Luke 18:1-8, Jesus teaches us how to win the legal battle, which must precede the military battle if we are to succeed.

God is again portrayed as a heartless judge—that is not His real character, but it sometimes seems like it because He appears to be indifferent to our prayers. In this kind of situation, the delay is because God has to be righteous, even in His dealings with the devil.

God is the Lord and Judge in Heaven, but to fulfill all righteousness there must be a man on earth to prosecute the devil. In this story, even one weak widow woman is enough, providing she persists. Satan or one of his princes is the defendant. Our job is to prosecute him and declare that he no longer has any legal right to any person or any part of this world since Jesus has already purchased it completely by His blood. By this kind of prayer, we can call upon God to release angels to war with us and enforce the judgment already written, but it has to be done righteously.

In Luke 18:1-8, the widow "cried out for her legal rights"; forms of the Greek verb *ekdikeo* (meaning "to vindicate, retaliate, avenge") are used four times in these eight verses. Jesus makes the point that even an uncaring, unrighteous judge would probably give in just because of the widow's persistence. If that is true, then how much more will our heavenly Father give full legal rights to those who cry out to Him day and night? (See Luke 18:7.)

God the judge is already on our side and has longed from the first moment to give us the verdict. But He has to act righteously, and satan has to be given the chance to defend himself against a prosecuting Church. Satan and his angels will accuse the brethren and try to discredit, intimidate, and discourage the witness. Is there sin? Is there any real faith? Is there perseverance? Do we value our lives more than the cause of the Kingdom?

If we are righteous and if we persevere, we will certainly win the case. If we quit before the final verdict is given, satan will get away with it even though we have a perfect legal case. We must persist until the case is finished, and the verdict is given. Once the judgment has been obtained, God can then legally release angelic hosts to work with mankind to enforce the heavenly court order.

Jesus tells this parable so that we should learn how to pray and not to faint (see Luke 18:1). He asks a final pertinent question in verse 8: "When the Son of Man comes, will He really find faith upon the earth?" (Luke 18:8).

THE "MILITARY" BATTLE

The legal battles can be won by just a single individual or by two or three people who know how to intercede. However, when we come to the "military" battles, where we actually go against demonic forces to throw down their strongholds and remove their influence over our city or nation, then there is power in numbers. It is a corporate kind of praying, and prayer generals are needed to lead this kind of praying effectively. In this kind of warfare, prayer, warring praise, and the Scriptures are mighty weapons. We will sometimes be led to go to specific physical locations and drive out the demonic powers who have ruled there from their demonic strongholds. If we command them with authority and faith, then they will have to flee from us.

When we press right through to win a legal battle, angels can then be released to go to war with us to enforce the judgment already given. However, the human agency must not stop praying and thus remove the legal ground for the angels to act. When Michael and Gabriel were wrestling with the princes of Persia and Greece, Daniel's prayers were essential. In the middle of the battle, Gabriel was sent to strengthen him so he could continue praying (see Dan. 10:10-21).

When we have already won the legal battle, then the whole dynamics of the "military" war change dramatically, and we see a real breakthrough. Many bound people are released from satan's captivity to turn to the Lord, and a great harvest can be reaped. The devil and his forces are put on the run because of the power of the angelic hosts that are released to fight with us against them.

Look also at Judges 7:9-23, Second Chronicles 20:17-25, Psalm 149:1-9, and Isaiah 30:29-32. These great Old Testament passages, which have been recorded especially for our instruction, describe amazing victories that were won by the power of warring praise alone. The enemy was totally routed and fled because of powerful, warring praise. The Spirit is anxious to teach and train us to be effective in this kind of prayer warfare.

WAIT IN JERUSALEM UNTIL YOU ARE CLOTHED UPON WITH POWER FROM ON HIGH

Luke finishes his Gospel with the following exhortation in Luke 24:49, "And behold, I am sending forth the promise of My Father upon you; but you are to stay [or tarry, or wait] in the city until you are clothed with power from on high" (Luke 24:49 NASB). The verb *stay* here is *kathizo* in Greek, meaning "to seat down, to settle, to set," that I described to you earlier in this book. Jesus is indicating that you have to become a Christian who knows that you have been raised with Christ and are already comfortably and rightfully seated with Jesus on His throne far above the heavens. You have to be confident of your calling and of your ability and authority to rule with Him; you must realize that you are definitely and permanently clothed with power from on high. Jesus was basically saying, "Don't go anywhere until you get this, and it has really become your experience!"

You need to understand what God has done for you in the resurrection so that you become clothed with power from on high. Otherwise, you won't be any use to Him in establishing the Kingdom.

The great passage on prayer in Luke 11 ends with the Church, as the stronger force, attacking satan or any major demonic principality that is likened to the strongman. This Kingdom Church is able to disarm him and rob him of all his possessions.

P. 63

The city just needs someone to mouth and cry out to see transformation

Humble is denial of self (disinterest in self) and a burning passion for God. It is the denial of self in order to magnify the person & purposes of God.

Establish your own secret place, go alone, shut My door and have your own time with God, really getting to know Him as your Father. The power of everything else you P.75 do will be decided by private prayer time you have alone with God everyday

If you and I do... ...up and...
limited government ideals, this turn to statism will i...
will inherit.

The Heritage Foundation offers a wiser wa...
from President Obama and the liberal leadership i...
honesty back to the markets. One that gets our ec...
gimmicky tax rebates and pork-barrel spending.

Heritage is also urging policymakers to g...
just the easy things like pork barrel projects, but...
increasingly dominate the federal budget.

Heritage reminds government leaders an...
the financial industry is thoroughly dwarfed by t...
entitlement spending will cost our nation in year...

Our nation has to get a handle on these p...
promising way forward.

Chapter 9

THE KINGDOM IN JOHN'S GOSPEL

THE NATURE OF THE KINGDOM

John mentions the Kingdom of God by name only twice, when Jesus exhorted Nicodemus to be "born again" so as to enter the Kingdom (see John 3:3-5). However, John does record how Jesus referred to His Kingdom. He explains its nature and its sphere when Jesus was bearing witness before Pilate (see John 18:36-38). He explains that His Kingdom is "not of this world." If the Kingdom had been of this world, Jesus said that His disciples would have fought in a natural, military way. But the Kingdom's true purpose was to have a powerful, transforming influence upon this world: first, by winning the war in the spirit realm and casting down and cleansing the contaminated lower levels of heaven; then, by powerfully and progressively influencing the earth from a cleansed heaven, so that God's will is increasingly done on earth; finally, by taking over the whole earth and transforming it.

LOVE IN THE KINGDOM

While Luke emphasizes the warring power of the Kingdom and the person of the Holy Spirit, John emphasizes the love of the Kingdom and the person of the Father. By entering the Kingdom at an individual level, we can have an intimate personal relationship with the Father and really know Him on a daily basis, just as Jesus did.

John mentions the Father by name about 150 times in his writings and refers to Him many more times. He speaks many times of the love between the Father and the Son and of the Son's joy in obeying the Father because of that love. John invites us into the same relationship as coequal sons of God through His amazing grace. We are then called to obey the Father to the same degree that Jesus did. We need to be motivated to obey, not only by reverential fear, but much more so because of the love that flows between the Father and any true son.

The Kingdom can only truly function on earth through the benevolent dictatorship of God operating through His delegated human authority. It is a totally submitted relationship to the Father, but because it works through love, it becomes a matter of great joy. Otherwise, it could become very legalistic, distorted, authoritarian, fearful, and overbearing. Now let's look more carefully at John's Gospel and his letters.

John uses the phrase "the Kingdom of God" twice in John 3:3-5, where we are told that we must be born again of the water and of the Spirit in order to enter the Kingdom of God. John is writing his Gospel around A.D. 92-95[1], over 30 years after the other three Gospels. The first three synoptic Gospels were written to evangelize different groups of people. Matthew was written primarily to the Jews to convince them that Jesus was their Messiah, the King of the Kingdom for whom they were eagerly waiting. Mark was written primarily to the Roman world to convince them that someone much greater than Caesar had come and was truly worthy of all worship. Luke wrote primarily to the Greek world to prove that Jesus was that perfect Man for whom they were eagerly looking.

Thirty years later, around A.D. 93, during his exile on the Isle of Patmos, John was moved by the Spirit to write this fourth Gospel. It was not written primarily to evangelize the world. It was written to wake up the Church, to get them into their inheritance, and to urge them to go to war spiritually and become the victorious Kingdom people that God intended them to be.

YOU MUST BE BORN AGAIN

John alone uses the phrase "born again." Peter twice mentions something similar in First Peter 1:3 and First Peter 1:23 when he talks of being born of the "incorruptible seed" of God. A similar phrase "born of God" comes a number of times in John's first letter, and he is the only one to use this term. It is very clear from these writings that this phrase "born again" is not referring primarily to someone who has just had their sins forgiven or has "been saved" in the usual evangelical meaning of the phrase. It is referring to someone who has come powerfully into the Kingdom and whose life has been totally transformed as a result.

According to First John, those who have been born of God are no longer living in defeat but in victory over sin (see 1 John 3:9). They know the love of God and have great love for the brethren (see 1 John 4:7). They have power over the world; they have overcome the devil, and he cannot touch them (see 1 John 5:4,18). These, according to the Word of God, are the marks of someone who is truly "born again."

This phrase "born again" has been greatly devalued by the evangelical world. We need to use it the way John used it in order to produce the right kind of "born again" people who are truly in the Kingdom, living under God's rule, and forcefully advancing the Kingdom against all the opposition of the devil.

KNOWING THE FATHER

John's Gospel emphasizes the relationship of the Son with His Father. Because of the love they have for one another, it is His great joy to obey the Father and to do the Father's will perfectly in everything. Yet at the same time, we are told that Jesus feared (or reverenced) His Father. We need to ponder these things in order to learn how to live in the same relationship with our Father God.

If we preach the Kingdom without the loving fatherhood of God, the Kingdom can seem very severe and harsh. But when we see the Kingdom in terms of a loving Son joyfully obeying a loving Father, then it becomes a delight. It was a wonderful relationship for Him, and Jesus did not find it hard to live in the Kingdom. It is clear in John's Gospel and letters that after Pentecost John himself had come to experience the same relationship. The words that John uses are absolutely amazing at times. For example, in First John 1:3, he tells us that he now "has fellowship" with the Father and with the Son. He now has the same relationship with the Persons of the Godhead that They have among themselves; he now literally shares Their common life. He cries out, "Truly our fellowship is with the Father and with His Son Jesus Christ" (1 John 1:3).

This is a staggering statement for anyone to make: the Father loves the Son, the Son loves the Father, the Holy Spirit loves them both, and now I have been taken into that same love relationship and fellowship with Them. That is what John was claiming. Several times in John's Gospel, Jesus used the same language: The Father loves you in the same way the Father loves Me...and I love you the way I love the Father...come and abide with Us in that love...We (that is the Father, Spirit, and Son) love you, and We will come and make Our permanent dwelling place with you, if you love Me and keep My commandments (see John 14:20,21,23).

So we are being invited to come into fellowship with the Triune God by grace as equal sons of the Father, and we live with the Father in the same way that Jesus did. You and I are not still miserable sinners "saved by grace." You and I have been emancipated by grace into the same relationship with the Father that Jesus had. That is the key to powerful prayer. You must get this truth into your spirit because it will transform your life in every way (see John 16:23-27).

THE SPIRIT SHOWS US THE FATHER

In 1965, just after I was baptized in the Holy Spirit, the Spirit of God visited me in a very definite way; He showed me the Father and the love the Father had for me. This stiff, old, British Baptist was totally melted by that revelation and ran around his

135

study with excited, hysterical joy, crying out, "He loves me! He loves me! Yes, He loves me!" That was 1965, and I have never gotten over that experience. It gets more real and deeper all the time. That was when it began—when I discovered that God loved Alan Vincent personally, and not just lost sinners in general!

God is not interested in just saving souls in an impersonal way. He wants to love us and have a personal relationship with us. He wants to know us, and He wants us to know Him and love Him the same way the Persons of the Godhead love each other. He wants to mend our broken relationship with Him fully. He wants that relationship to be so mended that the relationship we have with Him by grace is much better than the relationship that Adam enjoyed with God in his innocence before he sinned. He wants our relationship to be the same as the one that Jesus had and still has with the Father. It's staggering, almost unbelievable, but it's true!

You have to ask yourself these honest questions: Do I know the Father the way Jesus knew Him? Do I really know that the Father loves me the way He loves Jesus? Do I want to know Him like that? Will I pay the price to get there?

When you come fully into this relationship, your security is in that relationship—not in any position you may hold, or any work that you do for Him. If I never preached or did anything in public again, it would not trouble me at all because my security and my fulfillment are in my relationship with Him. Much of the competitiveness in the body of Christ is caused by insecurity through the lack of the knowledge of this relationship. To totally obey someone who loves you so much is not a hard thing to do; it is always absolute joy.

So I love my Father, and my Father loves me. In fact, He loves me so much that He loves to manifest Himself to me. It seems that He has trouble keeping His hands off me! That may sound strange, but there are certain experiences we can have with God which almost defy verbal explanation. In my case, God's manifest presence can sometimes become so intense that it is as if He physically wraps His arms around me, and then I just melt in those wonderful arms.

Just after my first great experience with God, I was lecturing in the Institute of Printing Technology in Mumbai. I was teaching a science class, and I was writing some chemical formulae on the chalkboard. I had a large group of very respectful students taking down their notes. I wasn't in some great church meeting with an incredible atmosphere; I was just writing chemical formulae on a chalkboard in a college classroom. Suddenly, God just came and wrapped His arms around me in the middle of this lecture, and I could not continue. I was completely overwhelmed with the love of God. I said to Him, "Not now, Lord, you're spoiling the lecture." He didn't seem to care. He just wanted to love me. This is the wonderful relationship I now have with Him.

INTIMACY AND FEAR GO TOGETHER

Yet, at the same time, there is an appropriate reverence. This love does not lead to a wrong familiarity or lack of reverence, but there is a fear that goes with this love. The balance of this is very hard to describe, but what I am talking about is perfectly portrayed in the life of Jesus. He deeply loved His Father and yet reverenced Him at the same time.

I reverence God. He is the Almighty Creator of Heaven and earth. He's the Creator of everything seen and unseen. Myriads of angels worship Him, and I also stand in awe or fall on my face before Him in adoring worship. Sometimes it is love that motivates me, and sometimes it is fear that motivates me. The apostle Paul talks about these two things within a few verses of each other in Second Corinthians 5. In verse 11 he says, "Knowing therefore, the terror of the Lord, we persuade men" (2 Cor. 5:11). In verse 14 he continues, "For the love of Christ compels us" (2 Cor. 5:14). It urges us, or pushes us on in some powerful way. So Paul also had this double motivation, the fear and the love of God were compelling him always to do the will of God.

Let's now come to Jesus, at the end of His ministry. In His last great teaching, usually called the Upper Room discourse, which we read of in John chapters 13-17, Jesus is having His last evening with His disciples. The next day He will die on the cross. This is His last chance to speak intimately with His beloved disciples. Obviously, if you knew that you were going to be executed tomorrow and that this was your last evening with your family, you would not spend your time speaking about trivial things. You would concentrate on the most important things. So, it is interesting to see the things Jesus focused on in this discourse.

His major theme was the great coming of the Holy Spirit, the Helper who could only come to them if Jesus departed. This was such an important event that Jesus frequently called it "that day." When "that day" came, they would have fantastic, new revelation of the Scripture, they would be empowered, and then all kinds of wonderful things would be accomplished through them. However, one of the most important things Jesus told them was that when the Spirit came He would "show them the Father." In John 16:25 Jesus said, "These things I have spoken to you in figurative language; but the time is coming when I will no longer speak to you in figurative language, but I will tell you [or show you] plainly about the Father" (see John 16:25).

The tragedy of this generation is that very few have a satisfactory experience with their human fathers. Many have no idea what good fatherhood is like, even in natural terms. To know the fatherhood of God is far greater than the best of human experiences, but it is incomprehensible until the Spirit comes.

Jesus tried to explain it in words to them, in the best figurative language He could find, but that explanation did not bring them the real revelation. I feel the same thing while writing this book. I want you to pray for a revelation of the Father by the Holy Spirit that will produce the same effect in you as it did in me all those years ago. Women, just as much as men, need a healthy, glorious revelation of what the real fatherhood of God is like. This is the absolute foundation of the Kingdom.

THE KINGDOM OF GOD RUNS ON FATHERHOOD

God designed the Church to run on fatherhood. God has designed society, politics, government, and indeed all human relationships to run on fatherhood. We don't need professional politicians so much as we need fathers. And God so designed the natural family that it only really works with proper fatherhood. In fact, in the Greek language, there is no separate word for family. The Greek word used for family is *patria* which means a sphere of someone's fatherhood. Without functioning fatherhood, there can be no real family. That is how fundamental this is. We have a generation that is bereft of fatherhood and deprived of the security and love of a real family. Apart from salvation, to truly know the Father is the greatest need in every human being's life. That is why the last words of the Old Testament are a promise that God will send the spirit of Elijah to restore fatherhood (see Mal. 4:6). There cannot be a manifestation of the Kingdom of God without true fatherhood.

A KINGDOM OF SONS

We cannot enter the Kingdom except we enter as a son who willingly and lovingly obeys his Father. We are told in Romans 8:15 and Galatians 4:6 that when the Spirit of God comes He will come into our hearts crying, "Abba, Father." *Abba* is a Hebrew word of intimacy like "daddy" in English. The Greek word *pater* for father is a word of respect, recognizing the authority and headship of the father of the family. So, we have both the concept of intimacy and the concept of reverence in the cry of the Spirit. The Spirit of God has come to reveal the Father to us as one of His main purposes. In Romans 8:15 one of the names for the Holy Spirit is "the Spirit of adoption." He cries, "You are my very own son." Now you, by the same Spirit, can cry back in response, "Daddy, Father."

Galatians 3:26 says, "You are all sons of God through faith in Christ Jesus." For those who are not familiar with Greek, this word *son* or *huios* does not have a male only gender connotation as it does in English and many other languages. It is emphasizing the relationship, not the gender. You have to put a prefix on the Greek word for son in order to make it restrictively male or female. In Greek you can have male and female "sons of God," but the phrase "daughters of God" is not used even once in the New Testament. In the next two verses (Gal. 3:27-28), Paul goes on to say that in this respect of sonship there is neither Jew nor Greek, slave nor free, male nor female but we are all one in Christ.

Many Scriptures that we have thought to be men's domain are equally applicable to both men and women in Christ. There are a variety words that come across masculine in our English translations that are not restrictively masculine in Greek. The word *"anthropos,"* although masculine, is often used to represent the whole human race, male and female in the same way we use the word "mankind" in English. When talking of a man in particular the distinctly male word *"aner"* is used.

In a similar way the word *"brother"* (*adelphos*) is used to represent both men and women who are siblings of the same family. Frequently the word *"brother"* or *"brethren"* (*adelphos*) is used to address both men and women in the church, as we see in First Corinthians 14:23-26: "Therefore if the whole church comes together in one place... How is it then, brethren? Whenever you come together each one of you has a psalm...."

Occasionally *brethren* is narrowed down to refer to men only, in which case the Greek says *aner* (a distinctly male word). It is interesting to note the occasions where *aner* is used. Here are some examples: "Therefore brethren [adelphos], seek out from among you seven men [aner] of good reputation..." (Acts 6:3); "God...now commands all men [anthropos] everywhere to repent.... He will judge the world in righteousness by the Man [aner] who He has ordained" (Acts 17:30-31).

As we become sons of God, we become mature, we become like our Father, and we become heirs of all our Father has given us in Christ whether we are male or female. Until this revelation comes, we are not able to live fully in the Kingdom, and we certainly cannot advance the Kingdom.

Jesus was deeply concerned that His disciples should have this revelation. Similarly, the apostle Paul in his letter to the Ephesians, after setting forth all the glory and power of this Kingdom, writes, "For this reason, I bow my knees before the Father, from whom every family [*pas patria*] in heaven and on earth derives its name" (see Eph. 3:14-15 NIV). So, Paul also wanted us to have the revelation of family through fatherhood, and to live exactly like Jesus, as a son extravagantly loved by his Father—as a son knowing his Father, loving his Father, fearing his Father, joyfully obeying his Father, and as a result being determined always to do whatever the Father says.

Jesus said that His very food was to do the will of His Father (see John 4:34). In essence He was saying, "I do nothing of my own initiative. What I see the Father do, I do with Him in the same way." John 5:30 suggests that Jesus heard in His spirit, just like us, all the various sounds and voices in the spirit realm, but He never made a mistake in hearing His Father's voice. He said, "As I hear, I judge, and My judgment is righteous" (John 5:30). What a statement! Jesus was saying, "I have never missed my Father's voice, not even once. I have never heard the voice of my Father God and confused it with something else. I've always heard the Father perfectly, and I've always done His will perfectly." Jesus gave the reason that this was possible. He said, "...because I do not seek My own will but the will of the Father who sent Me" (John 5:30). That is the Kingdom, and that is how God has called us all to live in it.

So without the revelation of fatherhood there cannot be any real understanding of the Kingdom. Once we have comprehended His overwhelming love in that relationship, then living under the rule of this loving Father is not hard, but is utter and complete joy. If you have never had that revelation, then you need to pray for it. Then God will come to you, as He came to me and to many others, and show you the Father. I have seen so many lives, of both men and women, transformed by that revelation.

THE PRIVILEGES AND RESPONSIBILITIES OF SONSHIP

Galatians 3:26 tells us that we "are all sons of God through faith in Christ Jesus." There are four main aspects to actually living as a son of God rather than as an immature babe.

1. Sons Have a Relationship

If we are going to advance the Kingdom, it is very important that we understand the importance of our relationship as sons to the Father. Jesus taught us how to pray Kingdom prayers. It is all there in Matthew chapter 6:

> *Our Father in heaven, hallowed be Your name. Your Kingdom come. Your will be done on earth as it is in heaven. Give us this day our daily bread. And forgive us our debts, as we forgive our debtors. And do not lead us into temptation, but deliver us from the evil one.... For if you forgive men their trespasses, your heavenly Father will also forgive you. But if you do not forgive men their trespasses, neither will your Father forgive your trespasses* (Matthew 6:9-15).

Understanding Jesus' relationship to the Father will dramatically change not only the way we pray, but also our understanding of how we can forcefully advance the Kingdom. Because of His work on the cross, we have been brought into this same glorious relationship of sonship with the Father. In the Galatian letter, we read that the Spirit is in us crying out, "Abba, Father!" (see Gal. 4:6). In fact, it is impossible to pray effectively without this revelation. Once we have this revelation we can learn to pray like Jesus and see the same 100 percent success in our prayer life because the Father will always hear and answer the prayer of His sons.

2. Sons Have Rights

We must learn that there is all the difference in the world between being a petitioner and being a son. If you pray as a petitioner, you might get an answer. But if you pray as a son, your Father must hear and answer you. That is why Jesus said that if you are going to learn to pray, you must start with a relationship and be able to say from the heart, "My Father..." Then you can expect your Father God to answer every one of your prayers just as He did for Jesus.

Please understand this: sons have a relationship, and they have rights. Fathers have to answer sons, and fathers have to provide for their sons because sons have a claim upon their fathers. Jesus said that if evil fathers know this, how much more will your heavenly Father give good gifts to those who ask Him? (See Matthew 7:11 and Luke 11:13.)

When Jesus stood outside the tomb of Lazarus, He prayed as a son. He cried out with a loud voice, "Father, I thank You that You have heard Me. And I know that You always hear Me..." (John 11:41-42). Jesus didn't speak loudly because God was deaf, but because He wanted the people around Him to hear and understand why He always got His prayers answered. When a son prays to a father, the father must answer. If he does not, he is not a father.

3. Sons Have Resources

I learned another related lesson about being a son of God in Mumbai in 1965. In 1963 Eileen and I went to Mumbai as "Faith Missionaries." We did not receive a salary from Gospel Literature Service where I was working, and we did not receive any support from any mission organization. We just trusted God to supply our need. I was taught by others that I therefore needed to pray earnestly every day for God to supply the needs of my family.

One day I was relaxing at home, watching Eileen iron some shirts. She came to one shirt belonging to our son Duncan and pointed out it was frayed at the collar and needed replacing. Right away, I said, "Get him a new shirt. He needs it." God immediately spoke to me and said, "What kind of Father do you think I am?" I replied, "What do You mean, Lord?" God said, "Well, look at the way you treat your son. He doesn't even know he needs a new shirt and already you have made provision to get him one without him having to ask you even once. He doesn't have to get on his knees and plead with you. You just see his need and supply it. Have I not said in My Word that before you ask I will already have provided for you? So why do you treat Me like this? Stop crying out to Me every day in this way. From now on, just thank Me. I will always be faithful and supply your every need even before you ask, because I have promised that I will be a Father to you."

Since then I have never petitioned God to supply my needs. Since then I have never prayed to have my basic needs met. Now, I just thank my Father because He is faithful. I know I am His son by grace, and He will always meet my needs. Now I can concentrate on praying for other people and other things rather than for myself. I do not need to pray for myself. My Father loves me, and everything my Father has is mine. Amen!

If you really believe that, you do not pray like a petitioner, but you pray like a son. Sons have a relationship. Sons have a right to be answered. All that the Father has is available to the son. That is Kingdom living.

4. Sons Have Responsibilities

The fourth thing we need to see is that you cannot have the privileges of sonship without the responsibilities of sonship. My son had the privileges of sonship, but he also had the responsibilities of sonship. He had to obey me and do what I told him to do because he was my son. You cannot have the relationship and the privileges of sonship without accepting the responsibilities, which means you must be obedient.

Let's look again at Jesus' prayer outside of Lazarus' tomb. Jesus had earlier taught His disciples how to pray as sons and say "Our Father" to Almighty God (see Luke 11:1-4); He now deliberately modeled the prayer of a son for His disciples and all who were gathered to mourn for Lazarus. In essence, He was saying, "Listen! There's a rotting corpse in the tomb. I've already asked My Father to raise Lazarus from the dead, and He has already heard Me and said, 'Yes.' So I'm just going to the tomb now to speak that answered prayer into physical manifestation."

Jesus did not strive in His prayer. He prayed in a loud voice so that everybody could hear, "Father, I thank You that You always hear Me" (John 11:41). He did not just pray about the situation; He had already prayed privately and got His Father's answer. Instead, in obedience as a son, He spoke one simple sentence of command! He did not speak hesitantly or hopefully, "La-La-La-Lazarus, c-c-come out." He already knew that His Father would raise Lazarus. As a son of obedience, He just spoke a word of firm, certain commandment, "Lazarus, come out!" and Lazarus immediately came forth.

ENDNOTE

1. The precise date of John's Gospel is uncertain, but many scholars such as Hendrickson, Berkhof and Thompson quote Ireneus and Clement, who were disciples of Polycarp, a young man who became a disciple of John the apostle after his release. They place the writing of John's Gospel around A.D. 95-96 in Ephesus. He probably had written the Book of Revelation about A.D. 92, while still in exile. The three letters of John are usually dated shortly before his release from Patmos around A.D. 95. In Second John 12 and Third John 14, John is joyfully anticipating his imminent release. The Gospel of John was then written shortly afterward.

Chapter 10

THE LEVELS OF THE KINGDOM

Now I want to look at the actual coming of the Kingdom in the New Testament. The Lord has shown me that there were different levels at which the Kingdom came into the Church, and they all appeared within the first 30 years. It was not until the final phase came that Europe was shaken to its foundations and became the first Christian continent in the world. When you look at the global Church today, you can see all of the phases functioning simultaneously to different degrees in different places.

There is still a sizable group of Christians who do not believe in the possibility of the Kingdom coming to any degree until after Christ's return. They are programmed to believe there is nothing we can do but accept the worsening situation in the world today.

In their view, it is only after His second coming that anything will change, and only then will His Kingdom be manifested on the earth. But I am primarily writing to those who have seen the Kingdom at least in some measure. As a result, they are motivated to see the Kingdom come with power and so hasten the day of the return of our Lord Jesus Christ.

I find it hard to be dogmatic as to how much we will be able to accomplish before the glorious appearing of our mighty King and how much He will do Himself after His return to complete all things. But there are many promises to encourage us, and there are great rewards promised to those who are found busy about our Master's business of establishing His Kingdom at His return. So even if He takes us by surprise, biblically, it is still the best way to be occupying our time on earth until He comes.

LEVEL 1: THE JOHN THE BAPTIST PHASE— PROCLAMATION WITHOUT MANIFESTATION

Proclamation without manifestation simply means that someone can talk about the Kingdom and to some extent tell us what it should look like, but they cannot make it actually happen. When John the Baptist began his ministry, the first words out of his mouth were "Repent, for the kingdom of heaven is at hand!" (Matt. 3:2). While John the Baptist could proclaim the Kingdom vigorously, he never saw any manifestation of the Kingdom, and he never entered into the Kingdom while he was on earth. He was never able to demonstrate the Kingdom of God or see it manifested with power through his ministry. That is one reason why Jesus said, "The least in the kingdom of God is greater than John the Baptist" (see Matt. 11:11).

At this level, it is a powerless, theoretical, proclamation of the Kingdom. There is no manifestation of it on earth and no authority over the demonic principalities and powers that resist its manifestation. It is dangerous to rebuke major demonic strongholds without the power to overcome the demons that subsequently come against you. John the Baptist was bold enough to speak plainly concerning the evils of his day, but he was not powerful enough to cast demonic spirit powers down and bring about political, religious, and social change.

In my opinion, most evangelical and charismatic churches are living in what I have come to call "John the Baptist" Christianity. They can deplore the evil of our day and speak against it, but they can't change it or overcome it. What's even worse is that when they do try to overcome demonic powers through spiritual warfare, political activism, or some other means, they don't win. Instead, the demonic powers overcome them, and they run away wounded and defeated.

The first example of this kind of battle in the Old Testament occurs when Elijah came and rebuked King Ahab and Queen Jezebel for their evil, immoral, and idolatrous behavior. Jezebel was controlled by a spirit that was a mighty ruling principality, behind many of the great heathen empires. It was not just Jezebel who came against Elijah; the high-ranking demon who controlled her was outraged that this bold prophet dared to speak against it. As a result of this confrontation, Elijah suddenly went into a deep depression. He then ran away, wished for his own death, and never came back again into his full warring, prophetic ministry (see 1 Kings 19).

An almost identical thing happened to John the Baptist when he came against King Herod and his immoral relationship with

Herodias. The Scriptures say that John came in the power of the spirit of Elijah (see Luke 1:17). It was the Elijah spirit in John engaging the same high-ranking demonic spirit in Herodias. John the Baptist did not win that battle either. He was defeated and ended up in prison. But what was even worse was the total depression and disillusionment that came upon him.

He was the first person to declare who Jesus really was. In the first chapter of John's Gospel, he declared very boldly that Jesus was God's Son, the Lamb of God who takes away the sin of the world (see John 1:29). John also declared that He was the one who would baptize with the Holy Spirit and with fire (see Matt. 3:11; Luke 16). He had incredible revelation, and it was a powerful declaration. He had been preaching and telling the crowds, "I indeed baptize you with water unto repentance, but He who is coming after me is mightier than I, whose sandals I am not worthy to carry" (Matt. 3:11). When John was asked to baptize Jesus, he said, "I need to be baptized by You, and are You coming to me?" (Matt. 3:14). He knew who Jesus was. He knew Jesus was the Messiah, the Bridegroom of the Church. He knew Jesus was the one the prophets had spoken about for centuries. Yet in Matthew 11, you find this same John in prison, totally disillusioned, and asking the following question of Jesus: "Are You the Coming One, or do we look for another?" (Matt. 11:3). What a question to ask!

Looking back over several decades of ministry, I could make a list of men I have known over the years who have suffered this way. They were courageous and bold enough to speak out against the wrong things in their day, but because they were not properly equipped for the demonic counterattack that followed, they became casualties rather than victors. Those who are still alive no longer have an effective ministry and are doing very little except licking their wounds in semi-retirement.

It almost happened to me once, so I know a little of what it feels like. These people give up and start to talk "John the Baptist" talk. They say, "Maybe I will find something else to live for. The Kingdom of God is not what I thought it was. The Kingdom has not come as powerfully or as quickly as I thought it should. The powers of darkness seem to be getting stronger, and the Kingdom of God doesn't seem to be having much effect upon them. This Kingdom stuff is not changing my world; it is not changing my city. Maybe I should look for something else."

These are the symptoms of John the Baptist Christianity. Many Christians are carrying this disease right now, and as a result much of the Christian world is living in that kind of disillusionment. It is nothing more than deep disappointment resulting from the inability to make things come to pass that they once knew and believed to be true.

Two things particularly mark this powerless phase of the Kingdom:

1. John Did No Miracles

John 10:41 says, "John performed no sign, but all the things that John spoke about this Man were true." He accurately taught who Jesus was and described everything about the Kingdom perfectly, but could not demonstrate its power. This is description without demonstration. That is "John the Baptist" Christianity. You accurately teach the truths about the Kingdom, but without any power and without anything miraculous happening. Let me say this clearly: *If your ministry is without power and there are no miraculous manifestations of the Kingdom, you are not really in the Kingdom of God.*

2. John Was Not That Light

In John 5:35 Jesus testified about John the Baptist saying, *"John was a lamp that burned and gave light, and you chose for a time to enjoy his light"* (John 5:35 NIV). Jesus affirms that John the Baptist was a lamp that burned and gave light. But notice the way the word "light" is used in John 1:4. John the apostle begins by speaking about Jesus, *"In Him was life, and the life was the light of men"* (John 1:4). We are told very plainly that the life of Jesus was "the light" that came into the world.

The life Jesus lived before men is described as the light of men. Then in verse 6, the apostle John's testimony concerning John the Baptist begins, "There was a man sent from God, whose name was John. This man came for a witness, *to bear witness of the Light*, that all through him might believe" (John 1:6-7). Now notice verse 8 very carefully, *"He was not that Light, but was sent to bear witness of that Light"* (John 1:8). John the Baptist was able to point to Jesus as the Light of the World. John the Baptist himself was *a* burning light, but we are told very clearly that he was not *that* light.

Because John the Baptist could not live a life like Jesus, he could not be that light. He was *a powerful light*, bearing witness to the true light, but he never became *that light*. However, when Jesus spoke about Himself, He said, "I am the light of the world. He who follows Me shall not walk in darkness, but have the light of life" (John 8:12).

Amazingly, when Jesus spoke of the Church, He said exactly the same things about the Church that He said about Himself.

He said to the Kingdom Church, "*You are the light of the world*" (Matt. 5:14). When He pointed to John the Baptist he said, "No, he is not that light. He is a great light, but he's not that light." But when He turned to the Kingdom Church, He said, "You are that light!" The true Kingdom Church is clearly called to be that light and live a life just like Jesus.

Some evangelicals like to say, "Don't look at me or my life: I am just a sinner saved by grace. I can't show you anything supernatural in my life or my works. Don't look at me; look to Jesus." While it is true that of ourselves we can do absolutely nothing, once we are indwelt by God, He has declared that He can do amazing things through our surrendered humanity.

THE KINGDOM IS POWER

First Corinthians 4:20 says, "for the kingdom of God is not in word but in power." If you go through the New Testament, there is a tremendous group of Greek words for power. These words are all derivatives from the word *dunamai*, "to be able, to have power." The nouns are *dunamis* ("power, might, strength"); *dunastes* ("a ruler, a potentate"); *dunatos* ("strong, mighty, powerful"). Then there are two verbs: *dunamoo* ("to make strong, enable"); and *dunateo* ("to be able, to be powerful"). These are all words of power. These words in their various forms occur over 350 times in the New Testament. It is interesting to see how these words are translated. One hundred sixteen times they are translated simply by the English word "power."

One of these six words is often used to describe God and what He can do. But the New Testament uses exactly the same six words almost an equal number of times to describe Kingdom

Christians and what they can do! The Word puts us and God into the same category once the power of the Kingdom has come into us by His Spirit.

Fifty-four times *dunamai* is translated as "able," which also means "powerfully capable." We are told God is *able* (dunamai) to do exceedingly abundantly above all we can ask or think according to the *power* (dunamis) that works in us (see Eph. 3:20).

Twelve times *dunatos* is translated as the word "possible." We are told "with God all things are possible [dunatos]" (Matt. 19:26), and we are also told "all things are possible [dunatos] to him who believes" (Mark 9:23). There is no doubt that God can do it, but then the New Testament says the same thing about the believer. What is possible for God is possible for the believer provided he or she is correctly related to God, filled with His Spirit, and is in His Kingdom doing His will.

This was never said about John the Baptist. He could point to Jesus, proclaim Jesus, and admire Him, but there was no way he could become like Him and do His works. However, when the Scripture turns from John the Baptist to a Kingdom believer, it begins to say the same things about the believer that it has been saying about Jesus, provided the believer is filled with His risen life and lives the same life of obedience.

The trouble is that most of the Church does not believe it. Most Christians are quite content to be "John the Baptist" Christians. They are content to teach accurately things concerning Jesus, but they do not attempt to live like Him. What is the good of teaching these things accurately when you can't live that way? There is a power in the Kingdom that brings us into the actual practice of what we believe and teach.

Look particularly at John's first letter. He's writing to the believers in Asia and particularly to the church in Ephesus. They were not advancing the Kingdom at all. They were just holding on while all kinds of demonic fury were coming against them. John wanted so much to strengthen and steady them. In his first letter, John uses the Greek word for fellowship (*koinonia*), which has two important dimensions to its meaning. First, it means "*to be joined together in a common life*." So, here's a paraphrase of John's words in First John 1:1-3: "I, the Father, and the Son, all have one common life. It is the eternal life of the eternal God. We first saw it in Jesus. We touched it. We heard it. We looked intently upon it. This same eternal life that is the life of the Father was manifested to us in the Son, and we're now able to show it to you. We write these things to you that you may come and be joined together in a common life with us. We want you to come and participate in this one eternal life of the living God. For truly our fellowship (our common life), is with the Father and with his Son, Jesus Christ."

Can you imagine Jesus, after He was anointed, just walking around for weeks doing nothing supernatural? No! So start thinking of yourself in the same way. If you can learn how to deeply draw on that life, then you will powerfully manifest that life. If I do not see something miraculous working through me frequently, if not every day, then I must ask myself, "What's wrong with me?" I know it is never me doing the miracles. I know I'm just a channel for God to work through. But if many days pass without God flowing through me to glorify His Name, then something is wrong with me. There are vast needs everywhere, so I must ask myself the question: why is God not using me to meet those needs?

157

Most of the Christian world doesn't even believe this. If we get sick our first instinct is to go and get some natural help or at best go and get someone else to pray for us. My wife and I never do this. If she wakes up with some excruciating pain, then I lay my hands on her, and expect her to be healed right away. The same is true in her response to me. We just live this way. Whether it is cancer or a backache, it is all the same to God. Whether it is a financial need or any other need, there is all sufficient power in our living God. Again and again we have seen God immediately answer.

The second meaning of the word *koinonia* is *"to be joined together in a common purpose."* God has one intention, one passion that overrules every other passion. Jesus taught it very clearly, and we sing about it frequently. His passion was and still is to see His Kingdom come on earth and His will be done on earth as it is in Heaven. Everything else is secondary to that one primary passion. The Father wants to see Jesus, the King of the Kingdom, glorified over the whole earth. That is His passion. So if I am having fellowship with God, I will be joined together with Him in the same purpose. Because God is a fanatic about these things, I am a fanatic about these things. I am not a bit interested in who wins the World Soccer Cup or the NFL Super Bowl. I cannot waste my time on such unimportant stuff. I want to see His Kingdom come!

Most of the evangelical world believes we will get eternal life, but only after we get to Heaven. I would rather be empowered now, because then I can do something about this sin-sick, needy world all around me. Once I get to Heaven, I can only be a spectator to what other people are doing on earth. I can cheer them on, but I cannot participate with them. I would rather stay on earth and be part of the victorious advance of the Kingdom. I have no desperate anxiety to get to Heaven prematurely. God and I have a job to do on earth. We are in fellowship together. We share a common life, and we share a common purpose.

John the Baptist never lived that way. While he prepared the way for Jesus and spoke about the coming Kingdom, he was not able to minister *in* the Kingdom—or see widespread transformation. In the end, the dark, demonic powers of his day attempted to wear him down in doubt and disillusionment, prompting him to ask Jesus, "Are You the Coming One, or do we look for another?" (Matt. 11:2). Jesus sent John's disciples back with these words: "Go and tell John the things which you hear and see: The blind see and the lame walk; the lepers are cleansed and the deaf hear; the dead are raised up and the poor have the gospel preached to them. And blessed is he who is not offended because of Me" (Matt. 11:4-6). Jesus reassured John with a testimony of His Kingdom works, and He said of him to the multitude, "Among those born of women there has not risen one greater than John the Baptist" (Matt. 11:11).

What John sought to do by his dedicated, natural zeal was probably a thousand times better than what had been accomplished by any other natural man or woman. We are told that he was anointed with the Holy Spirit from his mother's womb, so he was not without the Spirit. But he was not in the Kingdom. It says he was born of a woman, but he was not yet born from above. What we see in John the Baptist is the best that anyone in that pre-Kingdom category can be.

Jesus gave him great honor but also clearly declared the limitation of such a lifestyle and such a relationship. Jesus was saying that the least person who is truly in the Kingdom of Heaven is greater than John the Baptist (see Matt. 11:11).

Jesus had to wait for John the Baptist's ministry to finish before he could bring the Kingdom in with power. So let's agree that we don't want to live in "John the Baptist Christianity." Let's agree that we don't just want to be part of a Church that can accurately teach the truth concerning Jesus and yet not be able to do any miracles in His name. We are here to change our world.

LEVEL 2: JESUS WITH THE POWER OF PROCLAMATION AND MANIFESTATION ON EARTH

We have already seen how in the beginning Adam and Eve, living in obedience to God in their innocence, were the first real manifestation of the Kingdom on earth. Once they stepped out from obedient dependence into independence, they left the Kingdom of God and from then on only had their own ability, strength, and wisdom to live by. They immediately became victims of the devil. The devil took control of them. They were forcefully subjected and became prisoners of the kingdom of darkness. Because they had been given the responsibility to rule over all creation, satan could, through them, establish his kingdom over all the earth, corrupting and perverting everything God had made.

Remember: *satan cannot work on earth without human beings cooperating with him.* Most people do it unconsciously, but a few people are so deceived that they consciously work for satan. God could have made the decision to wipe out the whole kingdom of darkness and start again. Instead, He decided that He would give mankind the opportunity to voluntarily come back into the Kingdom and once again live under the rule and government of God. He would then bring the whole of creation back into Kingdom order and purity under man's delegated authority. In order to do this righteously, it was necessary that mankind be saved by a man and that the Kingdom of God in this world be reclaimed from the devil by a man.

In Isaiah 59:15-21, God declared that He Himself would become the man: "He saw that there was no man, and wondered that there was no intercessor; therefore His own arm brought salvation for Him; and His own righteousness, it sustained Him" (Isa. 59:16). So in the great mystery of the incarnation, God shrunk Himself into the limitations of the same humanity that Adam had before he sinned. For that to be righteous, it was necessary that He be born of a woman. We are told categorically in Galatians chapter 4 that in order to accomplish this, He had to be born of a woman and born under the law (see Gal. 4:4). He had to pay the redemption price for all the sin of Adam's race and for all the sins of the Jewish people against the law of God.

JESUS BECOMES GOD'S FIRST HUMAN SON

The Greek word *huios*, usually translated "son," is the only word used for the Lord Jesus in regards to sonship. This particular word for son (*huios*) has three dimensions to its meaning. First, it has the idea of full-grown adult maturity; secondly, father-likeness; and thirdly, the receiving of a designated inheritance. In the culture of the Bible, you did not wait for your father to die to get your inheritance. To get your inheritance, you served your father in perfect obedience for 30 years. If on your 30th birthday your father declared he was well pleased with your obedience, then you were legally entitled to your inheritance. You could go to your father and say, "Father, I have served you with obedience for 30 years. Can I have my inheritance, please?" He was then legally required to give it to you.

Jesus had to fulfill the conditions of sonship, serving His Father with perfect obedience for 30 years, before the Father could legally pour out upon Him all the resources and power of the Kingdom. Only then would Jesus be free to use those resources legally upon earth. That was what Jesus was doing for the first 30 years of his life. For 30 years, He had to prove His obedience and fulfill all the just requirements of the law.

COMPLETE IDENTIFICATION

When Jesus came to His 30th birthday, He went immediately to the waters of the Jordan to be baptized by John the Baptist (see Matt. 3:13-17). He was not baptized to wash away His sins, since He had none. Nor was He burying His old man—because He didn't have one. He was not being baptized into a church because He was the Church. It was a baptism of identification into Adam.

As Jesus came and was baptized by John, the Father cried out from Heaven, "At last! I have a human Son with whom I am well pleased. He has served Me faithfully with perfect obedience for 30 years. I can legally confer on Him all the vast resources of Heaven. Son, all I have is Yours! There is not an angel or resource in Heaven that is not available to You! Because You are a man, You can legally call all those resources down to earth to empower You to establish the Kingdom of God." However, there was one additional test.

THE BATTLE OF THE WILDERNESS

On the heels of His 30th birthday, a great battle of faith occurred. Before Jesus could functionally move into His inheritance as a Son, He had to win a battle of faith in order to access those resources. So Jesus went into the wilderness to be tested by the devil.

We are told in Luke 4:1 that Jesus went into the wilderness full of the Holy Spirit, and in Luke 4:14 that *He returned in the power of the Holy Spirit.* Then He began His miraculous ministry. In no time at all, He was shaking the whole kingdom of darkness and giving us a demonstration of what happens to a man who, by faith, has really become the Son of God on earth. While He lived that life by faith, the power of God flowed through Him.

This also works for us, but there is no time requirement for us; we don't have to wait 30 years. Once you have been truly born again, you can become God's son by faith, with immediate, full access to your inheritance the moment you decide to believe it. It says in Galatians 3:26 that "You are all sons [*huios*] of God through faith in Christ Jesus." In this respect there is neither Jew nor Greek, slave nor free, male nor female, for you are all one in Christ Jesus (see Gal. 3:28). There is no ethnic, social, or gender divisions at all. It is simply a matter faith.

However, if the devil had the arrogance to test the faith of Jesus, what do you think he will do with you? He will try to get you to doubt so you never actually function as a son of God with power. Most Spirit-filled believers never move in power because they have never fought and won the battle of faith in the wilderness.

Jesus came to earth and began a war to restore all things (see Acts 3:21). In Matthew 11:12 we see Jesus as the first man to forcefully advance the Kingdom of God. That was the only way the Kingdom could be advanced and still is. It takes violent men to forcefully advance the Kingdom. And some of the most violent "men" I know are women. This is not a matter of gender but of sonship.

Jesus began the recovery by restoring what Adam had lost. Jesus had power and authority, but notice that at this level (prior to His resurrection), His authority was limited to earth. You find this phrase in a number of places in Scripture describing this limitation. Jesus said in Luke 5:24, "But that you may know that the Son of Man has *authority on earth* to forgive sins" (Luke 5:24 NIV).

During this second phase of the Kingdom coming to earth, we have the first man empowered with Kingdom authority on earth. Jesus had recovered what Adam had lost, but that authority did not yet extend into the heavenlies. While He was on earth, His authority was confined to Adam's original domain: the earth.

JESUS DELEGATES HIS KINGDOM AUTHORITY AND POWER

In Luke chapter 9, Jesus accelerated the advance of the Kingdom by empowering the 12 apostles to move in the power of the Kingdom. When I was pondering that years ago, I asked, "Lord, how did You do that? How did You empower them with the power of the Kingdom when You had not yet paid for their sins at the cross?" This is what the Lord said to me, "I used My Calvary credit card." Jesus claimed the power of Calvary in advance because He was already crucified and risen in the eternal realm of the Spirit. He was already credited with the full redemption price, which He promised to pay on the "due date" when He went to the cross.

STEPPING INTO THE ETERNAL REALM

Sometimes we have to get out of the structures of time and into eternity in order to understand spiritual things. The Bible tells us that Jesus was crucified before the foundation of the world (see Rev. 13:8). As we have already explained, although there was a historic moment in time when it happened, the power of the cross has always filled eternity. From any point in time, a regenerate man can enter eternity by his spirit man and grab hold of eternal things that are outside of time. They are already in eternity even if they have not yet happened in time. They have been spoken into existence by the eternal Word of God. In exactly the same way, by the spirit, a regenerate person can grab hold of things that happened long ago with an ever fresh now!

This kind of language is used in the Book of Hebrews. It speaks of Jesus as the permanently, freshly slain Lamb of God. Hebrews 10:20 literally says, "a new and living, freshly slain way." There is an eternal freshness about the cross that fills eternity and reaches from the beginning to the end of time. There never was or will be a need for any other sacrifice. From the beginning to the end of time, it fills eternity and is available to anyone who will believe!

The Word of God has the same eternal quality. God spoke at various times through the prophets, and then He spoke definitively through His Son (see Heb. 1:1-3). There were points in time when certain words were spoken. However, once a word was spoken, because of the nature of God's Word, it immediately became eternal. Once it has been spoken, God's Word hangs there, throbbing with eternal life in the spirit realm. His Word never gets old or irrelevant. At any point in time, anyone, through his spirit man, can get hold of anything God has spoken, because His Word is always freshly spoken in the spirit realm of eternity. With my spirit, I can step into eternity and grab hold of any word that God has spoken. I can grab hold of it and say, "This is mine." Then

I can bring it out of eternity into my time-space world, and suddenly it becomes manifested with present day power.

Jesus stepped into the eternal realm, obtained advance credit on what He would accomplish at Calvary, and was therefore able to send out the 12 under His delegated authority with the same power of the Kingdom that He had. He sent them out telling them to go heal the sick, cast out demons, raise the dead, and tell them the Kingdom of God has come (see Luke 9:1-2). They moved out, not only to preach the Kingdom but also to manifest the Kingdom. That was a great advance. At first, it was only Jesus, but then there were 13 moving out to preach and manifest the Kingdom on earth.

Jesus was still not satisfied. In Luke 10:1-9, He sent out the 70 as His delegates and empowered them with the same power. The 12 were to have a very specific ministry. They were to go only to the lost sheep of the house of Israel (see Matt. 10:6). But the 70 had no such restrictions. They were able to go anywhere with only one controlling condition. They had to go where He sent them, which was to every city where He Himself would come (see Luke 10:1). He didn't send them out as one large group but two by two. This minimum requirement of two is mentioned repeatedly in Scripture. If you want to take a city, how many people do you need? The biblical answer is two. Two means victory. If two of you can agree on earth concerning anything, it will be done for you (see Matt. 18:19).

MOVING IN HIS DELEGATED AUTHORITY

The 70 experienced this authority temporarily by fulfilling certain conditions. We tend to apply Scripture to everybody when sometimes it is restricted to a specific group of people and not intended for everybody. Sometimes, we need to note carefully who is being addressed, especially by Jesus. In Luke 10:1-21, He was not talking to the crowd but only to the 70. He appointed the 70 and sent them out two by two in the power of the Kingdom and told them that there was a great harvest waiting for them. He said this only to the 70 He appointed (who had fulfilled certain necessary conditions) and not to everybody who came to His meetings.

He also said to this specific group of 70, "Behold, I give you the authority to trample on serpents and scorpions, and over all the power of the enemy, and nothing shall by any means hurt you" (Luke 10:19). Many people who are living prayer-less, lazy, and sometimes sinful lives have taken this Scripture and expected to be victorious over the enemy. But it wasn't written for such people; it was only written for those who have fulfilled the conditions of the 70. It is very important that we fulfill these conditions if we want to see victory.

The 70 came back with great joy. They said, "Even the demons are subject to us in your name" (Luke 10:17). Jesus replied, "I saw Satan fall like lightning from heaven. ...Nevertheless do not rejoice in this, that the spirits are subject to you, but rather rejoice because your names are written in heaven" (Luke 10:18,20).

There were the 12, the 70, and Jesus, which made 83 in all. This growing number of people was moving in the power of the Kingdom and was having a profound effect on the kingdom of darkness. Nevertheless, in spite of all this, Jesus was still frustrated. In spite of this powerful manifestation of the Kingdom, very little was happening to change the religious, social, and political life of the city. In fact, in these respects, Jerusalem was getting worse, and the hearts of most of the religious leaders were getting harder. Out of jealousy, they were plotting to kill Him.

In Luke 9 and 10, Jesus got the 83 moving in the power of the Kingdom. In Luke 11, Jesus carefully taught on the kind of prayer life that leads to the casting down of the strongman. There are six levels of prayer mentioned that eventually bring us to the place where we can deal effectively with the strongman. As I have pointed out before, it is not *someone* who is more powerful than the strongman, but *something*. It is not a person; it is the Kingdom. The Kingdom of God is more powerful than any demonic strongman that rules over any region or city in the world. If we concentrate on bringing in the Kingdom, the Kingdom will destroy anything in its way. Nevertheless, 83 people moving in delegated Kingdom power on the earth was not good enough for Jesus. In His Spirit, He had seen something much more powerful and longed for that greater manifestation of the Kingdom to come.

THE FRUSTRATION OF JESUS ON EARTH COMES TO CLIMAX

In Luke 12, Jesus was still living in frustration over the level at which the Kingdom was being manifested. Signs and wonders were happening, demons were being cast out, and people were getting saved. However, the power controlling the city from the heavens was not the power of God's Kingdom but of satan's. The temple area in particular was the most demonized area of the city. The worst and strongest demons are usually found in religion. The nearer a religion gets to being a subtle counterfeit of the truth, the more deadly and dangerous it becomes. When Jesus came toward the temple, there was a terrible demonic response.

There was still a dark, demonic canopy ruling over the city of Jerusalem. Jesus never spoke to those demonic powers or addressed them while on earth. It was not yet time.

On earth, Jesus was impregnable to all the attacks of the devil. They could not touch Him at all (see John 14:30). He was doing a wonderful, destructive work to the demons who were operating on the earth. However, He was not yet empowered to deal with the demonic strongholds in the heavenly places. He was frustrated with this level of the Kingdom and longed for His baptism of suffering at the cross to be accomplished.

In Luke, Jesus expresses His frustration and declares His purpose in coming: "I came to send fire on the earth, and how I wish it were already kindled! But I have a baptism to be baptized with, and how distressed I am till it is accomplished!" (Luke 12:49-50). The Greek word *sunechomai*, translated "distressed," has the idea of being shut-in, constrained, restricted, and unable to move. It is like being tied as a prisoner. He is saying, "How tied and restricted I am until this is accomplished! I cannot wait for this baptism." What baptism? It is not the baptism in water, since that had already taken place. He was looking forward to the cross, to the baptism of suffering by which the power of the devil would be totally destroyed through the cross and the power of His resurrection would be released. Following His resurrection, a new powerful level of the Kingdom would come which would touch the whole earth. Then the full post-resurrection power of His Kingdom could come (see John 12:23-32).

Chapter 11

ALL AUTHORITY IN HEAVEN AND ON EARTH

LEVEL 3—JESUS WITH ALL AUTHORITY IN HEAVEN AND ON EARTH

After His baptism, Jesus could deal with any aspect of satan's work and activity on earth, but He did not yet have the authority to deal decisively with the demonic principalities and powers operating from their well-established strongholds in the heavenly realm. That was to come later.

Some confusing teaching has prevented a number of intercessors from gaining the victories they otherwise could have had. These intercessors have been taught that the Christian's sphere of spiritual authority is limited to the earth and that no Christian on earth has any authority to address demonic principalities in the heavenly realm. While that was temporarily true for Jesus during His earthly life, up until the time he died on the cross, it certainly is not true now. He is now risen and exalted and has all power and all authority in every realm of heaven as well as on earth.

Unfortunately, many still do not see Christians on earth as having any power or authority to deal with demonic principalities and powers in the heavenly realm, and they discourage other Christians from using their authority for fear of demonic back-lash. They limit themselves and those associated with them to the second level of the Kingdom.

THE RISEN CHRIST IS DIFFERENT FROM THE JESUS WHO LIVED ON EARTH

One thing I want to make clear in this chapter is the distinction between the Jesus who walked on earth and the risen Jesus who now reigns with all power and authority from Heaven. From the day He was anointed at His baptism, Jesus had authority to forgive sins and exercised authority over all the power of the enemy on earth. Mighty works with signs and wonders began to flow through Him. However, there was more to come.

Before Calvary, it was possible for Jesus to move on earth in the power of Adam's restored rule. In His earthly life Jesus was living the life of what the Bible calls "Last Adam" (see 1 Cor. 15:45). When we are studying these things, it is very important that we keep accurate and precise terminology. For example, Jesus is never called the Second Adam; He is called the Last Adam. He is also called the Second Man, but only after His resurrection. We are told that this Second Man is the Lord from Heaven and not of the earth at all. He also has no natural genealogy (see 1 Cor. 15:47;

Heb. 7:3-5). Now this Second Man is a completely different kind of man who has no ethnic connection with the First Adam or any of Adam's descendants. This one was never born of Mary, and never was a Jew.

Jesus on earth became the first man to move in the power of the Kingdom. He recovered the first Adamic level of anointing and authority and was able to rule over all things on earth. But Jesus was heading toward another battleground. He was going to enter into a realm where the first Adam had never been. The first Adam was never raised to be ruler of the heavens and the earth, because he failed the test of obedience. Authority in Heaven was never given to him, and even his authority on earth was taken from him after he had sinned.

As the Last Adam, Jesus came and reestablished the rule of God's Kingdom on earth, but it came into immediate conflict with satan's kingdom which was already established. After His resurrection, having proved His obedience so totally and gloriously, the Father could righteously promote Him to dimensions of authority that the first Adam had never experienced. However, certain things had to be accomplished first. Jesus as the great Kinsman-Redeemer still had to settle the great debt of sin that was owed by Adam's race. That was completed on the cross when He cried out in triumph, "It's finished; there is nothing to pay!" (See John 19:30.) He then immediately dismissed His spirit and died, having completed that assignment. Until His death He was called the Last Adam, but after His resurrection He became the Second Man.

From the First Adam, the rays of sin and death went forth and touched every part of creation on the face of the earth. All men, all women, all animals, and all plants were infected, damaged, and corrupted by sin which spread to cover the whole of God's creation. The totality of all the sin of Adam's race over the face of the whole earth from the beginning to the end of time was brought to a vile concentrate which Jesus drank on the cross, and it all became part of this one man, Christ Jesus, as the Last Adam.

THE CUP HE DRANK

It is good sometimes to sit down and ask God for some understanding of these things. Why did Jesus shrink from the cross? What was so absolutely terrible? Was it the physical pain? No! What was troubling Him most was that His perfect, sinless humanity was going to be made filthy and foul with all the sins of Adam's race. Just think of everything down through the history of humanity. Think of every wicked thing that has ever been done. Think of all the violence and brutality. Think of all the abuse, sex perversion, and racial hatred. Think of all the cruelty and greed.

All the sin from the beginning to the end of time and from the very perimeters of creation was brought to a concentrate. It became like a thick, dark soup of iniquitous evil. That was the cup that the Father gave His Son to drink. He shuddered and shrank from being polluted by something so foul and filthy, but He did not refuse to drink it.

Some years ago, I was ministering at a conference in Africa. One of my jobs at that conference was to minister in what we called the "pig pen." This was where all the badly demonized people came to get the demons cast out of them. A man came to that conference in desperate need. He cried out for salvation.

I had never met anyone like this man in all my life. He was filled with sexual demons in a way that I had never seen before. He just lusted and craved for sexual intercourse with anyone and anything all the time. He had been with many women and many men, and now apparently he was trying to find fulfillment with animals. This demonized man came crying out for salvation. So another man and I took on the task of getting all these demons out of him. As the demons were coming out of him and manifesting the foulness of who they were, they seemed to pollute the very atmosphere, and I felt myself being contaminated by all this filth. For a brief period, I actually felt what it was like to be sexually perverted, and I felt what it was like to be homosexual. There were hundreds of these demons in him, and some of that polluting filth came upon me.

We went on for hours, and we were getting tired. One particularly strong demon was very stubborn and refused to move. So I just got on my knees with the other man, and said, "Come on, let's just pray." I can still remember that experience and how Jesus so richly manifested himself. As I was on my knees, I felt something like wonderful, soft, cashmere wool just brushing across my face. I somehow knew it was the garment of Jesus. I could feel His arms come around the two of us although I could not see anything. He was standing between us with His arms embracing us. At that moment, the demon in the man cried out, "He's come!" I said, "Who's come?" The demon said, "The Lord! Can't you see Him?" I said, "No, but I can feel Him." Then this demon said, "All right, Lord! We're going!" Instantly they all were gone, and it was over.

I walked away from that encounter feeling as if I had been soiled with something so foul and filthy. I went to the shower and poured gallons of water all over me trying to wash off this feeling of filth. I said to myself, "That was just the demons and filth in one man." They came onto me superficially, a man who is by no means perfect, and yet I found the whole experience completely revolting.

It made me think what it must have been like for Jesus to actually have all the sin of Adam's race come upon Him. I cannot really comprehend what it must have been like for a man as pure and holy as He to be made so filthy. The Bible says that Jesus "bore our sins in His own body on the tree" (1 Pet. 2:24).

He Who Knew No Sin Became Sin

In addition, not just the acts of sin, but the totality of the depraved sin nature of Adam's race was brought to a focus in the Last Adam. It says in Second Corinthians 5:21, "For He made Him who knew no sin to be sin for us." It was not just all the acts of sin, but also the very nature of sin somehow became part of Him. When that happened, He became millions of times more foul and filthy than any other human being that has ever lived. He willingly became the garbage can for the sin of the whole of Adam's race.

At that point in time, it was impossible for a holy Father God to remain in fellowship with His Son. God the Father had to withdraw from His Son because He was so foul and filthy with sin. A gap as wide as hell came between Father and Son. In His agony and His distress He cried out, "Oh, My God! My God! Why have You forsaken Me?" (See Mark 15:34.) When He needed His Father most, He lost all contact and connection with Him because of the sin. All He had for company were jeering demons, crying out,

"We've got Him! We've got Him!" and mocking evil men saying, "Ha! Ha! Ha! He saved others, but He cannot save Himself. Why don't You come down from the cross and we will believe in You" (see Mark 15:31-32). Not only was there such spiritual and psychological agony, but the excruciating physical pain was beyond comprehension.

THE GREATEST FIGHT OF FAITH

Yet, deep down inside something began to happen in Jesus' spirit. He was not living in the experience of His circumstances, but He was living by faith in what the Scripture said. Deep within His spirit, He began to make a raw confession of faith while there was no evidence in His circumstances. By faith He declared, "You have not left Me!" Then He began to cry out the most incredible confession of faith that has ever been recorded anywhere, "But You are holy, enthroned in the praises of Israel. Our fathers trusted in You; they trusted, and You delivered them. They cried to You, and were delivered; they trusted in You, and were not ashamed" (Ps. 22:3-5). Whenever I read Psalm 22, I end up in tears because I cannot get over this mighty warrior man and the power of His fighting faith. Even when He was utterly alone going through the agony of the cross, He still had amazing faith.

Before He went to the cross, He had already obtained His resurrection by faith through the travail in the Garden of Gethsemane (see Heb. 5:7-8). There on the cross, He was wrestling for other things: He was fighting for the nations and claiming them as His inheritance according to the promise of God in Psalm 2:7-12. He was seeing the church and claiming multitudes of liberated believers dancing and worshiping because of what was being accomplished on Calvary. He saw the total destruction of all the power of the evil one (see Col. 2:15). He cried out in triumph in Psalm 22:27-31.

It Is Finished!

On the cross, and not in the tomb, Jesus completed all that was necessary to pay the debt of Adam's race. Isaiah 53 tells that it was the Father who was meting out all this punishment upon Him. Every drop of sin had to be righteously paid for, not just forgiven. The Father poured out upon His Son the full price of His wrath until every last sin was paid for.

Jesus, not only paid for all the sins of Adam's race, but He also paid the full purchase price to redeem all of physical creation back from the devil so that he no longer had any legal claim over even one square inch of this earth. It was not just the Holy Land that God was after, but the whole world. He cried out, "I came to send fire on the earth, and how I wish it were already kindled! But I have a baptism to be baptized with, and how distressed I am till it is accomplished!" (Luke 12:49-50).

Then there came a great cry from the cross, "It is finished!" We know from Matthew's Gospel in particular that this was not a cry of pain but a cry of victory. It was the cry that a gladiator made when he made the killing thrust in a fight! "Ahhhhhh! I've got him. It's finished!" That's what Jesus was saying, "It's finished! I've got him!"

The word Jesus used was *teleos*. This word was used in accounting. If you had debts that you were unable to pay and someone graciously came on your behalf and paid the full price, the creditor would write the same word over the stack of bills, *teleos*—it's finished. Nothing to pay.

Jesus cried out, "It's finished! There is nothing more to pay!" At that moment, John's Gospel says, Jesus dismissed His spirit. In the temple, at the same moment, the veil that blocked the way into the Holiest of All, was ripped apart from top to bottom. We are told in Hebrews that this signified that the way into the Holy of Holies was now open.

The Roman centurion, who was in charge of the execution, was a man who had probably killed many men in battle and crucified many criminals. He was tough, hard, and not normally moved by a crucifixion. However, he had never seen anyone behave like this before. He saw a man who was totally in charge of his own execution. Jesus Himself selected the moment that was appropriate for Him to die, dismissed His spirit, and was gone.

It says in Matthew and Mark that the centurion was standing right in front of Him, and having seen the way in which Jesus died, he went to his knees and said, "Truly, this was the Son of God!" He is laying His life down voluntarily and choosing for Himself His own moment to die (see Matt. 27:54).

THE TRAVAIL BEGINS

His body was then taken down from the cross and carried to the tomb. I want you to get this absolutely clear. Sin was already fully paid for before that sin-laden body was taken down from the cross and that sin-invaded soul went down into the tomb. We are dealing with mysteries here, so I cannot be too dogmatic, but according to other Scriptures, the soul of the Last Adam went down into the depths of hell (see Acts 2:31). His spirit went immediately to be with His Father. At some point, His body just disappeared. Then there was a period of three days before the new Second Man walked triumphantly out of the tomb.

The next thing I want you to notice is revealed by looking at three Scriptures.

First, go to First John 5:4-6:

> But whatever is born of God overcomes the world. And this is the victory that has overcome the world—our faith. Who is he who overcomes the world, but he who believes that Jesus is the Son of God? This is He who came by **water and blood**—Jesus Christ; not only by water, but by water and blood. And it is the Spirit who bears witness, because the Spirit is truth (1 John 5:4-6).

Notice that He came by *water* and by *blood*.

Second, come with me to John 16:20-22 where Jesus is speaking to His disciples,

> Most assuredly, I say to you that you will weep and lament, but the world will rejoice; and you will be sorrowful, but your sorrow will be turned into joy. A woman, when she is in labor, has sorrow because her hour has come; but as soon as she has given birth to the child, she no longer remembers the anguish, for joy that a human being [full-grown adult] has been born into the world. Therefore you now have sorrow; but I will see you again and your heart will rejoice, and your joy no one will take from you (John 16:20-22).

I've given you the actual literal meaning of the Greek in brackets. It was a full-grown, adult man that was "born" in the tomb and came forth on resurrection morning.

Third, come to John 19:30, *"And bowing His head, He gave up His spirit."*

The authorities did not want the bodies of those crucified to remain alive on the Sabbath Day. This was the ultimate act of religious hypocrisy. They wickedly murdered Him, and yet they were still so particular to maintain their religious rules that they asked Pilate to have the soldiers break their legs so they would die quickly and not pollute the Sabbath.

> *Then the soldiers came and broke the legs of the first and of the other who was crucified with Him. But when they came to Jesus and saw that He was already dead, they did not break His legs. But one of the soldiers pierced His side with a spear, and immediately **blood and water** came out* (John 19:32-34).

How does He come? *By the water and the blood!*

The soldier ripped open the side of Jesus, and out came blood and water. This is what I want you to see. Several mighty things are happening sequentially. Jesus came to that cross as the Lamb of God to take away the sins of the world. That was accomplished when He cried, "It is finished." At that very same moment, the veil was torn in the temple, and the way into the Holiest of All was now open.

So what are the three days all about? Jesus told His disciples in John 16:21 that when He was in the tomb something else powerful would be happening. He said that He would be like a woman in travail, giving birth to something new. What He was saying was that what He would give birth to was not a resurrection of the Last Adam. That one who died filthy and foul with sin would never rise again. But immediately once sin was paid for, He would be like a woman in travail and would be in agony with birth pangs because He would be giving birth to something entirely new. While He was in the tomb for three days, He was giving birth to a whole new creation of man that never was and never would be part of Adam's race.

THE NEW MAN COMES FORTH

This new man was not created like the First Adam—by putting together the dust of the earth and breathing life into him. Neither was this man like the Last Adam who was supernaturally born of a virgin woman. He went through the normal birth process, was born under the law, and was circumcised on the eighth day so that He might be the Kinsman-Redeemer of all men. This one, after He had died, went through three days of mysterious, spiritual, creative travail, and then walked out from the tomb as a full-grown, totally new man in a glorious, new resurrection body. He Himself, in His resurrection, was the first fruit of His own womb and the beginning of a totally new creation, a glorious new genealogy of men who never were part of Adam's race.

THE ALLEGORY OF THE CREATION OF EVE

Go back for a moment in your mind to the way God created woman. You know the story. God created many wonderful creatures. They were all lovely and friendly before the Fall, even the lions. It must have been great fun. Animals can be wonderful companions. Those of us who love dogs know how much an animal can capture your heart. In our family, we have had two wonderful Labrador dogs. I had a tremendous relationship, particularly with one of these two dogs. We understood each other perfectly. I loved her very much, and I was very sad the day she died. But I never felt like marrying my dog! Wonderful as they are, they are just not the same as women.

Adam enjoyed the created animal world, but none of the creatures were suitable for him or were able to complete him. What God did when He made woman was a prophetic act, a powerful allegory of what would happen on the cross thousands of years later. He put Adam into a deep sleep, opened up his side, and took out a rib. In the Hebrew, it is worded this way, "from the bone, he built the woman." Then Adam awoke from his deep sleep, and here, according to one of my Hebrew scholar friends, the Hebrew is hilarious. Adam opened his eyes and saw this fantastic creation for the first time. Something he never experienced before began to happen inside of him, and he instantly fell in love with this woman. This apparently is what Adam literally says in the Hebrew: "This is it! This is it! Bone of my bone and flesh of my flesh" (see Gen. 2:21-23).

The reason it was done in this way was to give us an allegorical picture to help us understand what was happening in the tomb. Not only did Jesus the Lamb of God pay for the sins of the world, but then, after His death, He went on to be a mother in travail who gave birth, through His side, to an entirely new creation of men.

THE LAST ADAM AND THE SECOND MAN

First Corinthians 15:45-47 gives us clear teaching on this. The Last Adam was of the earth. But the new Man is the Lord from heaven. He is the Second Man, who was neither born of Adam nor of woman. He was never contaminated with the sin nature. It was a different humanity altogether. In the travail of the cross, after sin was completely dealt with, God in Christ immediately went into labor to bring forth the Second Man. When that soldier ripped open his side, it was like a surgeon performing a cesarean on the very womb of God.

What happens when a woman begins to give birth? The first thing is that her water breaks. Then blood and water gush out together. Through the dead corpse of Jesus, God was in labor to give birth to something new. The tomb of Jesus was like a maternity labor room. There were three days of labor to bring forth this new man. On resurrection morning, the full-grown new man, who had nothing to do with the man who died on the cross, came forth.

When Peter and John ran into the tomb, they found the grave clothes that had been wrapped around the body, including the cloth that had been wrapped around His head like a turban, totally undisturbed (see John 20:3-10). It was as if the crucified body they placed in the tomb had vaporized, passed through the grave clothes without disturbing them, and had simply disappeared.

What walked out of the tomb was not the raised body of the man who had been crucified, because that body had completely disappeared. Instead, He was an entirely New Man with a completely different genealogy. He never was contaminated with sin and never was a part of Adam's race. Adam's race finished with the death and burial of our Lord Jesus Christ. The Last Adam never rose from the dead. Instead, he and all his kin were eternally terminated, put to death, in that act of Calvary. What walked forth from the tomb was a new man.

Satan had never had any power or claim over Him. To this new man was given a totally new authority. Jesus as the Last Adam recovered the authority of the first Adam to exercise government *on earth.* During His earthly life, Jesus often said things like: I have power on earth to forgive sins. I have power on earth to cast out demons. I have power on earth to heal sicknesses. But the first words of this new man who walked out of the tomb, this glorious, new Second Man who is called the Lord from Heaven were: *"All authority has been given to Me in heaven and on earth"* (Matt. 28:18).

Look at the Scriptures in First Corinthians 15:47-49: "The first man was of the earth, made of dust; the second Man is the Lord from heaven. As was the man of dust, so also are those who are made of dust; *and as is the heavenly Man, so also are those who are heavenly"* (1 Cor. 15:47-48). Verse 49 literally translated reads, *"As we have borne the image of the man of dust, let us also* [right now] *bear the image of the man from heaven."* In verse 49, in many Greek manuscripts the verb *bear* is in the present imperative. The Majority Text has "let us also bear." That means it is a commandment, and the point of time is now. It is not in the future tense. It means we must do it now! Sometimes, the translators of our English Bible water down what the Bible literally says because they have not experienced it and do not understand it. They sometimes relegate to the future what God says is available to us now.

The moment the risen Christ appeared and spoke to His disciples, He first dealt with their unbelief, and then He said, "All power in heaven and on earth has been given to me. Now you go and make disciples of all nations!" (See Matthew 28:18-19.)

During those three-and-a-half years of earthly ministry, the second level of the Kingdom, Jesus saw successes and victories.

But there were also many counterattacks. Most Christians and churches who have seen something of the power of the Kingdom live at that second earthly level of the Kingdom. They see some wonderful things happen, but they also see many setbacks. It is much better than living at the John the Baptist level, but you sometimes wonder whether you are winning or losing.

There was no obvious, outright victory during Jesus' earthly ministry. At the end of three-and-a-half years, Jerusalem was more wicked in its social, religious, and moral life than it had been at the beginning. Large crowds would turn out to the special healing meetings, and they were excited to be touched in their bodies. But when it came to real discipleship, only a few were prepared to pay the price. At the end of three-and-a-half years, even with all those mighty miracles and all His amazing teaching, Jesus had a committed church of only 120. It was not much better than many of us are doing.

The raising of Lazarus was an incredible miracle, which took place in Bethany, near Jerusalem. A rotting corpse walked out alive from the tomb. What effect did that have on Bethany and Jerusalem? It generated enough new interest that even the Greeks began to seek after Him, but primarily it produced more jealousy in the religious leaders and a more determined, sinister plot to kill Him. During His earthly ministry, Jesus had not yet been given authority in the heavenly realm. He could not yet deal with the demonic spirits that were ruling over Jerusalem from their heavenly strongholds.

The second level is the level at which many churches are moving in the power of the Spirit today. They are seeing a number of people healed, demons are being cast out, and a few salvations are taking place, but there are also some setbacks and defeats. Even though they are seeing some people gloriously transformed, the city is not really changing. In fact, in most places, it seems to be getting more wicked and darker all the time. The religious system is not moved, the social and moral conditions continue to deteriorate, and the political leaders are not changed. The groups that are seeing the Kingdom and manifesting its power still seem irrelevant to what is seen as the power and life of the city.

As Jesus left the city of Jerusalem for almost the last time, He cursed a fruitless fig tree which immediately withered and died. This was a powerful prophetic sign that cannot be adequately dealt with in this book. It is discussed in my previous book, *The Good Fight of Faith*, and I will address it as it relates to the Kingdom of God in a further volume on the Kingdom.

The Scriptures record that just before Jesus had ascended back to His Father He commanded his disciples to "sit down" until they had been clothed upon with power (Luke 24:49). The obedient 120 of His disciples spent the next ten days in the Upper Room in a powerful "one accord" prayer meeting. Many things went on during those days that are not recorded. When they came out on the day of Pentecost after the Spirit had fallen upon them they were totally different in many respects.

Also the city into which they suddenly burst out was radically changed. The same multitude that had gathered only a few weeks earlier to demand that Jesus be crucified (see Matt. 27:22-23) began to cry out in terror and repentance as Peter preached to them. As a result 3,000 gladly received his word, were baptized and added to the church (see Acts 2:36-38, 41-43). A little while later a lame man was healed (see Acts 3:1-8). He began to leap and praise

God. It was quite a miracle, but it did not compare to a rotting corpse walking out of the tomb alive as Lazarus had done a few months earlier.

When Lazarus was raised it only produced hostility in the city and a stronger determination to kill Jesus. But now, when this man was healed by Peter, the whole city went crazy and another 5,000 men (plus an unknown number of women and children) turned to the Lord. In the culture of the Jews at that time it was customary to only record the number of men and not bother to give any number of women and children. There are a number of examples of this, such as the feeding of the 5,000 men, besides women and children (see Matt. 14:21). It was probably a crowd of at least 20,000 who were fed on that day.

There were an unknown number of girls, who are not counted or recorded, born to Mary as well as four named sons through her husband Joseph after Jesus had miraculously come forth from her virgin womb before Joseph "knew" her (see Mark 6:3).

For these reasons it is estimated by several historians and commentators that, following the day of Pentecost, the church in Jerusalem grew rapidly to about 20,000 people within two years.

What had happened to bring about this change?

It was the casting down of the demonic powers that had ruled over Jerusalem and controlled the politics, the judiciary and the dead religious system which held the people captive in their minds through fear and deception so they could not respond to even the preaching and the works of Jesus.

Once He was risen, Jesus now had all power in the heavenly realm as well as on earth, He could now empower his disciples to wrestle with these demonic powers and cast them down and thus give us a model to follow for every other city on earth. Paul taught this to the Ephesian church (see Eph. 6:11-13). Later when John the apostle returned from exile he quickly showed them how to deal with the ruling spirit of Diana or Artemis and the city was quickly liberated and transformed.

In our own experience in Mumbai and in the stories of many recent revivals from Wales, to Azusa Street in the U.S., from South Korea, to South Africa, in Argentina and Brazil and many other places, a group of warring intercessors have wrestled in a similar way with demonic principalities and powers and have suddenly seen a miraculous breakthrough in many cases.

The demons that rule over cities are powerful, and when they are thrown down, the city radically changes. But then you discover there are even greater levels of demonic rule. There are principalities and powers that have authority over regions, nations, and even whole continents (see Eph. 6:12). The church then had to learn how to deal with that next level of demonic power, and it took the church a few decades to learn how to fight and win at that level of spiritual warfare.

I am sure you would agree that it is much better to live at this third level of the Kingdom where we move in the power of the resurrection and can invade the heavenly realm rather than being limited to only exercising authority on earth. What happened in Jerusalem can happen in your city when you learn how to move in the power of the risen Christ and attack those principalities and cast them down.

Most of the church on earth is not in this third level of the Kingdom. That is why we do not see many cities being taken. But that is changing, and it will continue to change!

THE NEW GENEALOGY MULTIPLIES

Jesus in His resurrection was the first to be born again from that womb as a mighty, glorious new man. In Colossians 1:15,18, there is a word in the Greek (*prototokos*) that has the idea of being the firstborn or first-begotten. It says, "He is the image of the invisible God, *the firstborn over all creation*...and He is the head of the body, the church, who is the beginning *and the firstborn from among the dead*, so that in everything he might have the supremacy" (Col. 1:15,18, literally translated). He was the first one to come forth from that womb to be the firstborn or first-begotten of this glorious, new genealogy of men and women from Heaven. We who are called are also raised to live that same new life in Him.

Romans 8 says, "For whom He foreknew He also predestined to be conformed to the image of His Son, that *He might be the firstborn among many brethren*" (Rom. 8:29). So it wasn't just Jesus who was to become this glorious, new Lord from Heaven by His resurrection, but He was pioneering the way for all of us to come into that same new humanity.

You will notice in most English versions that some words are in italics. Whenever you find italics in your English Bible, it means those words were not in the original Greek text. They have been inserted by the translators because they think it makes better sense. Usually, it does not, and it is good to cross them out. That is not tampering with the Word of God. You are just correcting the translators' mistakes. Romans 6:5 literally reads in the Greek, "If we have been united with Him in a death like His, certainly also *we are His resurrection.*" Most translations put the reality of the resurrection into the future. But it is not future; it is now. The English translations usually put in this phrase, "*we will* *be in the **likeness** of His resurrection"* which takes away the force of what is being said. They speak of "likeness" instead of actual reality and postpone to the future what is intended to be ours right now in the present.

In the city of Mumbai, India, there was is a certain market area where you could buy all kinds of things very cheaply, but you had to be careful because many things for sale there were either counterfeit or stolen. There was a stall where you could buy what looked like beautiful Schaffer pens for only $5.00 each. So I bought one of these pens. Stamped on the side of the pen were the words "Made in U.S.A." But it wasn't the real U.S.A. It stood for the Ulasnagar Sindhi Association, a group of villages in the Sindh area where they made these counterfeit pens. If you picked one up it was in the likeness of a Schaffer pen, but it was not the real thing. The words were the same, but when you tried to use it, the pen would break in a short time and be useless.

In a similar way, many people speak the language of the resurrection, but it is not real. Even some translators of our Bibles treat it as a theological concept with no present experiential reality. Therefore, they change the wording of our Bibles to say that we will be in the likeness of His resurrection one day, but not now. But the Bible actually says, "we already are His resurrection." The risen man, Christ Jesus the Lord, began a completely new genealogy of mankind, who have never sinned and have never had any part with satan. By the grace of God we are now part of that genealogy.

This truth comes so many times in the writings of Paul that it is hard to select one particular reference. It is the main theme of Romans 6–8 and is strongly taught in Colossians and Ephesians. A good example would be Romans 6:5 which literally says, "If we have been united with Him in a death like His, certainly also we are [or will be] His resurrection." This is described by some theologians as either a conditional present or conditional future. So which is it? The answer is both! It is a future tense that immediately becomes present once the condition is fulfilled, but it remains endlessly future until the condition is fulfilled.

Let me try to give and example to clarify this. I live in San Antonio, Texas, which is famous for its outstanding basketball team the San Antonio Spurs.

Imagine they are about to hire a new player to further strengthen their team and they present to him a five-year contract. Over five years let's say its value is $75 million.

If he signs the contract and binds himself to be totally under their authority and agrees to go where they say and play as and when they say and attend all training sessions faithfully etc., then immediately, once he has signed the contract, the money becomes a guaranteed present reality. But until he signs the contract, the money remains only a future possibility. Fulfilling the condition of signing the contract makes all the difference.

In a similar way, we must first be united with Him in a death like His, which was a moment by moment life of total death to self and a life of total obedience, even to death on a cross. The moment we fulfill this condition then at the same moment we will actually become His resurrection.

WE BECOME AMERICAN CITIZENS

A few years ago, the Lord impressed upon my wife and I that we should become American citizens. We had been living in America for about ten years when the Lord said, "I want you to take American citizenship," and He showed us very clearly why this was necessary. At the time we began this process, it was not possible to have dual citizenship. That meant we would have to renounce our British citizenship in order to become Americans.

By the time we completed all the formalities, the laws had changed. British citizens are now allowed to have dual citizenship. However, the wording used during the U.S. naturalization ceremony had not yet been changed. So in October 2001, my wife and I stood before a Federal Court judge, and we each took a solemn oath before this judge. First of all, we formally renounced our British citizenship. We were no longer British, but American. The second part of the oath stated that as loyal Americans we would take up arms and fight against any enemy that came against our nation. No pacifism was allowed. The third part of our oath stated that if the enemy that came against America proved to be the nation of our former citizenship, we would still fight as loyal Americans against them.

I found this ceremony deeply moving, emotionally and spiritually. I immediately began to see a powerful spiritual allegory in what I was doing. I saw that in a very similar way, by my natural birth, I had been born as a citizen of the kingdom of darkness through my ancestor Adam. When I was born again, I needed to renounce that citizenship and receive my new citizenship in the Kingdom of God. My loyalty now went totally to the Lord Jesus Christ. I could not be a pacifist, but I had to be ready to fight any enemy that came against Him and His Kingdom.

The American Travels to India

Shortly afterward, I got my new American passport. In the 1960s and '70s I had lived in India for 13 years as a foreign resident with a British passport. Since leaving in 1976, I have continued to minister in India at least once or twice every year. I must have passed through Indian immigration more than 100 times as Alan Vincent, the citizen of the United Kingdom. I was quite well known in India, and when I would arrive, the immigration officer would take my passport and type my name into the computer. Immediately, pages of data would come up detailing my former visits and what I had done in India. The immigration officer would get more and more serious as he read all of my Christian activities over the years. I could see him thinking very hard, "Are we going to let this guy in again?" So I would pray hard. He would sometimes go to a higher-ranking official, and I would pray even harder. He would finally come back, reluctantly stamp my passport, and let me in again. I would breathe a sigh of relief and continue on into India.

In January 2002, I arrived in India for the first time as an American and presented my new passport, which read "Alan Vincent, Citizen of the United States of America." The official clicked the keys, and not one word against me came up on the computer. I was a completely new creature without a single word written against me, and I was welcomed without any hesitation.

Spiritually, which passport do you carry? Which citizenship do you confess? We are told that if we have been united with Him in a death like His, certainly also we already are His resurrection. As part of His resurrection, you are a new creation; all your past sinful life has been wiped away. Your new man is not part of Adam and has never been a part of satan's kingdom; he has no power over this new you. The devil may try to say to you, "Oh, you're still mine! You're still one of my citizens," and he may try to give you a list of all the sinful things you once did. You must say in response, "That's not me! That guy is dead! He was crucified with Christ. He was buried and will never rise again. You are dealing with a totally new person who is now risen with Christ and has all power and all authority with Christ in Heaven and on earth. Look, here is my new Kingdom passport. In fact, since my resurrection with Him, Jesus and I own everything, and I'm His authorized delegate. So don't try to mess with me now!"

WE ARE AMBASSADORS OF CHRIST

Years ago, we went with our two small children into the upper east corner of Assam to Nagaland, a part of India touching China and Burma. There was a civil war going on at the time, and no foreigners were permitted there, but I had been invited to go there and speak in a series of conferences. God had opened the door to give me this opportunity to preach in this strategic area.

We came to the Calcutta airport and presented our papers and tickets. The official said, "You are foreigners. You can't go there." He said, "Even Indians are not allowed into this area without special permission." I said, "I have to be there tonight because I have been invited to speak at a series of meetings." He insisted, "You cannot go. You can go back to Assam House in Calcutta and try there, but they will never give you a permit." I sat down on a chair nearby and said, "Lord Jesus, You and I own this airline; they cannot refuse me. That territory where I am going also belongs to You. If You are sending me there as your ambassador, then they can't keep me out. I claim my rights of ownership and my rights of citizenship to go into this area." When I couldn't think of anything more to say, I just continued praying in tongues.

When it came to departure time, the plane did not take off, instead, there was a big commotion as some important officials came through the lobby. A very nice gentleman emerged from the crowd and came to the check-in desk. I overheard the conversation and discovered that this gentleman was the personal secretary of the Chief Minister of the State of Assam. The Chief Minister needed to fly to the same place we were going. They had sent a message, "Hold the plane because the Chief Minister is coming." They rearranged the seating in the plane to make the first few rows into a private cabin for the Chief Minister and his staff. They took a great big red carpet and rolled it out to the plane. Then a military band came in readiness to play for the minister as he walked to the plane.

I still do not know why, but just then, as I was standing by the desk still praying in tongues, the personal secretary of the Chief Minister turned to me and said, "Is there anything I can do to help you?" I said, "Sir, we need to be on that plane. I have to be in Gauhati tonight to preach at a large Christian conference, but apparently we don't have the right permit." He said to the man at the desk, "Give me a piece of paper," and proceeded to write us a personal permit to travel anywhere within Assam without hindrance. He put the Chief Minister's stamp on the notice, signed it with a flurry, handed it to me, and said, "This will take you anywhere." I said, "Thank you, sir!" We were then permitted to be seated in the plane and were treated with the honor that ambassadors of the King deserve.

The risen man Christ Jesus passed through the heavens to His throne, far above all rule, powers, lordships, principalities, dominions and names, both in Heaven and on earth, in this age and also in the one to come (see Eph. 1:20-21; Col. 1:15-18). We must believe this! The risen Lord Jesus is different from the Jesus that moved on earth before His death and resurrection. The Jesus on earth was the Last Adam, but the risen Lord Jesus is the Lord from Heaven. The Jesus on earth recovered all the power that was lost by Adam, but His authority was confined to earth. The risen Lord Jesus has all power and all authority in Heaven and on earth, now and forever more!

In His earthly life, Jesus was "born of a woman, born under the law" (Gal. 4:4). The purpose was to "redeem those who were under the law that we might receive the adoption as sons" (Gal. 4:5). In His earthly life according to His natural genealogy, Jesus was a Jew. As a result, we are told, salvation is of the Jews (see John 4:22). Do you see what is being said here? God chose to make the Last Adam ethnically a Jew so that through this Jew, by His death and sacrifice, the whole of the world might be saved. When it comes to paying Adam's debt and dealing with Adam's sin, when it comes to the Jesus on earth before His resurrection, we are dealing with Jesus the Jew.

What you must also see is that the one who walked alive out of the tomb on resurrection morning was not a Jew but the Lord from Heaven who is without genealogy. In His risen life, He is without father or mother, without beginning or ending of days (see Heb. 7:3). He is no longer the Jew, but He is the Lord from Heaven (see 1 Cor. 15:47).

According to the Majority Text, in First Corinthians 15:49, the Greek verb *phoreo* is in the present imperative tense and would more accurately be translated: "As we have borne the image of the

man of dust, let us also *now* bear the image of the man of heaven"
(1 Cor. 15:49). Paul carefully says something several times in his
epistles: Jesus, *according to the flesh*, was of the Jews (see Rom. 9:5).
He used the phrase, "according to the flesh" as someone Jesus was.
Now, He is no longer of that flesh. Now, He is the Lord from
Heaven. Paul said, "Even though we have known Christ according
to the flesh, yet now we know Him thus no longer" (2 Cor. 5:16).
He was saying, "I don't know Jesus after the flesh anymore. In-
stead, I now know Him, according to the spirit, as the Risen
Christ who is the Lord, Savior, and King!"

PAUL, A TOTALLY NEW CREATION

Paul also describes a man he once knew called Saul who was a
crazy, demonized Pharisee who hated Christians. He was so evil
and full of religious demons that he was the worst of sinners. Nevertheless, God saved him and delivered him. That terrible person,
Saul the Pharisee, died with Christ. He counts his natural genealogy as dung (see Phil. 3:5-8). Now, says Paul, just like Jesus, he is
from Heaven. He is now in the Kingdom where no one has an
earthly genealogy. Instead, we are all of this one, new nation, the
Kingdom of God, where none of these things exist. When this
revelation really came to the Church, it was able to move into an
even greater level of the Kingdom.

Chapter 12

THE KINGDOM IN ACTS

THE MAIN THEME IS THE KINGDOM

After He was risen from the dead, Jesus' primary concern was to teach His disciples concerning the Kingdom of God (see Acts 1:3-5). This was His main theme over the 40 days from His resurrection to His ascension. Acts chapter 1 says, "to whom He also presented Himself alive after His suffering by many infallible proofs, being seen by them during forty days and speaking of the things pertaining to the Kingdom of God" (Acts 1:3). Jesus did not go out publicly to demonstrate His power as the Risen Christ. He made no public appearances at all. Instead, He spent the entire time with His disciples convincing them that He was truly risen, and then He opened their hearts to the most important passion of

His heart, the Kingdom of God. It was going to be their job to forcefully advance that Kingdom. In His three-and-a-half years of ministry, He had given them an example, and they would need to follow that example exactly.

What He did for three and a half years in Judea, they were now to go and do all over the world. Then they, in the same way, were to train others to be the same kind of Kingdom disciples. He did not say to His disciples, "I'm going back up to Heaven ahead of you. Just pass the time until I come to take you home. Isn't it nice to have all your sins forgiven and know that one day you are going to be with me in Heaven? Just have fun and fellowship until I come!" These were not the burning issues on Jesus' heart. The primary issue was the Kingdom.

CLOTHED WITH POWER FROM ON HIGH

Acts 1:4 reads, "And being assembled together with them, He commanded them not to depart from Jerusalem, but to wait for the Promise of the Father, 'which,' He said, 'you have heard from Me'" (Acts 1:4). It is impossible to advance the Kingdom unless you've been baptized in the Holy Spirit. They could not go out and do anything until the power of the Spirit came upon them.

THE KINGDOM ONLY FOR ISRAEL?

After Jesus' resurrection, the first 12 apostles were still focused on restoring the kingdom of Israel in a natural way. In Acts 1:4-7, they respond to Jesus' command to wait in Jerusalem until they received the "Promise of the Father" by asking, "'Lord, will You at this time restore the kingdom to Israel?' And He said to them, 'It is not for you to know times or seasons which the Father has put in His own authority'" (Acts 1:4-7). They still only saw "the kingdom" in terms of their own nation, ethnic Israel. Although their own prophets had clearly said that the Kingdom was for all nations, they still saw the prophetic Scriptures in a very limited way. To them, Jesus had come as the Messiah to fulfill prophecy literally. They believed that a son of David would come and reestablish David's physical throne and restore the glory of his former physical kingdom. They were expecting Jesus, as their Messiah, to throw off the Roman yoke and bring about a literal restoration of Israel in military and political terms, restoring it to the way it was under David and during the early years of Solomon.

Jesus had already challenged this concept by asking the Pharisees and scribes who the Christ (or Messiah) really was. He then quoted Psalm 110:1 and asked, "How then does David in the Spirit call Him Lord?" (Matt. 22:43). In other words, if Christ is literally David's son, why then did David call him Lord? (See Matthew 22:44, Mark 12:36, and Luke 20:42.) He also said that because they had rejected Him as their King, the Kingdom would be taken from the Jews and given to another "nation" bearing the proper fruit (see Matt. 21:43).

Jesus had already made it clear that His Kingdom was not of natural Israel or of this world system (see John 18:35-37). Having risen from the dead, He made it very clear that His disciples were not to be witnesses just to the Jews, but were to reach out to all nations, even to the uttermost parts of the world (see Matt. 28:18-20; Acts 1:8). Nevertheless, it seems that His disciples could not escape the mindset of the Jewish people, which had existed for many generations, that the Kingdom was only for ethnic Israel and that other nations could only come in through the door of natural Israel by first becoming practicing Jews.

WITNESSES TO THE ENDS OF THE EARTH

It was never God's intention to bring ethnic Israel back as a nation to be His Kingdom exclusively. Hundreds of years earlier, after they had left Egypt, Israel had been invited to be the founding members of something much bigger, the Kingdom of God. It would fill the whole earth and touch all nations, but they refused to obey (see Exod. 19:1-6).

This glorious Kingdom could not be restricted to a mere 8,000 square miles of the Holy Land; it was destined to fill the whole earth. This Kingdom of the whole earth was to be His inheritance. Jesus said, "Go into all the earth…preach the gospel to every creature…be My witnesses not only in Jerusalem and Judea but also to the uttermost parts of the earth…make disciples of all nations…" (see Matt. 28:18-20; Mark 16:15; Acts 1:8).

He said in Acts 1:8, "but you shall receive power when the Holy Spirit has come upon you; and you shall be witnesses to Me in Jerusalem, and in all Judea and Samaria, and to the end of the earth." After He said this, Jesus ascended into Heaven.

THE KINGDOM RUNS OVER THE WALL

The Spirit fell on the day of Pentecost, and the power of the Kingdom was let loose from that day forward. In those first few years, Peter was the main instrument that God used. But, after a short time, the message of the Gospel could no longer stay within the boundaries of the Jews in Judea. In the early years of the Church, God shook them out of their Jewish nest by allowing persecution. Philip, the first evangelist, was forced by circumstances to preach the Kingdom of God in Samaria with amazing results (see Acts 8:4-13).

Peter was compelled by supernatural events to go to the house of Cornelius and preach the Kingdom for the first time to Gentiles. He and all the Jews who were with him were amazed when the Spirit fell upon these Gentiles just as He had fallen upon the disciples on the day of Pentecost (see Acts 10:1-48; Acts 11:12-18).

At about the same time, we read about a zealous Pharisee named Saul. At that time, he was a highly demonized, religious fanatic. This man thought, "I'm going to destroy this movement of Christians if it's the last thing I do!" But he was powerfully converted, completely turned around, and became the great apostle Paul. The Gospel of the Kingdom could no longer stay within Jewish boundaries, so it just ran over the wall like a mighty river and invaded the Gentile world.

Paul was very clear from the beginning of his ministry that preaching Jesus and the Kingdom to the whole world was his calling and his mission. From the beginning, Paul saw the Kingdom clearly in all its multicolored, multinational glory, encompassing all races, all classes, and both genders. He did not simply preach Jesus as a Savior from sins; He preached the Kingdom of God and the things concerning Jesus in the light of that Kingdom (see Acts 14:22; 19:8; 20:25; 28:23,31).

Living in the Kingdom Requires Military Obedience

Acts 1:2 states that "until the day when [Jesus] was taken up...He had by the Holy Spirit *given orders* to the apostles whom He had chosen." He did not give them suggestions; He gave them orders or commandments. In the Greek, *commandment* is a military term. I did some counting in the New Testament concerning this word and found that Jesus commanded His disciples hundreds of times. Scripture also says many times that Jesus obeyed His Father's commandments, using the same military term for His obedience.

If you have ever been in the military and you are given a commandment by a superior officer, you know that there is only one acceptable response. You just say "Yes, Sir!" and do it. It doesn't matter whether you agree with the order or whether you like it or not, you just have to do as you are told—immediately! You can't say, "Sir, I'll do it later when I have time," or "I'm watching a very interesting football match. I will just watch to the end and then I'll do it, Sir." You wouldn't say such a thing to an officer in the military. Nor would you say, "Sir, are you sure you know what you are saying? It doesn't seem like a good idea to me. I don't really agree with that, so I'd like to think about it."

There is a military style, "Yes, Sir!" attitude in the Kingdom that we need to comprehend and cultivate. Jesus gave hundreds of commandments to His disciples, particularly to the apostles. I think the main reason He chose them to be apostles was that they learned how to immediately say, "Yes Lord!" to everything He said. It wasn't their ability, but their obedience that qualified them. He gave them commandments by the Holy Spirit, and they learned to obey every order that He gave to them.

TO HAVE AUTHORITY, YOU MUST BE UNDER AUTHORITY

Years ago, during the reign of King George VI in Great Britain, I did military service and went through a military boot camp. Those who were particularly obedient during basic training and showed good leadership qualities were transferred to officer training. Those who went on to officer training found that the training did not become easier but even more severe. If one of the team members worked independently or rebelled under pressure, then he was taken off the course. He was considered unsuitable officer material. Many men in officer's training cracked under the pressure. However, those who got through to the end, working with the team, and perfectly obeying the word given to them through delegated authority, were considered good officer material.

During all of this training, we only learned one basic thing—obey the word! Obey the one set over you with the king's authority. While those officers were in training, they never gave one order; they just obeyed.

When your obedience was proved and you were seen to be a man under authority, then you graduated as an officer. Only then were you allowed to give orders. After that, for the first time you were given a squad of new recruits, and you began to give orders and lead them through their basic training. They would all obey instantly, not because of the volume with which you spoke but because of your authority.

Here is the principle. There was no authority in the words you spoke unless you yourself were under the authority of the king.

Because you were under his authority, whatever you said carried his authority.

THE CENTURION EXAMPLE

Luke teaches this same principle in Luke 7:1-9. Through his military training, a Roman centurion, not a religious Jew, was the first to understand the power and the authority of the Kingdom of God in Jesus.

The centurion had a sick servant, and he sent to Jesus saying, "Lord, you don't need to come to my house. Just speak the word, and he will be healed. Your words have authority" (see Luke 7:6-7). Luke tells us how the centurion knew that. He said:

> "For I, too also am a man placed under authority, having soldiers under me. And I say to this one, 'Go!' and he goes; and to another, 'Come!' and he comes; and to my servant, 'Do this!' and he does it." When Jesus saw these things, He marveled at him, and turned and said to the crowd that was following Him, "I say to you, I have I not found such great faith, not even in Israel" (Luke 7:8-9).

The centurion knew he was a man under Caesar's military authority, and he recognized that Jesus was a man under God's divine authority. The centurion was saying, "I've learned the power of being under authority. Servants and soldiers obey me because I am under the authority of Caesar. My sphere of authority is the military. I can command soldiers and servants, but You are a man under the authority of Almighty God. Because of the authority You are under, You can speak, and whatever You say will happen. You serve Almighty God. He has authority over all demons and sicknesses, and over the wind and the waves. You can speak with authority into these situations, and they have to obey You because of the authority You are under."

Jesus marveled at this man. He is the only man who ever made Jesus marvel. He was not a Jew, and he was not religious; he was a Roman soldier. Yet Jesus said of him, "I've not found such great faith in all of Israel." It is amazing how religious people think they can be disobedient, and it doesn't matter. I don't know why this is. If people treated their secular employers the way they treat their church leaders, they would be fired immediately. If we tried to behave in the military the way we behave in the church, we would be shot, jailed, or at least dismissed from service. We need to learn to come under authority.

Jesus could not find that kind of faith in the Jewish people, but He found it in a Roman soldier. Jesus was the first manifestation of the Kingdom, and the power of the Kingdom was released through Him because He lived as a man under the authority of His Father God.

INDEPENDENCE AND POWERLESSNESS GO TOGETHER

Just imagine that the centurion is tired of being in the military. He is tired of getting up at 5:30 A.M. each morning, shaving, putting on his uniform, and going on parade at 6:30 A.M. He is living in Judea when he could have been living in Rome with much better shops and much better schools for his children. Why was he in Judea? Because Caesar put him there. He was a man under authority. He could not choose anything, not even the place where he lived.

Imagine him saying, "I've had enough of this army life. I'm going to resign." He writes a letter of resignation, "Dear Caesar, it's been good to be in your army, but it's time for me to move on. Please accept my resignation effective next month." His resignation is accepted, and finally that wonderful day of release comes. At last he is free! "Wow!" he says, "now I can do whatever I like. I'm going to stay in bed until 9:00 A.M.; I won't shave, and I will put on some dirty, old jeans. I'm going to shuffle around and do whatever I like as a free man. No one is going to tell me what to do anymore."

Then on his first morning of "freedom," he realizes that all of his servants are gone because they were Caesar's servants. The chariots have all disappeared because they were Caesar's chariots. So, he's on his own. There's no one there to cook his breakfast, and he begins to think, "I'm not so sure that this is such a good way to live."

He has to go to the store himself and buy his own groceries. As he is carrying his bag of groceries home on foot, he sees one of the soldiers from his old platoon. He thinks, "That man has obeyed me for years. He has always done exactly what I told him to do." So the former centurion cries out, "Hey, soldier, come here and carry these bags!"

What do you think the soldier would say to him? He would say, "Get lost! Why should I obey you now?" While the centurion was under authority, he could order these soldiers, and they had to obey him. When he stepped out from under that authority into independence, he immediately lost all his authority.

Many Christians have no authority because they themselves are not under any authority. The Jews could not cast out demons because the real issue was obedience to Christ, not

Bible knowledge, learned methodology, traditional ceremony, or religious activity.

Jesus, the founder of the Kingdom, the first man manifesting the Kingdom, was recognized by that centurion as a man under authority. Of all the disciples who followed Him, the thousands who came to His healing meetings, and the thousands who had their stomachs filled miraculously, there were only a small number of people who were really prepared to obey Him. In the end, there were only 120 of them. Among those 120 were the 12 apostles, the 70 that Jesus sent out, and a number of women. Their main qualification was that they knew how to obey His orders, and, as a result, they shook the world. If we are willing to be that kind of person, then God can do through us what He did through them. Jesus gave them orders, like military commandments, through the Holy Spirit, and they learned to obey with a "Yes, Sir!" military attitude.

THE KINGDOM ALWAYS CAUSES CONFLICT

Acts 14:21-22 says, "When they had preached the gospel to that city and made many disciples, they returned to Lystra, Iconium, and Antioch, strengthening the souls of the disciples, exhorting them to continue in the faith, and saying, 'We must *through many tribulations enter the Kingdom of God*'" (Acts 14:21-22).

Whenever the Kingdom is preached, it always causes a spiritual war to break out, and there is conflict. Always! This can often become violent, and the Kingdom will always bring persecution, particularly by religious people. Always! It is a principle you find in Scripture and in practice. You must not quit but fight back, not carnally against flesh and blood, but with the true spiritual weapons and with even greater spiritual violence than has been used against you. In this way, in the Book of Acts, they forcefully advanced the Kingdom.

Paul came to Ephesus in Acts 19 to a small group who knew only "John's baptism" and we read from verse 6:

> And when Paul had laid his hands on them, the Holy Spirit came upon them, and they spoke with tongues and prophesied. Now the men were about twelve in all. And he went into the synagogue and spoke boldly for three months, reasoning and persuading concerning the things of the Kingdom of God (Acts 19:6-8).

So how long did Jesus teach on the things regarding the Kingdom of God after He was risen? 40 days! How long did the Apostle Paul teach on the Kingdom? Three months! We are not going to cover the whole subject adequately in just one book.

In Acts 20:25, Paul went on to say, "And indeed, now I know that you all, among whom I have gone *preaching the kingdom of God*, will see my face no more." Paul here is speaking to the elders of Ephesus. How long was Paul in this city? Three years. The entire time that Paul was among them, he was teaching and preaching to them about the Kingdom of God. He continues in verse 27, "For I have not shunned to declare to you the whole counsel of God" (Acts 20:27). In three years Paul completed the task and was able to say, "I have fully taught you all the things that are profitable. I taught you everything necessary." Unfortunately, I don't have three years, but I hope I can get enough of the Kingdom into you to make you hungry, passionate, and sufficiently equipped to begin to forcefully advance the Kingdom wherever God has placed you.

THE KINGDOM COMES TO ROME

Right to the end of his ministry, even during those last few years of his imprisonment in Rome before his execution, Paul had only one theme and one burning passion.

> So when they had appointed him a day, many came to him at his lodging, to whom he explained and solemnly testified of the Kingdom of God, persuading them concerning Jesus from both the Law of Moses and the Prophets, from morning till evening.... Then Paul dwelt two whole years in his own rented house, and received all who came to him, preaching the Kingdom of God and teaching the things which concern the Lord Jesus Christ with all confidence, no one forbidding him (Acts 28:23,30-31).

In the Philippian letter, Paul refers to his years of detention in Rome. In Philippians 1:12-13, he marvels at how God is using his circumstances for the furtherance of the Gospel. Those years in Rome allowed Paul to preach the Kingdom of God and teach concerning Jesus to the whole praetorium, and many officials and politicians at the heart of the Roman Empire turned to Jesus. In Philippians 4:22, he sends greetings from the saints of Caesar's household.

Paul's imprisonment was part of God's plan to conquer the whole Roman Empire. Through this faithful witness, God was preparing the way for the Kingdom to come fully. Thirty to 50 years later a mighty harvest was reaped from the Kingdom seed that Paul sowed which was destined to change the world. God would replace the Roman Empire with the Kingdom of God throughout all Europe.

May God give us similar doors of opportunity into the political arenas of the capital cities and the governments of our nations in this day. May we, like Paul, sow the seed of the Kingdom at every opportunity and then have the patience to pray and wait for harvest time, for we will reap if we do not faint.

Chapter 13

THE KINGDOM OF GOD AND THE KINGDOM OF HEAVEN

I now want to explain some differences between the terms "The Kingdom of God" and "The Kingdom of Heaven."

THE KINGDOM OF GOD

We have already seen that the phrase the "Kingdom of God" is emphasizing a relationship with God where we joyfully live under His benevolent despotic rule.

The Kingdom of God essentially is a relationship of love between an individual and our Father God in which He is obeyed perfectly. We saw it for a short while in Adam before he sinned. We saw this restored again to earth in the person of Jesus Christ. All that His life was and all that He was able to do was empowered through that Kingdom relationship. When He healed the sick and cast out demons, He said that this was the Kingdom of God which had come amongst them. The Kingdom of God has the power to undo everything that the kingdom of darkness has established in its absence. The Bible speaks several times regarding the end of the age and about the restoration of all things. The Kingdom of God is the instrument through which that restoration takes place. So what Jesus was really saying was, "Just live like Me, and you will become the Kingdom of God. Then the works that I do, you will do also, and even greater works than these you will do because I go to the Father. Then the Spirit who has been working though Me will be able to come to you and work in exactly the same way through you" (see John 14:12). We must not live a mediocre Christian life but aim to live just like Jesus.

Although this is clearly what the Bible teaches, much of the Church is so unfamiliar with this teaching that it sounds to them like heresy. They say, "Are you claiming to be like Jesus? That's blasphemy!"

And our reply can be: "No, I'm just going to give my humanity to the Holy Spirit the same way that Jesus did. I'm going to relate to the Father the same way that Jesus did. Once the blood of Jesus has done its mighty work in me, then God is able to work through my humanity in the same way that He worked through the humanity of Jesus. Nothing is going to be impossible for the Spirit who is in me. So, I expect to live this way. The Kingdom is a matter of both obedience and relationship."

The Bible states that God is perfect love, perfect goodness, perfect wisdom, absolute power, perfect righteousness, perfect knowledge, perfect light, perfect truth, indestructible life, etc.

I suggest you make a list of all the things the Bible says God is and then make a list of all the "I AM" statements of our Lord Jesus Christ. You'll be amazed at how much they overlap and at the all-embracing completeness of the list. The Bible summarizes this with these words, "As for God, His way is perfect; the word of the Lord is proven [or flawless]" (Ps. 18:30). The Hebrew word for perfect here is *tamiyn*: "without blemish, perfect, complete, full, sound, whole." To do His will perfectly or completely is fullness for us. To do less than His perfect will is to go from perfection to imperfection, with its consequent loss. We are not living in His Kingdom properly if we are not doing His will as perfectly as we know how. We will find the same perfection increasingly flowing through us as we develop that same life of obedience. Just as God is absolutely perfect, to obey Him perfectly causes that same perfection to be manifested in our lives and in all the environment over which we have authority and influence.

Once the Kingdom is working properly in us, we can then begin to impose it on our society, bringing about glorious change. Although everybody will enjoy its benefits, it doesn't take everybody to make it happen, just a militant minority.

THE SPHERE OF OUR GOVERNMENT

Every one of us has a sphere of government to some degree. If you are a single individual, you have government over yourself and over your world. If you are a father, you have a family over which you have government. If you are married to a wonderful wife as I am, you have the headship of the government that the two of you represent. Together, in right relationship, my wife and I have had the authority to extend the Kingdom over our

215

whole family. All our children grew up secure within the Kingdom that we produced by our joint submission to Jesus. Our obedience not only affected us, but it also affected and protected our children.

When Adam sinned, it affected all of creation because it was all within his sphere of authority. So when you disobey, it doesn't just affect you; it affects all those who are under your authority. Because my wife and I, after salvation, have always lived within the Kingdom of God, we have always had authority, and the devil has never been able to touch our kids. Now we have wonderful grandchildren, and they are in the Kingdom. As they get older, they are catching fire for Jesus, and God is beginning to do fantastic things through them. The devil cannot touch them because they are in the Kingdom.

IF THE KINGDOM WOULD ONLY COME TO OUR CITIES

Our own family is where we start; once you see the power of the Kingdom, you begin to see what could happen if all the churches in a given city would come together under proper government within the Kingdom. It would then be simple for God to take that city. Independence is a luxury that no one can afford. It is so destructive. If a pastor and the elders of a congregation would let the Kingdom truly come into their relationships, then everyone within their sphere of authority would be protected by the Kingdom that they would be able to establish. You cannot have disasters, tragedies, splits, and divisions in a church where the government and the Kingdom are properly established.

THE KINGDOM HAS ITS OWN ECONOMY

The entire time we lived in Mumbai, there was about 40 percent unemployment in the city. But in our church, because we were in the Kingdom, we had a different economy. Nobody in our church was permanently unemployed because we had authority in our sphere to see to it that each person was gainfully employed. We taught our church members to live and work with the excellent work ethic of the Kingdom, so that everyone wanted to employ them. After an employer had taken one or two of our people, he or she would come to us and say, "If you have any more of your people needing jobs, let us know; we have jobs waiting for them."

The Kingdom of God is powerful and practical concerning our everyday lives. If we get into the Kingdom, all that we have authority over is then protected by that Kingdom. If we live in independence, then we and all that we have authority over will be subject to attacks from the devil. That is too big a price to pay. This is why the devil is able to do so much damage to Christians.

THE KINGDOM OF HEAVEN

The phrase "The Kingdom of Heaven" is emphasizing the environment that is produced when God's will is perfectly done, whether it is by angels or by mankind. It is obedience to God that produces the environment of Heaven. That is the first sense in which we can look at the Kingdom of Heaven. Obedience produces heaven, and disobedience produces hell. It really is that simple. If you are living a hell of a life, it is a measure of your disobedience. Sorry, but that's the truth, and we need to get real. Obedient people do not have a hellish life; they have a heavenly life. Tremendous peace comes because it is a foundational part of the Kingdom.

Peace Is the Environment of the Kingdom of Heaven

There are some tremendous one-line statements about the Kingdom in Scripture. For example, "The kingdom of God is not eating or drinking, but righteousness and peace and joy in the Holy Spirit" (Rom. 14:17). Our family home is a house of peace. It is a place where God rules. He is worshiped, loved, and obeyed in our house. No demon would ever dare come near the place. The presence of God is always there, and it is wonderful to come into that atmosphere. People walk into our house and feel it. I'm talking about tradespeople who don't even know God. They walk in and say, "Boy, this house is wonderful. There is such a peace here." Air-conditioning engineers, painters, and tradespeople have felt the atmosphere of our house and been impacted by just stepping inside it.

One time a painter came into our house with a big radio/cassette player ready to play his noisy pop music as he painted. Fortunately, we already had a great praise and worship CD playing as he came in. He said, "That is beautiful music. This house has such a feeling about it. It's so full of peace. It's wonderful. I enjoy working here. How can I get a copy of that CD?" This is the Kingdom of Heaven. It has become the environment of the house because the house and all who live in it are submitted to the authority of God. You go to some homes, and the kids are peaceful, happy, content, and quiet because the environment is the Kingdom of Heaven. In others, it is just the reverse.

If we could get all our Christian families to live this out practically, we would see a constant harvest being reaped, just by people coming into our homes. Most people are not anti-God; they are just lost. They are looking for something, but they don't know what it is or where to find it. This is the first understanding of the Kingdom of Heaven. It could be your life. It could be your home. It should be true in the church and of everything over which we have authority.

THE KINGDOM OF HEAVEN IS THE ULTIMATE SEAT OF GOD'S THRONE AND AUTHORITY

The second thing I want to emphasize regarding the Kingdom of Heaven is its role as the ultimate seat of God's government. In Scripture, God is portrayed again and again as sitting on a glorious throne, surrounded by light and worshiped by multitudes of angels. We are told several times that God's throne is located in what is called "Heaven itself" or sometimes "the third heaven." It seems there are layers in the heavens. It is said of Jesus that when He rose from the dead, He "passed through the heavens" (plural) and then came into "heaven itself" where He sat down at the right hand of God (Heb. 4:14; 9:24). The idea of a plurality of the heavens is frequently mentioned in biblical language.

SATAN HAS INVADED AND POLLUTED THE LOWER LEVELS

It is also clear that the lower levels of the heavens have been invaded and polluted by demonic powers. The Book of Hebrews speaks about God cleansing the earth and also the lower level of the heavens. They both needed cleansing. It seems there are demonic powers and principalities who have discovered that their warfare and influence on earth become more effective if they carry out their activity from strongholds in "heavenly places." Jesus, as the glorious New Man after His resurrection, said that all authority in Heaven and on earth had been given to Him. Paul speaks several times in Scripture of wrestling with demonic principalities and powers that are located in the heavenly places (see Eph. 3:10; 6:12).

There is also clearly a realm beyond and above the contaminated layers of heaven where God dwells and rules in unpolluted glory and with undisputed authority. The term Kingdom of Heaven is also used to describe that sphere of rule and government, somewhere far above the earth, where God sits in glorious, undisputed power and majesty.

We are told in Ephesians 6:12 that we are to wrestle with demonic principalities and powers. Where do we wrestle with them? In heavenly places. We have to deal with those lower levels of the heavens, where the rule and influence of darkness bears down strongly upon the earth, so that the glory of God's heavenly realm may, with mounting power, pierce this murky veil, shifting the atmosphere of earth so that we increasingly live and minister under an open heaven.

You can sometimes feel this very strongly over certain cities. It seems like a canopy of demonic darkness hangs over the city. When you start to deal with that canopy of darkness, you can turn that heavenly realm from darkness to light and from the power of satan to the power of God. Then people begin to respond very differently to the preaching of the Gospel. It says again in Ephesians chapter 1 that the throne of Jesus is far above all principalities and powers in the heavenly places (see Eph.

1:20-21). The Bible calls that ultimate Heaven, where God dwells, "heaven itself" (Heb. 9:24) or "the third heaven" (2 Cor. 12:2). However, the Bible never directly describes or defines an actual first or second heaven.

There is some teaching going around concerning the first and the second heavens, which is not based on anything that the Bible actually says, and this must be regarded as mere speculation rather than biblical truth. All we know from Scripture is that there is a third heaven which is a place of uncontaminated glory, and it is the seat of God's rule and authority. It never has been, and it never will be penetrated or polluted by any demonic darkness.

WE MUST LEARN TO CLEANSE THE HEAVENS

If we are going to bring the Kingdom functionally into our society, we have to learn to deal with that contaminated heavenly realm. The only way we can enter that heavenly realm is through spirit activity. In spirit, I can sit with Christ in heavenly places even though my body is on earth. I have pondered this for years and have tried to pray over exactly what this means. We are dealing with things beyond our understanding, and maybe one day God will give us more light, but we don't need to understand fully in order to obey God.

Even with our present understanding of this material world, we know it is possible for two physical worlds to exist in the same space without being aware of or interfering with each other. It is a matter of the frequency of vibration of the particles that make up the molecules. They could, theoretically, pass through each other without either becoming aware of the other's existence, and yet, at the same time, they would each seem solid and real enough to anyone within either of these two worlds. There are spiritual laws and powers, as well as physical laws, that work in these realms of earth and heaven. We need to learn how to harness them more effectively for the advance of the Kingdom of God and for the destruction of the kingdom of darkness. We must be willing to let God teach us like little children how to behave in these realms in order to bring the Kingdom in.

OBTAINING AN OPEN HEAVEN

When we are dealing with any city, we must be aware of the heavenly dimension over it as well as the earthly dimension. We must accomplish certain things in the heavens before there can be any manifestation on the earth. Dealing with the heavenly realm changes the environment in which we are able to function spiritually. I will talk more about this when dealing with the gates of the city in the sequel to this book.

Some years ago, my wife and I had some contact with Dr. David Yonggi Cho, the well-known Korean pastor. We visited his church for the first time in the late 1970s. The church had a huge membership. Eileen returned six months later to find it had continued to grow rapidly. We were privileged to see that church in those days as few others have seen it.

The power of that church is in its prayer life, which is centered in Prayer Mountain. Prayer Mountain is located outside the city and is dedicated to permanent prayer. It has existed as part of the church from its early days and has never been just for that one church. Prayer Mountain is for the whole city, for the nation of South Korea, and for all nations.

PRAYER MOUNTAIN

In 1958, Dr. Cho began with five people. There was himself, his wife, his mother-in-law, and two other people. The church in the city was small and struggling, and a congregation of 50 seemed like a dream. Nevertheless, they persevered in the way God showed them. From its early days, it was a church founded on prayer. Early on, they established a permanent place of prayer out on a mountain about one hour's drive from the city, and this became "Prayer Mountain." No food was served; only water was available. It was assumed that everybody came to fast and pray. When Eileen visited, they were meeting in a tent and later moved to a permanent building. By the mid-1980s, there were about 10,000 people there most of the time.

This powerhouse of prayer has transformed that city. They bombarded the demonic strongholds continuously from Prayer Mountain and cleared the heavenly realm. Now, because of the many years of Prayer Mountain's ministry, there are more than 3,000 churches in the city of Seoul, and many of them have become very large.

I have listened to David Yonggi Cho preach. He is a good preacher and a wonderful man of God, but it is the power of prayer clearing the heavens that makes things happen on such a massive scale. I have heard Dr. Cho say several times, "When I preach in my own church, I preach under an open heaven. When I go to any other place, I may pray for hours before the meeting and never experience the same freedom because there is not the same open heaven."

When I attended his church meetings, the main building then held about 25,000 people. It was filled seven times on a Sunday. It was an organizational miracle to get one crowd out and the next crowd in within 30 minutes, seven times each Sunday. Everything ran precisely to time; the worship was good, the preaching was good…everything was good. However, what was fantastic was what happened at the end when he gave an invitation for people to come forward to receive Jesus. Thousands responded, and they did so every Sunday.

PRAYER OPENS HEAVEN

During the 1980s when we were there and the church was around 200,000 members, the average number of salvations recorded each Sunday was around 10,000 people. I went into the church offices and asked, "What happens to all these people?" They kept meticulous written records in those days, and they could show through their records that between 7,000 and 8,000 people were established in home groups within the church each month. Then I asked, "What about the rest?" Through the same careful records, they could show me that many others had become established in other churches. They seemed just as happy that people were established in other churches as in their own church. They said, "In the last month we recorded about 350 who did not continue, but the rest are firmly established in other churches somewhere else." They could show me the records of each individual and how they matured and developed. I was amazed at what I saw.

I had never seen anything like it in my life, but we should see similar exploding growth around our nation as we establish similar places of prayer. It is in prayer meetings like this that we learn to clear the heavens. Luke 3:21 says that while Jesus prayed, the heavens were opened. It was as if the dark layers of the contaminated heavens were parted for a few moments, and a clear corridor between earth and the unpolluted third heaven was established. That is the way I see it in my imagination. When we learn to pray like that, the principalities and powers who rule this present darkness from their heavenly vantage point can no longer stay on their thrones. They are cast down and the way into Heaven itself is opened.

We need to see the Kingdom of Heaven as a place of government and rule over the affairs of this world. We are told that if we want to see anything happen on earth, it must already have happened in Heaven. Jesus said that what you bind on earth, will be, because it already has been bound in Heaven. And whatever you loose on earth, will be, because it already has been loosed in Heaven (Matt. 16:19; 18:18, literal translation).

An important part of our prayer life is to bring the rule of God into those polluted heavenly realms until they are cleared and become the Kingdom of Heaven. When that is accomplished and a permanent Kingdom of Heaven atmosphere is maintained over a city, then there comes a totally different responsiveness by the people in that city because they are now living under that canopy of the Kingdom of Heaven instead of the kingdom of darkness. We saw this happen in Mumbai years ago, and it continues to this day.

When you go to some cities, you can feel the canopy of darkness, and it is all you can do just to breathe spiritually. Sometimes as you pray, you can feel the moment when it cracks, breaks, and begins to change from a hellish to a heavenly environment. The people living under that canopy begin to respond differently because of the change of kingdom in that heavenly realm.

This is something we must learn to do through our prayers. When we learn to do this properly and effectively we will be working under an open heaven. It won't just affect a particular local church but will affect the whole Church in the city. To pray this way, you must have a passion for the city. We have established such a prayer center in San Antonio where we live: the San Antonio Apostolic Prayer Center. It is for the whole city. Anybody can come and pray there, and our passion is to see every church in the city grow as we see the heavens open and the Kingdom of Heaven established over our city.

Chapter 14

THE KINGDOM PROPHESIED
IN THE OLD TESTAMENT

Throughout the Old Testament (beginning in Genesis and proceeding through the Pentateuch, through all the Books of Poetry, the Psalms, and the Prophets), there are many direct and powerful references to the coming Kingdom. Some are connected directly with the birth of Jesus and do not refer to His second coming at the end of this age. Some of the most obvious and glorious are in the Book of Daniel and in Isaiah (and reference has already been made to some of these in this book). Once the Spirit had come and opened the understanding of the first apostles, light suddenly streamed into all the Old Testament writings. As a first priority, after His resurrection, Jesus began to carefully explain the things concerning Himself in all these Scriptures. This was the primary weapon He used to deal with their inability to understand. He was then able to cast their chronic unbelief out of them.

CHRIST ON EVERY PAGE OF THE OLD TESTAMENT

Now let's come back to First Corinthians chapter 10:

Moreover, brethren, I do not want you to be unaware that all our fathers were under the cloud, all passed through the sea, all were baptized into Moses in the cloud and in the sea, all ate the same spiritual food, and all drank the same spiritual drink. For they drank of that spiritual Rock that followed them, and that Rock was Christ. But with most of them God was not well pleased, for their bodies were scattered in the wilderness. **Now these things became our examples,** *to the intent that we should not lust after evil things as they also lusted. And do not become idolaters as were some of them. As it is written,* **"The people sat down to eat and drink, and rose up to play."** *Nor let us commit sexual immorality, as some of them did, and in one day twenty-three thousand fell; nor let us tempt Christ, as some of them also tempted, and were destroyed by serpents; nor complain, as some of them also complained, and were destroyed by the destroyer.* **Now all these things happened to them as examples, and they were written for our admonition, upon whom the ends of the ages have come.** *Therefore let him who thinks he stands take heed lest he fall* (1 Corinthians 10:1-12).

As Paul predicted, these Old Testament Scriptures are becoming particularly relevant as we come to the end of the age. We are told two things when we read the history of God's dealings with Israel. First, it is an example and a warning for us. We are told here, "For they drank of that spiritual Rock that followed them, and that Rock was Christ." The rock they spiritually drank from was Christ.

Christ was already actively present among them even in those days. When He was born on earth through Mary, it was the beginning of His physical life as a man, but not the beginning of His existence. He had already appeared to Abraham and was made known to both Abraham and David as Melchizedek, the great Eternal High Priest of the New Covenant (see Gen. 14:18-19; Ps. 110:4). Through His pre-incarnation ministry to them, they lived as New Covenant believers in Him and His perfect sacrifice by faith for hundreds of years, long before He became a physical man on earth.

Paul is saying that we must learn from their example. If we do what they did, we will get the same judgment from the same God. God was not pleased with them, and He will not be pleased with us if we do the same things. In spite of their confession, "all that You say, we will do," in Exodus 19:7-9 and again in Joshua 1:16-18, they were blatantly disobedient.

The second thing we are told in First Corinthians 10:11 is that these events were types (Greek *tupos*) or allegorical shadows or pictures of the spiritual reality that they represented. All of these Old Testament Scriptures are an example and a warning to us to be careful. However, they are also types or allegories. They are powerful spiritual pictures of great spiritual truths.

JESUS OPENS THEIR UNDERSTANDING

When Jesus was raised from the dead and met two disciples on the road to Emmaus, He was "hidden from them" so that they did not recognize Him. They were in deep depression and thoroughly disappointed. They said:

> The things about Jesus of Nazareth, who **was** a prophet mighty in deed and word before God and all the people, and how our chief priests and leaders handed him over to be condemned to death and crucified him. But we **had hoped** that he was the one to redeem Israel (Luke 24:19-21 RSV).

Notice the past tense of their speech. They were utterly discouraged and completely disillusioned. They thought, "We are not going to see this mighty Kingdom that we thought would come. Jesus is dead, and it's all over. Our leader is gone, and now we are completely finished. We are going home in utter disappointment."

Jesus rebuked them saying, "O foolish men, and slow of heart to believe all that the prophets have spoken!" (Luke 24:25 RSV). Which prophets was He talking about? Obviously the Old Testament prophets, since the New Testament was not yet written. Jesus then took the Law, the Psalms, and the Prophets and expounded everything in these books concerning Himself to His disciples (see Luke 24:27,44). He showed them Christ on every page of the Old Testament. Their hearts were burning within them as He opened up the Scriptures to them. When we read the Old Testament and its stories, history, and ancient prophecy, they become, through the Spirit of Christ, present-day spiritual revelation. Then these Scriptures begin to throb with power and life and become relevant for our particular day.

OLD TESTAMENT SCRIPTURES IN THE NEW COVENANT

I think it's totally wrong to divide the Bible into two watertight compartments called the Old Testament and the New Testament. So much of what we call the Old Testament is speaking powerfully by revelation about the New Covenant. Some teachers today are encouraging believers to blatantly disobey Scripture because it is so-called "Old Testament." "Oh, that's Old Testament," they say. "We don't have to listen to that any more. It doesn't apply to us today."

But Jesus said this in Matthew chapter 5:

> Do not think that I have come to abolish the law or the prophets; I have come not to abolish but to fulfill. For truly I tell you, until heaven and earth pass away, not one letter, not one stroke of a letter, will pass from the law until all is accomplished. Therefore, whoever breaks one of the least of these commandments, and teaches others to do the same, will be called least in the kingdom of heaven; but whoever does them and teaches them will be called great in the kingdom of heaven. For I tell you, unless your righteousness exceeds that of the scribes and Pharisees, you will never enter the kingdom of heaven (Matthew 5:17-20 NRSV).

For example, some will say, "Where in the New Testament are we told to raise our hands, shout, and conduct extreme and extravagant worship? Where does it say that? The answer is "It's in the Psalms!" Then some will say, "But that's Old Testament." No! It is New Testament. David wrote most of those Psalms in the tabernacle of David, which was fully New Testament in its faith and practice.

The theology of most of the Book of Psalms is in fact New Testament theology. Once the tabernacle of David was raised, David lived as a New Testament believer. The Son of God did not come into existence when He was born of Mary. He has always existed, and He appeared a number of times to people in the Old Testament. The cross is a historical event, but at the same time, the cross is a timeless, spiritual event filling all of eternity. The Bible tells us that Jesus was foreordained and crucified before the foundation of the world.

UNDERSTANDING TIME AND ETERNITY

In order to reap the full harvest of spiritual truth, we must come to some understanding of time and eternity and how they differ and yet relate. For this reason, this concept is found in many of my teachings, including my previous book, *The Good Fight of Faith*.

The Bible tells us that when God created all things, there was a moment when time began. We are also told that there will come a moment at the end of the age when an angel will declare the end of time, and then time will be no more.

Imagine the passing of time, in this physical time space-world in which we live, as a long line. At one end is the beginning of time, and at the other end is the end of time. Between the beginning and end of time is the whole history of the human race. Somewhere on that line, Jesus was born of a woman. Christians have divided time into two parts, before and after Christ. On this timeline, Abraham was born approximately 2,000 years before Christ was crucified, and Alan Vincent was born approximately 2,000 years afterward. Approximately 4,000 years divide Abraham from Alan in terms of time.

Then try to think eternally using your spirit man and not your natural mind. Eternity is not just a long time going on for thousands and thousands of years. In eternity there is no time at all as we presently know it. It is an ever-present "now" going on forever. Think of eternity like a circle. It doesn't have a beginning or an end. It's not a straight line; it's a circle, and at its perimeter, you can go on traveling around it forever. Once you step inside eternity, you are in all of it at the same moment. It is one, great, eternal now, and you can touch any or all of it simultaneously.

Once we are born of the Spirit and our spirit man comes alive, we can step from time into eternity. We receive a new faculty that the Bible calls "faith." It is the ability to believe or take hold of what God has said without needing to perceive anything with our natural senses. That is one of the great benefits of being born again. Although we continue to live naturally in time, in the spirit we can also enter eternity. We can step from time into eternity where there is no time. There is no past, present, or future. There is just an everlasting, great, eternal now.

The natural habitat for God and the angels is eternity, but God can step into time when and wherever He chooses. Abraham lived 2,000 years before Christ in time, but once he was justified by faith, he became a New Testament believer and was able in spirit to step into eternity. He was able to meet Jesus in the person of Melchizedek, and embrace the cross because it was already "now" in the eternal realm. In eternity, the blood of Jesus Christ was already eternally and freshly shed for him. Therefore, Abraham could experience the power of the cross and be saved by the Blood of that perfect Lamb as a New Testament believer 2,000 years before it took place in time.

Alan Vincent is able to do the same thing 2,000 years after that historic moment in time, because in eternity it is still the same eternal now. The blood of God's Lamb is just as fresh for me today as it was for Abraham then. Therefore, Abraham and Alan can both meet Jesus in the eternal realm and have the same "now" encounter with the power and benefits of His cross.

King David lived in time approximately 1,000 years before Christ. Nevertheless, in spirit, he also was able to step into eternity and embrace the power of the cross. As we read Psalm 22, we are forced to conclude that David must have had a vision of Jesus being crucified in which he saw every detail of it as if he was an eyewitness to the event. He wrote it all down in his wonderful Psalm 22 approximately 1,000 years before it took place in time.

Because of this revelation, David, in his tabernacle, abandoned all the ceremony and sacrifices of Moses' law and became a New Testament believer 1,000 years before Jesus had been crucified in time. What he did was totally illegal according to Moses' law. In the flesh, as a descendent of Judah, he could not have been a priest to God. Nevertheless, in spirit he became a priest as part of the eternal Melchizedek priesthood and entered the Kingdom of God and the heavenly tabernacle. He enjoyed face-to-face fellowship with God and became a priest to God without any of the prescribed Jewish qualifications, sacrifices, or limitations.

This was possible because he saw, embraced, and received the power of the already sacrificed, perfect Lamb of God, which, as we are told, was crucified before the foundation of the world. He did not need any other sacrifice! As a result, he lived in face-to-face fellowship with God and did not die, but lived! He lived because he didn't come according to the covenant of law that God made through Moses, but according to the covenant of promise by faith that God made with Abraham and all his spiritual descendants, ratified through the blood of our Lord Jesus Christ who already "was and is" crucified in the eternal realm.

ONE DIVINELY INSPIRED WORD OF GOD

We have to recognize the inadequacies of some traditional "Old" and "New" Testament concepts of the Bible and see it as one Word of God. While it is truly historic, we must not be bound by "this time period" or "that time period." We must realize that there are eternal dimensions of God's dealings with man which transcend time. Long ago, as the children of Israel were walking in the wilderness, Jesus was there as the Christ saying, "Hey! Drink from Me!" He said almost exactly the same thing thousands of years later as He cried out to the crowd on the last day of the Feast of Tabernacles (see John 7:37). Anyone, at any time in the history of man, could have entered into the eternal realm and lived as a New Testament believer through the cross.

In John 8:56, Jesus said, "Abraham rejoiced to see My day." They said, "You are not yet 50 years old and have you seen Abraham?" (see John 8:57). Jesus said, "Before Abraham was, I AM." Jesus was saying, "Oh, Yes! Abraham rejoiced to see My day. Abraham saw it, embraced it, and said, 'Hallelujah! I believe it.' He lived in a face-to-face relationship of friendship with God through the power of the cross."

Jesus could have said, "I was there as the great Melchizedek, and Abraham and I were having fellowship together long, long, ago. I gave him the bread and the wine of the New Covenant, and he gave me a tithe of everything by faith."

In a manner of speaking, spiritually, Abraham had his own love feast experience and broke bread with the Lord 2,000 years before it took place in time in the Upper Room with His disciples.

When you see this, you begin to understand that all these things were written for our instruction, and they are particularly relevant for those who live at the end of the age. We need to understand the allegories and truths of the Old Testament. We need to come and meet the Spirit of Christ on the Emmaus road. We need to attend the Emmaus Road Bible School where Jesus Himself opens up all these Old Testament Scriptures so that they burn within us in the same way they burned within the first disciples.

Then we can see that Christ and the message of the Kingdom are on every page of the Old Testament. It is not just history, but is written for our instruction, particularly for those on whom the end of the age has come.

Chapter 15

The Counterfeit Kingdom

The Counterfeit Often Comes First

Sometimes our wrong prayers are answered to teach us a lesson. Sometimes God's people have to first taste the false and be burned by it before they will genuinely desire the true. Jesus, speaking of the Kingdom, said that some do not immediately desire the new wine for they have tasted the old and say it is better (see Luke 5:36-39).

Moses had prophesied that the Israelites would one day have a king, and he warned them about the dangers of having the wrong kind of king (see Deut. 17:14-20). However, up until the time of Samuel, God's people had never had a king. The first king of Israel was named Saul. He was not God's choice but the people's choice.

God allowed them to have their own way in order to teach them some lessons.

If you pray earnestly about something that is not God's will and insist that God answer you, be careful! God may finally let you have your way, but it will be to your detriment. He may let you have your way, and you will learn the hard way if you stubbornly persist in praying the wrong prayers.

Jesus was much wiser when He prayed. The thought of becoming filthy with all the sin of Adam's race was so repulsive to Him that He could barely handle the weight of it. It was not the pain of the cross, but the dirtiness of sin coming upon Him that so revolted Him. He cried out, "Oh, if it's possible, let this cup pass from me. I don't want to do this. It's so unbelievably foul and filthy." Then He quickly said, "Nevertheless, not My will, but Your will be done" (see Matt. 26:39). He was not going to pray a foolish prayer and resist His Father's will.

Sometimes, we pray foolish prayers. We ask God to give us things so earnestly that in the end He gives us what we have been asking for, knowing that it will be painful for us. He allows this in order to teach us a lesson. There are many examples of this in Scripture, and many examples that I know of personally.

Because I've seen this happen to others many times, I am now scared of getting my own way. I really want only the will of God. It so terrifies me that I now say, "Lord, I don't want my own will, only Your will in everything!" Sometimes you can wrongly pray for someone to stay alive instead of dying quickly and peacefully because it is God's time to take them home. You need to learn to pray the right prayers when people are coming to the end of their life. It may be God's time for them to go to be with Him. Your prayers can sometimes keep them alive against the best plan of God. These wrong prayers can make the whole death process a long, drawn-out misery of pain and suffering instead of the dignified, joyful exit it should have been.

Hezekiah got his prayer answered. He did not want to die at that time (see 2 Kings 20:1-6). He had experienced a glorious, kingly reign; he was at the peak of his spiritual success, but he was falling into the sin of pride, and it was God's time for him to depart before he became badly corrupted. He cried out desperately not to die, and God answered his prayer. He eventually lived 15 years longer than he should have lived. As a result, he became proud and boastful over his success and made a terrible compromise with the Chaldeans. Manasseh, one of the most evil kings in Judah's history, was born to Hezekiah in that time period. Manasseh did terrible destruction to the purpose and people of God. It would have been much better for Hezekiah to have died on time. Then these things would not have happened, and Manasseh would never have been born.

Sometimes God uses you for a ministry, and then your time for that ministry is over. Make sure you get out of the way when it is God's time! If you stay there too long praying for God to bless you when you are supposed to move out of the way, you can become the main obstruction to what God is planning to do next.

WHEN A MOVE OF GOD HAS RUN ITS COURSE—LET IT DIE!

Years ago, I knew a great man of God who had been used powerfully to bring back lost truth to the Church. I once heard him say publicly, "The people used by God in His last move often become the main opponents of the next move of God because they think that their move of God was the last and final move. It's usually not the final thing but another step toward God's perfect plan to bring in the fullness of His Kingdom." This man suffered a lot for the truth that God used him to bring back to the Church. He suffered much persecution from people who had been part of a previous move of God. Many others, including myself, received so much from him. His revelation was not the final revelation but a great step along the way.

In 1965, when I received the baptism in the Holy Spirit and began to speak in tongues, this same man cut me off immediately. He would have nothing more to do with me because he rejected "this tongues nonsense." Unfortunately, he fulfilled his own word and became an ardent opponent of the next move of God. So I prayed then, and I still pray now, "Lord, I never want to do what I saw that great spiritual father do. I never want to get in the way of Your next move. When it is time for me to move out of the way, I want to have ears to hear what You are saying and the grace to quickly move out of the way. I never want to oppose anything new that You are doing because I don't understand it or immediately like it."

SAUL ESTABLISHED A FALSE KINGDOM

In the Bible, we have such an example in King Saul. God gave the people what they asked for. Saul was known as the man who was head and shoulders above everyone else. In natural terms, Saul represented the best of natural ability, the best of natural gifts and natural intellect. He was the people's choice. At first, when the people called him to be the king, he went and hid (see

1 Sam. 10:22). He didn't even want the job. I used to think, "What a humble man. He didn't even want the job."

I asked God, "What happened to this humble man that he became so proud?" One day God said to me, "That never was genuine humility. The thing that made Saul hang back was not humility but the fear of failure. He didn't want the job because he was not sure he could do it successfully. It was not true humility but fear and insecurity mixed with pride. He was so afraid that he would not look good before the people that at first he was afraid to try."

Once he got the job of king and discovered that he could do it and that all the people admired the "great King Saul," he changed his mind and began to say, "Oh, I like this. When I walk by, the people bow before me and admire. I'm enjoying this!" Once he got a taste for prominence and popularity, it became like a drug, and he could not live without it.

I have met people like that, and I have seen movements like that. I am not going to cover this in detail, but we need to understand what these "Saulish" tendencies are so we can make sure that they are not in us. In this last century, some previous movements of God deteriorated into elitism, exclusivity, and pride. They became bound in laws and traditions of their own and fossilized to become a "Saulish" house that opposed the next move of God.

The Pentecostal movement in some countries is a typical example of this. Almost every new move of God in the history of the Church, after a time, has become historic and respectable and lost its fire. These movements become like the house of Saul that does not want "the house of David" to come and take over.

Saul was not only an individual, but he also produced a house that was called the "house of Saul." A strong leader will produce an entire movement that will carry his or her genes and have his or her character. Those with Saulish tendencies will produce a "house of Saul" that has powerful momentum—because religious demons will eventually invade and take control of any house of Saul. Even after the founding leader dies, the house will often continue in the power of its own momentum, sometimes for many years afterward.

CHARACTERISTICS OF THE HOUSE OF SAUL

Saul Never Really Sought the Face of God

Saul never had a real, personal relationship with God. He knew how to put on a convincing religious act when necessary, but it wasn't real. This was no different from certain professional ministers today who put on their professional ministry clothes and start a religious show. You can see and sense that they are merely putting on a religious act in public. In their private life there is no passion for God, there is no real seeking of His presence, and there is no desire to know Him or walk with Him.

If one of these ministers wants to do something, he or she may say, "Let's all pray and ask for God's wisdom," but in reality, it's just a religious pretense. He or she has already made up his or her mind. The only role that God can play is to help him or her accomplish that plan. He or she is not really looking to hear God and do His will. The "prayer" is just an empty, religious formality. Watch out that you don't follow a man or woman like this or get these Saulish tendencies in you.

If you are looking for a leader to follow, first mark the relationship that person truly has with the living God. Saul didn't need God or want God in any personal way. Oh sure, he wanted God's help, but only as far as it helped Saul accomplish his plan, "Oh God, bless me and help me. But please don't get in my way. I know where I am going and I know what I want to do. Just help me to get there, and even if you don't, I'll still manage somehow to get there on my own."

David Sought After God

David was the real king of God's choice. David's passion was to have a personal relationship with God. He could not live without that relationship. He didn't want to do anything his way; he wanted to do it God's way.

Saul fought with the Philistines all the 40 years of his reign and never won a decisive victory. When David came to the throne, he first went to God, and asked, "Do you want me to go and attack the Philistines?" (See, for example, Second Samuel 5:19.) He wouldn't move until God answered. When God told him to attack, David then asked, "What's the plan? How do we do it?" Each time God told him to go, God gave him a different strategy. The result was that David only attacked the Philistines three times, and they were totally destroyed as an effective fighting force. David occupied all their cities and put a garrison in each place. For the remainder of David's reign, the Philistines never attacked again. David established kingdom rule over them and then went on to subdue all his enemies. This happened because there was a totally different relationship between the king and his God.

Saul Added People to Himself

The second characteristic is the way these Saulish kings treat other people. It says in Scripture that when Saul saw a promising person he added that person "to himself" (see 1 Sam. 14:52). He was subconsciously saying within himself, "These men and women can help me to promote myself and my ministry." That was the bottom line with Saul. He only saw other people as useful to him in terms of getting his program fulfilled and his reputation enhanced. He had no interest in them as people but only in how they could serve his purpose. He only used people; he never really related to them personally.

So look for these Saulish tendencies. If you find any of them in yourself, then hate them the way God hates them. If these tendencies are in your church or in your network, and you find yourself serving a Saul, then consider whether you should stay there or not.

David Took Nobodies and Transformed Them

Because the Kingdom of God runs on fatherhood, if you have leadership responsibility, and men and women of ability come along to help you, then it should be a two-way street. They are there to serve you, but also you are there to serve them and develop them to the fullness of their gift and ministry.

A true father has more joy in his son's success than he does in his own success. If you are following someone and serving him or her, you must ask yourself, "Is this person a father or a demanding leader? What kind of heart does this leader have?"

More importantly, if you are a ministry leader with people following you, what kind of heart do you have? If you are a

David-hearted leader, you will produce ever-increasing ability, gift, and ministry in the people who are following you. They will get bigger and bigger spiritually in gift and in ministry while following you. David started with a bunch of men who were in debt, discouraged, and disillusioned. They were total zeros, but he turned them into mighty men of war who were incredible in their individual accomplishments. Those mighty men were proof of David's fatherhood.

Saul Was Insecure and Threatened by Greater Gifts

Another characteristic of Saul was his insecurity. When he saw another person with a greater gift than his own, it made him feel very insecure. That is why he had a problem with David. David was too successful for Saul, and his ability threatened Saul's security. Saulish leaders are like that. They like to have people serving them, but they will do everything in their power to keep them subject or inferior. I have known men like this. They lead large churches and large movements with thousands of people but are afraid to have leaders on their staff who shine with a greater gift in any area. They usually get rid of them because they are afraid they may outshine them and then usurp their leadership.

One day I was sitting with a group of well-known speakers at a large conference, and they were discussing how dangerous it was to let someone on staff preach regularly who had a great preaching gift because that person could steal the hearts of your people. They said that if you had to be away, it was better to pay a lot of money to bring in a visiting preacher.

That is Saul. David had an absolutely loyal heart toward Saul, but he was a threat to Saul because he was a better leader, had greater ability, and was more loved by the people. The people were saying, "Saul has slain his thousands, but David has slain his tens of thousands!" Saul could not stand that, so David had to go (see 1 Sam. 18:7-8).

Saul's Primary Concern Was to Look Good Before the People

The final thing that really concerned Saul was how he looked before the people. When Samuel finally came and told Saul that God was taking the kingdom from him because he had not been absolutely obedient, Saul said, "I have sinned; yet honor me now, please, before the elders of my people and before Israel" (1 Sam. 15:30). Saul still wanted to look good before the people. That was the most important thing to him. This kind of leader is more concerned with what the people think than with what God thinks.

David's Only Concern Was to Please God

David was different. When he was dancing before the Lord with all his might, his wife Michal, the daughter of Saul, despised him in her heart. She said, "Oh, how noble my Lord was before the people." She was being sarcastic. She was saying, "You looked like a fool in front of the people." Because she was Saul's daughter, she, like her father, was most concerned with what the people thought. David didn't care what people thought, but what God thought. David replied to her:

> It was before the Lord, who chose me instead of your father and all his house, to appoint me ruler over the people of the Lord, over Israel. Therefore I will play music before the Lord. And I will be even more undignified than this, and will be humble in my own sight… (2 Samuel 6:21-22).

The David heart is concerned with what God thinks. The Saul heart is concerned with what people think.

THE WRONG REASONS FOR WANTING A KING

Israel asked for a king for four wrong reasons.

1. Samuel's Sons Did Not Walk With God

Samuel's sons did not walk in the ways of God as Samuel did. This is one of the things that has frightened me, and it should frighten you. Eli was a mighty man of God, a great prophet, but what happened to his sons? They became apostate. Abinadab, the man who housed the ark of God for almost 70 years, was an incredible man of God. What happened to his son Uzzah? Samuel was a mighty man of God, a wonderful prophet in word and deed, but what happened to his sons? Moses was a great man of God. Did you know he had two sons? Most Christians cannot even name them. He had two sons who, as far as we know, never amounted to anything spiritually.

When I saw these Scriptures I said, "Dear God, I don't want that to happen to my sons." In Scripture, the inheritance frequently passed to spiritual sons and not natural sons. I think there are two reasons for this.

The first reason is that the father is so taken up with ministry that he neglects his own natural sons. The children become resentful toward God and the ministry because they see that the ministry has stolen their father. He never has time for them, so they come to resent God instead of love Him.

The second reason is a wrong familiarity with the man of God. Familiarity can cause natural sons not to appreciate the anointing and gift that their father carries. Other young men can see it, and they will do anything to get one or two hours with this wonderful man of God because they want what he can give them.

However, the natural sons almost despise what their father has and therefore do not run after him as other young men do. Therefore, God gives the inheritance to hungry, spiritual sons because the natural sons are not worthy to receive it. Moses' inheritance passed to Joshua and not to his natural sons. Eli's inheritance passed to Samuel, not his natural sons, and so on.

It is important for us to see this. If you are a father, particularly of teenage children, you should be careful not to cause them to miss their inheritance by neglect. If you are a child of a man or woman that God is using, be careful that you don't miss your inheritance because you don't respect and value your father's or mother's anointing as other people do.

The first reason the people looked for a king was the failure of Samuel's sons. The people looked for an alternative leader because they were not prepared to trust the sons of Samuel.

2. They Wanted to Be Like Other Nations

There is a tendency in the church to copy the world rather than set an example for the world. The things we do in the Kingdom should be more excellent than anything the world does. Unfortunately, it is often the other way around, but God is changing that right now. When Solomon brought in the kingdom, the whole world came to see it and were astonished by its excellence.

In the Kingdom, we should have the best architects, the best musicians, the best artists. Everything of God's creative heart should be at its best in the Kingdom. We tend to reject these things as worldly, but we need them desperately in the Church. All of the arts (such as drama, media, music, and the rest) are gifts from God and should be ten times better in the purity and glory of the Kingdom than they are in the world.

When we put on a presentation to glorify Jesus, it should blow people away. It should knock them out with its amazing glory. Just think about the fantastic celebrations of Jesus we could have if all the gifts were working together properly. Wouldn't it be fantastic if a celebration for Jesus was ten times better than anything the world could do? But the Church doesn't think like that. Instead, they think that the world is ten times better than the Church, and they just want to copy it. If that is your heart, you will choose the wrong king.

3. *They Wanted the King to Fight Their Battles for Them*

The Church tends to use paid professionals to do the work that the members of the Church should be doing. Their view of an evangelist is of someone who is hired to go and evangelize for us. But a real Kingdom evangelist is someone who motivates the whole Body to do evangelism. The idea that we have to employ professionals to do the work for us while we sit around watching is totally contrary to the Kingdom.

We don't want a king to fight our battles; we will fight them ourselves. The least in the Kingdom of God is greater than John the Baptist. Zechariah 12:8 says that in the Kingdom of God, the weakest will be like David, and united we will be like God! Imagine having a Church where the weakest is like David, the least is greater than John the Baptist, and we are also truly united. What could you do with a Church like that? Think of the power of such a Church. Come on! While we obviously need leaders to lead us, we don't need kings to fight our battles for us. Under apostolic leadership, with faith, unity, and proper organization, we ourselves will become a mighty warrior people, the terrifying army of the Lord.

4. *They Wanted the King to Hear From God for Them*

They wanted the king to hear from God for them because they did not want to pay the price of being intimate with God and hearing Him for themselves. In Hebrews 8:10-12, God says concerning the New Covenant, "they shall all know Me from the least to the greatest. And I will write my laws in their minds and their hearts. I will empower them with grace so they can do it" (see Heb. 8:10-12).

In my natural human body, every member is joined to another member by tendons and muscles. My fingers are joined to my wrist, my wrist to my arm, and my arm to my body. All these things are created to teach us spiritual principles. I could not function without those proper connections.

In addition, every member of my body is joined to the head. Messages from the brain go down a nerve allowing me to do complicated and wonderful things with my hands. Many parts of the Body of Christ are crippled because of their failure to be properly joined to the other members. Others are paralyzed because they are disconnected from the Head. It is essential to develop close relationships with the rest of the members of the Body of Christ in our city. However, it is not enough only to have natural relationships with each other, as some movements have so strongly emphasized. We must also be individually connected to our Head, the Lord Jesus. If we are not each properly joined to the Head, then we are paralyzed when it comes to doing the will of God.

There are many comparisons to the military in the Kingdom of God, but we must be careful not to take these analogies too far. Imagine an army where the general could have immediate, direct communication with every soldier. That would be far more effective than going through a ponderous military chain of command. When we go through a natural chain of command, mistakes are often made. To have proper relationships and properly delegated authority is absolutely necessary. However, when the general can speak directly and simultaneously to every soldier, as well as through his officers, it is even more powerful.

Imagine, just before an important battle, that the general could be in simultaneous, intimate communication with every soldier and say to each one personally "Men and women, we are going together to destroy this enemy! Let's go right now. Charge!!" I tell you, they would go to war with such force against the enemy that they would be invincible. Both connections are necessary. Without both working properly, a handicap prevents the body from working properly. If I have a dead nerve in my finger, it cannot work properly. It's paralyzed. Even though it is properly joined to my wrist, it cannot move as it should.

On the other hand, some people say, "I don't bother with human relationships. I'm just joined with Christ. I don't listen to men, just to Jesus." That person is like a wrist which is severed completely from the body except that it is hanging on by a thread of nerve. The nerve is not severed, but all of the tendons and muscles are severed. What use is that hand? It cannot do anything. This is a very precarious relationship. It is so easy to cut the nerve and completely sever the member. I have noticed frequently that when people only walk with Jesus and do not let anyone tell them what to do, it is not long before they are deceived, completely cut off from the Body of Christ, and destroyed by the devil.

THE KINGDOM IS TAKEN FROM SAUL

In First Samuel 15 the kingdom was finally taken from King Saul. In verse 17 Samuel says to Saul, "Although you were once small in your own eyes, did you not become the head of the tribes of Israel? The Lord anointed you king over Israel." Then he asks in verse 19, "Why did you not obey the Lord?" Saul responds in verse 20, "But I did obey the Lord" (1 Sam. 15:17-20 NIV).

It is amazing how many times people think they have obeyed the Lord when they have not. It is such a natural thing for us to do what we want that we are often not even aware that we are disobeying God in the process. What Saul did would seem to be a very reasonable thing to most people. He heard the word of God through Samuel but thought to himself, "That's a bit extreme, so I will just change things a little bit. We'll keep the best of the oxen and sheep and offer them as a sacrifice to the Lord. He ought to be pleased with that. We will also keep king Agag alive. So we will make a few amendments of our own which are obviously better, but the rest we will do."

It was 95 percent obedience, but God called it disobedience, and it was enough for Saul to lose the kingdom. Saul was unaware that he had processed God's will through his own intellect and had come to another decision. What he was really saying was, "I know better than God how to handle this situation." "But Samuel replied: 'Does the Lord delight in burnt offerings and sacrifices as much as in obeying the voice of the Lord?'" (1 Sam. 15:22). So, Saul was rejected as king of Israel. Now the interesting thing is that although he knew

God had rejected him, he still fought against David with all his might and tried to hang on to the kingdom for many years afterward. He still tried several times to kill David, and at least once he tried to kill him even after his own confession, "And now I know indeed that you shall surely be king, and that the kingdom of Israel shall be established in your hand" (1 Sam. 24:20).

In contrast, Jesus knew what most pleased the Father; before He ever became man, the Spirit of Christ had already declared what He was going to do with His physical body. It is stated in Psalm 40:6-8 and quoted in Hebrews 10:

> *Therefore, when Christ came into the world, He said: "Sacrifice and offering You did not desire, **but a body You prepared for Me;** with burnt offerings and sin offerings You were not pleased." Then I said, "Here I am—it is written about Me in the scroll—**I have come to do Your will, O God."** First He said, "Sacrifices and offerings, burnt offerings and sin offerings You did not desire, nor were You pleased with them" (although the law required them to be made). Then He said, **"Here I am, I have come to do Your will"*** (Hebrews 10:5-9 NIV).

First Jesus acknowledged that God neither desired nor was pleased by sacrifices and offerings, although the law required them to be made. Then He said, *"Here I am, I have come to do our will."* Can you see now why God could make this man king? He could give Jesus the Kingdom because obedience was the passion of His life.

The author of Hebrews also writes, "Though He was a Son, yet He learned *obedience* by the things which He suffered. And having been perfected [i.e., in the gamut of His human experience], He became the author of eternal salvation to all who *obey* Him" (Heb. 5:8-9).

Can you see the centrality of obedience in these verses? God can only really save people who will obey Him. That is the truth. When it comes to the Kingdom, God gives authority to those who obey Him. The Bible says that because Jesus was obedient even to death on a cross:

> *Therefore God also has highly exalted Him and given Him the name which is above every name, that at the name of Jesus every knee should bow, of those in heaven, and of those on earth, and of those under the earth, and that every tongue should confess that Jesus Christ is Lord, to the glory of God the Father* (Philippians 2:9-11).

Jesus was made King of the Kingdom because of His perfect obedience. Saul was 95 percent obedient, but God called that disobedience. He told Saul that he lost the kingdom because of his disobedience.

First Samuel 15:22 says, "Does the Lord delight in burnt offerings and sacrifices as much as in obeying the voice of the Lord?" (NIV). Which pleases Him more? The answer is obviously obedience. The verse continues, "For to obey is better than sacrifice, and to heed [or hearken] is better than the fat of rams." This particular word for hearing or heeding is a special word. It is hearing in a particular way. The picture is of a faithful servant, bending forward and listening very carefully to his master in order not to miss one word so he can obey perfectly. It has the idea of listening with the predisposition to obey before anything has been said.

It is not like a child who replies to his mother's calling his name, "What do you want?" In other words, "I'm not sure I'm going to obey you until I know what you want me to do." A person with real Kingdom hearing has already said, "Yes, Sir!" in his heart before he hears the first word of his directions. The purpose of listening is not to decide whether or not to obey, because that decision has already been made. The purpose is to listen intently so that I do not get one piece of instruction wrong because I want to obey my Master perfectly. Therefore, I listen to God very carefully. I hearken! "To obey is better than sacrifice, and to hearken is better than the fat of rams. For rebellion is like the sin of divination, and arrogance like the evil of idolatry" (1 Sam. 15:22-23 NIV). Listen to what God is saying here: To rebel against Him is the same as practicing witchcraft.

Do you think it would be acceptable to put a little Buddha statue in your bedroom and bow down to it? Of course not! But in God's sight, arrogance is the same as the worship of idols. There is no difference. There is no difference between them because in both cases you end up becoming possessed by demons. People who worship idols end up being demonized by the spirits behind the idols they worship. People who practice rebellion and arrogance end up being demonized by rebellious and arrogant spirits. When you take in what the Scripture says about these things and then carefully read all the things said about the Lord Jesus, you find that one of His great qualities was His obedience to His Father.

When Jesus says, "Follow Me!" or more accurately, "Imitate Me!" or "Mimic Me!" the main thing we must imitate is His obedience, because that is the power of the Kingdom. Disobedience caused Adam to fall and Saul to lose the kingdom. God chose to exalt Jesus Christ and give Him the name that is above every name because He was obedient even to death upon a cross.

Chapter 16

THE TRUE KING IS FOUND

Let's take a careful look at the kingdom of David, not simply because of its historical significance, but because the kingdom of David is the best biblical model of what the Kingdom of God is supposed to look like.

Many things about the kingdom of David illustrate the spiritual realities of the coming Kingdom of God. We were told many times in the Old Testament that when David's greater Son, Jesus, came, He would sit on David's throne and bring in the fullness of what David represented in allegory and shadow. The true fulfillment of this was to come, not through Solomon, but through Jesus. It was not Solomon but Jesus that God was talking about through the prophet Nathan in Second Samuel 7:1-17.

Particularly in his early years, Solomon completed the allegory of the Kingdom, but it was all pointing to the great Son of David who was yet to come. Once David's kingdom was established, its principles became definitive foundations for every other king who ruled over God's people. Every other king was measured by how much he did things like David. If he did things exactly like David, he was a good king (see 1 Kings 3:3). If he did not do it David's way, he was a bad king. The principles of David's kingdom were the measure by which the obedience of other kings to God's will was measured. When Jesus came and set up His Kingdom, the same principles were carried into the New Testament (see Matt. 21:9; 22:41-46). So, in a very real way, these things are written for our instruction.

If we want to see the Kingdom come, it must come in the way that the Bible has carefully explained. In the Bible, you will find that the kingdom of David has 77 long chapters devoted to it. There is no other subject to which so much time and so many words are given in the whole Bible. It is the most important thing as far as God is concerned. After David's kingdom passed away, the prophets kept referring back to it, saying that a time would come when that kingdom would be reestablished in the full glory of the New Covenant with David's Son sitting on the throne and ruling with an eternal power and authority.

DAVID IS THAT KING

Just a few days after rejecting Saul, God sent Samuel to find His choice for king, who was very different from the person the people had chosen. When people have experienced Saulish leadership and have seen what it does in the Church, they often understandably say, "I don't want to live that way anymore. I'm not going back to that ever again. I will not submit to any man ever again." Many wounds in the Body of Christ have been caused by Saul-like leaders.

Saul-like leaders abuse the people and make them serve their own interests rather than God's. Godly fathers don't wound people, but Sauls do. Godly fathers don't crush people, but Sauls do. Godly fathers emancipate people to become bigger, stronger, and more powerful in ministry than they would ever become on their own. But Sauls don't do that—they emasculate them instead.

In the Church in recent years, many people have been almost destroyed by various movements that had the spirit of the house of Saul. These people started with zeal and passion for Jesus and for His Kingdom but ended up wounded, hurt, discouraged, disillusioned, and out of the fight. They became disappointed. They became debtors. They became dismayed. These are the kind of people who came to David toward the end of Saul's reign. These are the sort of Christian people who are coming in to our churches today.

There is also a stream of people coming in from the world who have never been damaged by church life or Saulish activity, but they have been severely crushed by the devil in the world of drugs, sex, selfishness, and sinfulness, often exacerbated by a dysfunctional family life and a total lack of real fathering. Once they meet the true Father, they take off and grow under the care and fatherhood of a David-hearted leader.

DAVID IS ANOINTED KING

God decided to anoint David as king in Saul's place, and He said to Samuel in First Samuel, "Fill your horn with oil, and go; I am sending you to Jesse the Bethlehemite. For I have provided Myself a king among his sons" (1 Sam. 16:1-2). At Jesse's home:

> *Samuel took the horn of oil and anointed [David] in the midst of his brothers; and the Spirit of the Lord came upon David from that day forward. So Samuel arose and went to Ramah. But the Spirit of the Lord departed from Saul, and a distressing spirit from the Lord troubled him* (1 Samuel 16:13-14).

As David was anointed by God, the anointing lifted off Saul, but that did not stop Saul from fighting with all of his might to keep his position. As the Spirit of God was no longer with Saul, he began to cooperate with evil spirits instead to achieve his purpose. Can you see that fighting God's will as Saul did is blatant rebellion—as evil and demonic as witchcraft? What happened to Saul? He didn't just lose his God-given anointing; he became demonized; powerful demons were able to work through him against the purposes of God. That is absolutely frightening. I hope it frightens you as much as it frightens me so that you never want to get anywhere near doing such a thing.

THE TRAGEDY OF JONATHAN

Now look at First Samuel 18:1-5 because I want you to see something about Saul's son Jonathan. The story of Jonathan, in my view, is more tragic than the story of Saul. Jonathan loved David, and these two became knitted in soul. They made a covenant, not just once, but three times, and each time Jonathan initiated the renewal of the covenant. Nevertheless, Jonathan soon found himself in a most difficult position. He had a natural loyalty to his father and his father's house, yet he had made a covenant with a man who had become his father's enemy. By natural birth, he was joined to Saul, but by covenant, he was joined to David. The nature of Jonathan was to be absolutely loyal in his relationships.

Now I have seen something similar to this happen a number of times, and I want to warn you about becoming like Jonathan. You can compare Jonathan's situation to that of individuals who were brought up in a particular denomination. They may have received great light and instruction from that relationship. They may have been brought up under a particular spiritual father, or even their natural father. Nevertheless, what they were brought up in and what they were joined to for years is now proving to be part of the house of Saul. There is a new move of God's Spirit coming into the city, region, or nation, and God is now anointing new people who were nobodies with a new anointing like David's.

It is clear that God is with them, even though they do not currently have the buildings or the finances. They are being treated like outlaws by the established church and are being forced to live in spiritual caves. That was the situation then with David, and that is the situation many are now facing.

Saul's house was a luxurious palace with lots of servants, and it was well equipped. David was living in a cave, and none of the modern conveniences were there.

Jonathan knew in his spirit where the future was, and it wasn't with his father or with his father's house. As a result, there was a strong pull in Jonathan's heart, "Do I obey my natural loyalties and stay with my father, or do I obey the way the Spirit is pulling me and go with David?"

Now go to First Samuel 20:13. This is the second time that Jonathan and David make covenant. Here Jonathan is speaking to David at the end of verse, "and may the Lord Jehovah is with thee as He was with my father" (1 Sam. 20:13 YLT). Matthew Henry's Commentary expands this phrase: "May the Lord be with thee to protect and prosper thee as He had been formerly with my father, though now He has withdrawn."[1] Did you notice the past tense used here?

Jonathan continues:

> "And you shall not only show me the kindness of the Lord while I still live, that I may not die; but you shall not cut off your kindness from my house forever, no, not when the Lord has cut off every one of the enemies of David from the face of the earth." So Jonathan made a covenant with the house of David, saying, "Let the Lord require it at the hand of David's enemies" (1 Samuel 20:14-16).

Now go to First Samuel 23:

> Then Jonathan, Saul's son, arose and went to David in the woods and strengthened his hand in God. And he said to him, "Do not fear, for the hand of Saul my father shall not find you. You shall be king over Israel, and I shall be next to you. Even my father Saul knows that." So the two of them made a covenant before the Lord. And David stayed in the woods, and Jonathan went to his own house (1 Samuel 23:16-18).

JONATHAN FAILED TO MAKE THE BREAK

Jonathan knew exactly where things were going and what his role was supposed to be. His father had been anointed by God but was no longer anointed. His father had been placed by God as king of the kingdom, but that was now over. Jonathan's future lay in abandoning his father's house and coming to join David in the cave. If he had done that, he would have become second in the kingdom. But out of family loyalty, Jonathan never made that critical move. The tragic result was that Jonathan died with his father Saul instead, and he missed his destiny (see 1 Sam. 31:1-2).

Just imagine what could have happened if David and Jonathan had been partners in the kingdom. I do not think the house of Saul, after Saul's death, would have had any heart to fight the David and Jonathan alliance. They would have come together into immediate, loyal unity. With David as king and Jonathan beside him, the two houses would have flowed together to bring a great and glorious victory for God.

At this very moment there are many men in "houses of Saul" battling through these same things. They were brought up in some historic denomination. Some of their fathers were prominent leaders. In its day, that denomination was used by God, but because of recent disobedience, God has moved away from that house and is raising up another house. The house that God is raising up may not look very impressive yet. It may not have a lot of money. It may be meeting in an unsatisfactory, strange place rather than in a grand building. Nevertheless, there is such a presence of God there. Anyone who is alive can sense, "This is where God is. His Spirit is here." Those of a pure spirit who are still in the house of Saul are being pulled to join the David band, but they are battling within themselves over their divided loyalties.

In certain parts of America and Western Europe, there are new groups of churches forming within various historic denominations.

They are usually led by some wonderful, young, spirit-filled leaders who are on fire for God. The particular churches they lead are growing vigorously. These groups of churches within historic denominations usually have a particular person who has become like a Jonathan leader to them. Although brought up within the denomination, they are realizing that the church they still love has become a house of Saul. They are realizing that they cannot continue where they are because of the compromise and the wrong moral and doctrinal decisions that their denomination is making.

For example, some major denominations have been discussing whether to condone homosexuality and even allow homosexual men and women to become priests or pastors in their churches. They have been discussing whether to bless same-sex marriages and whether to liberalize divorce and re-marriage. Some have already passed laws permitting some of these things.

These Jonathan leaders who are ordained ministers within these historic denominations are in agony over these things, and they know they cannot continue with this kind of compromise. Their churches meet in wonderful buildings, but they all belong to the denomination. They have good salaries, excellent health care, and pensions provided for them. If they step out, they will lose everything. Some of these denominations experienced mighty moves of God in the past, but they have largely become dead and apostate. God is calling these Jonathans to leave their house of Saul and join David in the cave. Many are hesitating to do so because of the practical difficulties—but even more because of their loyalty and love for their historic roots.

JONATHAN DIES WITH SAUL

First Samuel 23:18 says, "And David stayed in the woods, and Jonathan went to his own house." I believe this was the moment that Jonathan should have made his break. Instead, he left David and went back home to his father. He never saw David again, and he never had another time of intimate communication with him. The next news we have is that Jonathan is dead beside his father, killed by the Philistines.

The lament of David over both Saul and Jonathan is hard to read without weeping. But spiritually this kind of thing is happening in North America and Europe right now. People are dying spiritually because they hesitate to cross over from Saul's house to David's house. They cannot find the courage to say, "I don't care what it costs. Even if I lose everything, I'm going to go with God and with what His Spirit is now doing." At the beginning, all the people who came to David were people who were destitute, in debt, or in despair. By the grace of God, David was able to reshape them into mighty warriors who were destined to lead a mighty army that subdued all God's enemies and established His Kingdom with power on the earth.

If Jonathan had gone with David, it would have prevented so much needless pain. The war that followed between David's house and Saul's house might never have happened (see 2 Sam. 3:1). So much lost time and effort would have been avoided, and the Kingdom would have been immediately and powerfully established.

If you are not one of these people yourself, please join me and pray with all your heart for those who are in this agonizing situation at this present time. I don't want them to die with Saul. I want them to break out and be of significance in the Kingdom.

When the tragedy finally happened and Saul and Jonathan died together, David came to Hebron and was immediately anointed king by his own tribe (see 2 Sam. 2:4). It was the second of three occasions that David was anointed king.

DAVID'S THREE ANOINTINGS

In First Samuel 16:13 we read how David was anointed by the prophet Samuel at the direct command of God; yet, several years went by without his circumstances changing. In fact, things got worse, and the fury of the house of Saul against him became more violent than it was before. Notice how David handled these years. He was already anointed by God and knew what his destiny was, but his practical experience was very different. He spent those years being chased around the wilderness by Saul who, in a demonic fury, was trying to kill him.

David had two opportunities to finish this torment quickly by killing Saul. Even David's leaders misread these opportunities. They said, "This is the day of which the Lord said to you, 'Behold, I will deliver your enemy into your hand, that you may do to him as it seems good to you'" (1 Sam. 24:4). David is described as conscience-stricken after he secretly cut off the corner of Saul's robe (see 1 Sam. 24:5). And he replied to his men, "The Lord forbid that I should do this thing to my master, the Lord's anointed, to stretch out my hand against him, seeing he is the anointed of the Lord" (1 Sam. 24:6). Each time they encouraged him to take Saul's life, David said that he could not do it. Although he was being urged by other leaders, he wouldn't take that action against the formally anointed leader. David called Saul "the Lord's anointed" even though it was no longer true out of respect for the past anointing that was upon Saul.

When Saul discovered that David could have killed him but chose not to, he cried out in temporary repentance, "And now I know indeed that you shall surely be king, and that the kingdom of Israel shall be established in your hand" (1 Sam. 24:20). Yet in a very short period of time, Saul was back to his murderous tactics. David then got another opportunity to finish off his tormentor. His leaders were in essence saying, "Come on. This really is God's opportunity; kill him! You have the chance. Then you can take the kingdom. God has anointed you. You are king. This man is full of demons and opposing you. Kill him off, and get him out of your way." David again said no. He would not touch the Lord's anointed.

That was the heart and reverence of this man, which made him God's choice. As we pass through the difficult days of transition from Saul's house to David's house, we must be careful that we have the same spirit within us. If you are attacked, even in the media or the press, don't retaliate. Some of the men or women who will attack you have served God in a wonderful way in their day. They did a great job in the past. We cannot touch them. God must deal with them, not us.

DAVID CAME TO HEBRON

After the deaths of Saul and Jonathan, David first came to a place called Hebron. In Hebrew, this means "seat of association" or, possibly, "fellowship." In Second Samuel 2:4 we read how he was anointed by his own tribe, the tribe of Judah. At some point, the tribe of Benjamin joined the tribe of Judah, and these two tribes became the house of David. However, the other ten tribes did not recognize him as their leader. They were prepared to come and meet with him at Hebron, but they were not prepared to anoint him as their king.

Something similar to this often happens to a man or woman anointed by God for an apostolic ministry. Consider with me the situation of a man called by God to be a nation-changer or at least a city-changer. He cannot imagine why God has put His hand upon him in this way and has spoken powerful prophesies over him, but He has. He knows it, and other people close to him know it. There is a group of people, from his own house or local church, who willingly recognize that anointing. Right now, he is the pastor of a growing local church. But the call upon his life is much wider and more significant. His own church and people already know spiritually who he is, but the rest of the city is neither aware of it nor ready to recognize it.

That is probably the best situation you can find in most cities in the United States and in many nations around the world right now. A prominent pastor's own church recognizes who he is. Perhaps his own network of churches has recognized who he is. He is "having some fellowship" with other leaders and other groups of churches within the city where he lives. Nevertheless, the other city pastors don't recognize that he has an apostolic leadership that is beyond his own local house. They will come together for a period of fellowship and even cooperate to do some special event together, but when that event is over, they all go their separate ways.

That is Hebron. It is certainly better than competing or fighting with each other. However, the Kingdom cannot really be built with churches that only come together at a Hebron level. We are not exactly fighting each other, but we do not really work together either. We may meet once a month to pray for a little while. We may have a meal together and "have fellowship" before we go our separate ways. That is Hebron.

At Hebron, David had a measure of respect from the elders of the other tribes, but they did not recognize him as their leader and follow him. It was much better than being in the wilderness or in a cave, but there was still only a measure of recognition, and it was not possible to establish the kingdom from Hebron.

In a similar way, local pastors will say of an apostolic leader within their city, "He is a leader, but he is not our leader. We pray that God will bless him in what he is doing, but it's not our thing. We have our own program and our own people, and we are doing our own thing which we also pray God will bless."

Hebron is much better than being at war with one another, but Hebron is not the Kingdom. At Hebron, David could have built his own house and led his own tribe, but he could not come into the role that God wanted him to have.

DAVID RECOGNIZED AT LAST

David did not try to build the kingdom from Hebron for two reasons. First, it was the wrong place. Second, it was not yet the right relationship. He waited patiently for seven years; then things changed. Second Samuel tells us that "then all the tribes of Israel came to David at Hebron and spoke, saying, 'Indeed we are your bone and your flesh'" (2 Sam. 5:1). This was a great and amazing revelation, one that we all need to see.

We need to powerfully see that there is only one Body of Christ. There is only one Seed. We are all part of that one Seed and that one Body, whether we have acknowledged it or not. The tribes of Israel went on to say, "Also, in time past, when Saul was king over us, you were the one who led Israel out and brought them in; and the Lord said to you, 'You shall shepherd My people Israel, and be ruler over Israel'" (2 Sam. 5:2-3). So they had already known for years what God had said, but they wouldn't practically recognize him. Isn't that amazing? I've seen exactly the same thing happening in cities in the United States and many other countries.

Recently in one city in the United States, the city leaders asked me to come and address well over 100 pastors and their key leaders. They all recognized that I had a ministry to them. We had a fantastic weekend. Nevertheless, the moment I left the town, they all went their separate ways. While I was a visitor, they could all come together to receive my ministry.

What do you think would happen if I moved to that city to live there? Would all those pastors still have come to my meetings? No! They wouldn't do that if I lived there, because that would mean a permanent relationship, and I would be perceived as a threat to them. A temporary pretense of unity would no longer suffice. It would have to be the real thing.

While I was with them, one man stood out as the clear leader of the city, and two other men were clearly marked out as his right- and lefthand men. I could see the pattern absolutely clearly. So as I sat with a few of the more senior pastors over lunch, I asked them, "Who do you think God has anointed to lead this city apostolically?" They all gave me the same names that I had seen. I could see it, and they could see it too. So then I asked, "Why don't you recognize them and give them the authority to lead the city apostolically?" But they wouldn't do it.

DAVID COMES TO JERUSALEM

Now let's look again at Second Samuel 5:1-3. The elders of Israel finally came to David saying, "You were the one who led Israel on their military campaigns. God has already told us that you will shepherd His people Israel, and you will become their ruler."

Why did it take them years to do what they knew God had said? That is a good question but very hard to answer. However, once they finally got the message, things began to move swiftly.

Therefore all the elders of Israel came to the king at Hebron, and King David made a covenant with them at Hebron before the Lord. And they anointed David king over Israel. David was thirty years old when he began to reign, and he reigned forty years. In Hebron he reigned over Judah seven years and six months, and in Jerusalem he reigned thirty-three years over all Israel and Judah (2 Samuel 5:3-5).

Once he was recognized and anointed by everyone, David could at last do something. He moved immediately from Hebron to Jerusalem because he knew that the kingdom must be established from Jerusalem.

Remember First Corinthians 10:11, "Now all these things happened to them as examples, and they were written for our admonition, upon whom the ends of the ages have come." Can you see how relevant these Scriptures are to where many of us are today? It is just like reading today's newspaper as far as I am concerned, and we need to heed the warnings.

ENDNOTE

1. Matthew Henry, *Matthew Henry's Commentary on the Whole Bible* (Peabody, MA: Hendrickson Publishers, 2005).

Chapter 17

DAVID ESTABLISHES THE KINGDOM

In all, David took seven steps to establish the kingdom; however, we will deal only with those that apply directly to the subject of this book.

DAVID DEALT WITH THE JEBUSITES

If you go to the beginning of the Book of Judges it says, "Now the children of Judah fought against Jerusalem and took it; they struck it with the edge of the sword and set the city on fire" (Judg. 1:8). You would think from this, "Great! The city of Jerusalem is conquered and it is completely in the hands of God's people." However, come down to verse 21 and you will find an important "but" that qualifies the apparent total victory. We read, "But the

children of Benjamin did not drive out the Jebusites who inhab-
ited Jerusalem; so the Jebusites dwell with the children of Benjamin in Jerusalem to this day" (Judg. 1:21).

So the city was taken except for one area, which was the stronghold of Zion. In the stronghold of Zion, the Jebusites continued to
live and defy the conquest of God's people. It stayed that way until
Saul became king of Israel, and it continued that way throughout his
entire reign of 40 years, altogether more than 100 years.

But when David came to the throne, he must have thought,
*We can't have this! Right in the center of the capital city, there is a
stronghold defying the rule of God.* I imagine them taunting David
and saying, "Ha! Ha! Ha! David, you will never come in here!" All
the days before Saul, God's people lived with that indignity and
never dealt with it. Saul lived all his days with that taunting cry
and never did anything about it, but the first thing David said was,
"We can't have this!" He took the citadel of Zion and slaughtered
all the Jebusites.

PERSONAL JEBUSITES

What is this saying to us today? First, let's look at ourselves
personally. Before we came to Christ, many of us did sinful things
that we don't even want to talk about. We received Jesus as Savior,
and our lives were transformed in many ways—except for maybe
one thing. In one area of our lives, sin continued to reign, and Jesus
never became Lord. In my case, for a number of years, it was the area
of lustful thoughts. There was a stronghold in my mind of
pornographic pictures from the former life I used to live. I couldn't
get victory over it. It was like a Jebusite in my mind saying, "Jesus will
never come in here!" Some people have uncontrollable anger. Others

are compulsive spenders who can't control their finances and live in constant debt. Others are compulsive eaters and are unable to control what they eat. Some people can never get up in the morning and have a regular quiet time with God. Others have an irrational fear that controls them, like being petrified of flying.

You will never truly become a Kingdom person until that Jebusite stronghold within you is removed. The devil will often wait until leaders come to a level of success and prominence in ministry before he moves. All the time as they grow in popularity and stature, there is an unconquered area inside them where a Jebusite reigns. One day it will explode and destroy them if they don't deal with it.

Just imagine a massive military power with powerful weapons, jet bombers, fighter planes, great ships, and tanks. They seem invincible, but imagine that an enemy has been able to put a radio-controlled bomb in every single plane, ship, and tank. The enemy knows that at any time he chooses, he can push the button and blow up this great force. He is biding his time and waiting for the right moment. When this nation makes a great display of their military power, it looks very impressive, but the enemy is laughing. He knows that whenever he wants, he can push that button and destroy their formidable weaponry.

That is, unfortunately, the picture of a number of men and women in prominent ministry for Jesus Christ. They have never dealt with their Jebusites. Jesus has come into their lives almost totally. Most of their life has been transformed, but there is an area of failure and defeat right at the center of their life that they have kept secret and hope no one will find out about it. All the time there is some mocking demon within them saying, "Ha! Ha! Ha!

Jesus will never come in here!" The devil can also confidently say, "Any time I want I can push the button."

Think of the prominent names in Christian ministry who have fallen recently. Those things didn't suddenly crop up out of nowhere; there was something there from their earliest days that was never properly dealt with. They may have had a powerful gift as an evangelist with a mighty anointing, but at the same time there was a Jebusite of uncontrolled lust crying out continually, "Jesus will never come in here!" When the time was just right, the devil pushed the button, their ministry was destroyed, many people were wounded, hurt, and confused, and great dishonor came to the name of Jesus.

JEBUSITES IN THE CHURCH

We cannot build the Kingdom until we deal with the Jebusites. The Jebusites may not be in you personally, but they may be in the structure of the church or the ministry that you lead. Perhaps many things have become new, fresh, and exciting, but there is an area of the church with an old tradition that you have never been able to touch. You may still have democratic rule instead of Kingdom rule, and the church leaders or the congregation control the pastor by democratic voting.

You may have a powerful, carnal elder or deacon controlling the finances who has no faith at all, and he won't let the church become a generous, giving church. You may have a dear lady leading worship in the same old, dead, traditional way that she has led worship for years. You want to move her, but the old traditionalists say, "Sister Alice has been doing this for 25 years. We can't tell her to stop now!" Sister Alice may not seem like much of a threat, but anyone with a religious spirit who refuses to move with the Spirit of God will effectively impede the next move of God.

How can you move into the present move of God while keeping old traditions and not dealing with the Jebusites in the church? Oh, yes, Jesus has come to your church, and something new is happening, but there is a Jebusite at the center of your church, and no one has ever had the courage to confront it and kill it.

The church starts to grow, and it starts to be blessed. Everyone starts to feel this wonderful, new move of God. But, watch out! An explosion is coming. Maybe an elder or deacon has never really agreed with you or recognized you as the God-ordained leader. He never honored you, or gave you the place that God has given you in the church. He is one of the most influential members of the church, and all his relatives come to the church. They are the main financial supporters and carry a lot of influence. If you were to try to deal with this one, you would have trouble, and a serious setback with your finances and everything else. This group is not with you in the new move of God and is opposed to where you want to go.

However, it would be too painful to deal with it, so you leave this Jebusite undisturbed. You move on. You are just about to turn a big corner in the church's development when there is a crisis, and this man rises up against you. Because you've left him there undisturbed for so many years, he now has 200 people following him, and 400 people are following you. When it finally comes to the crunch, there is a painful ripping apart of the church. If you had dealt with it right at the beginning, all those years ago, it would have been painful but nowhere near as damaging as it is now.

YOU MUST DEAL WITH THE JEBUSITES

David said, "We cannot even think about establishing the kingdom until we deal with these Jebusites." We must have the same attitude. It could be personal. It could be in the traditions of the church or in the package of doctrines and beliefs we have held for years. It could be the role of women. It could be in our system of church government. If you don't deal with it, and just leave it alone, it will come back in much greater power later to destroy you. It may have been Saul's style of leadership to leave it alone, but David was not going to live that way.

David said the way to deal with the Jebusites was through the water chute, i.e., by the washing of the water by the Word (see 2 Sam. 5:7-9). In Ephesians 5:26, when talking of Christ and the Church, Paul says that Jesus cleanses her with the washing of the water by the Word, so that there is no spot or wrinkle or blemish anywhere (see Eph. 5:26).

One of my responsibilities as an apostolic father to some great men of God is to get into their lives personally and into the lives of their churches and deal with the occasional Jebusite. It is painful for them, and it is painful for me. But I would rather cause the pain now than see them destroyed later. So what do I do? I lovingly confront them with this area of their lives where some demonic power obviously has control and not Jesus. I don't do this in a judging way, but I come as a servant like Jesus. I wash them with the water of His Word, longing to cleanse them from this thing before it does them harm.

HONEST, TRANSPARENT
RELATIONSHIPS AMONG LEADERS

In John 13:1-15, you need to see and understand what Jesus was really doing when He washed the apostle's feet in the Upper Room. I believe He was getting them ready for the Kingdom which was about to come. They were all gathered together in the Upper Room to eat the Passover. Jesus took off His robes as a teacher and put on a towel as a servant. As they all gathered in the room, He knelt before Peter with a bowl of water, and Peter was embarrassed: "Lord, are You washing my feet?" (John 13:6).

You see, if you are going to have a real Kingdom church, you must have real relationships in the leadership where there is total transparency. I will never again have people on my leadership team who are not transparent. If I don't really know them and they don't know me, then I cannot totally trust them or work closely with them. Jesus did not correct Peter in private; He did it in front of the 12. On the other hand, it was not a public confrontation in front of all the believers either; it was within this private inner group of leadership.

What Jesus did next was a parable. It was an allegory, teaching a deep spiritual truth that He wants us to understand.

Peter, along with the others, had walked to this meeting. If you have ever lived in a society where people walk on dirt roads with bare feet or with open sandals most of the time, you know that their feet get very dirty. In India, many people do not wear shoes, and as a result, they have thick pads of skin on their feet. If you were to decide to wash their feet, it would be a big job because it would be hard to get all the dirt out of the deep cracks in their thick skin.

Jesus was essentially saying, "Peter, you have walked into an intimate time of breaking bread with Me." It was the first love feast, the first, wonderful New Testament fulfillment of the Passover. "But you also brought in the dirt of your past and of your present contact with this world. It's on your spiritual feet. I want to wash it out before we have this intimacy." Jesus came as a servant, not to find fault, but He lovingly wanted to get the dirt out of the cracks that resulted from the way Peter had walked. The condition of Peter's physical feet were an accurate picture of his spiritual feet.

When we walk with God and go about our daily business, many of us do pretty well most of the time, but there are certain impurities in the way we walk. There are certain habits we have and unconquered areas in our lives that defile the way we walk and do things. God wants to cleanse us from them by washing them away with the power of His Word. He is not against us; He is for us. But He wants us to walk the way He walked, so He must get the dirt out of our feet by first focusing our attention on these areas and then washing them clean with His Word.

Like Peter, it's possible to react in one of two wrong ways. You can refuse the washing altogether, "You're not going to wash my feet! And certainly not in front of these people." That is a Saulish character trait of not wanting to look bad in front of other people. That is the first wrong reaction. You won't let God get in and cleanse you. In public you pretend the dirt is not there, and you don't want anybody's attention to be drawn to it.

The second thing we can do, like Peter, is to overreact and collapse into complete self-condemnation because God has pointed out some area that needs cleansing.

> *Jesus said, "Peter, If I can't wash your feet, then I cannot have a relationship of intimacy with you." Peter responded, "Oh, in that case, then wash me all over!" Jesus lovingly replied, "For the most part, you are already beautifully clean through the Word I have spoken to you. You just need to wash your feet"* (John 13:6-11, paraphrase).

Spiritual Fathers, Like Jesus, Must Be Faithful to Spiritual Sons

Imagine that I have been staying in the house of a pastor who looks to me as a spiritual father, and I notice that he is irritable and bad tempered every morning. For the first hour, he is so grumpy that no one can talk to him. Imagine God shows me that as a spiritual father I have a responsibility to say something. In every other way he is fantastic; he just has a bad attitude in the morning. So I say, "Son, I need to have a little chat with you." I come in love, as a servant to wash his feet with the water of the Word so that the habit will not continue anymore. I want to help him to walk more like Jesus. I am not against him, but I am for him! I am not rejecting him or saying everything is wrong. I am just correcting this one little thing.

When someone lovingly points out a defect that needs to be corrected, you may react out of offense and say, "Oh, I'm going to resign! No one is going to speak to me like that." Or, you may go to the other extreme and say, "You're right, I'm just a failure; there's nothing good in me. I'm completely unfit for any leadership role. I had better lay down everything."

If someone comes to you with genuine, loving correction, don't be so extreme! They know that for the most part you are great! They can see Jesus shining out of you in almost every area of your life, which is why the one little thing looks worse in you than it does in most people. You are great; there's just that one little crack in the way you walk. Let's get it fixed.

Jesus said, "He who is bathed needs only to wash his feet" (John 13:10). There is a power in God's Word, a power in the washing of the water by the Word, which can remove every defect in our character and the way we walk on a daily basis. If we will believe it and let God do it, then we really can be changed in some of our deeply ingrained habits of behavior.

This was the point that Jesus was making. He knew they did not understand what he was doing at that point, but that they would understand it later. It was more than just an example of humility. He was essentially saying, "Listen carefully, I want you to understand something. You also need to lovingly wash one another's feet. You need to be the guardian of your brother's and sister's purity in the way they walk. Don't you dare do it in a judging, condemning way. You must come on your knees in love as a servant with the sole motive of releasing them from this hindrance that is spoiling the way they walk." You must come as a servant, just as Jesus did.

To me, this is the New Testament equivalent of dealing with the Jebusites. In all of the leadership teams that I have ever led as a spiritual father, we have had this kind of relationship. I love my sons enough to wash their feet. I teach them the right way to wash one another's feet. And, with the proper respect and love, they have the freedom to wash my feet. In that way, we will have no Jebusites in the house or dirty feet at our love feasts. In that way, we can build the Kingdom!

DAVID BROUGHT BACK THE ARK

Now let's look at some more of the steps that David took to establish the Kingdom. David's real passion was to bring back the ark of the covenant. The ark of the covenant had several different titles. We are told in one place it was called "the ark of the covenant of the God of all the earth" (Josh. 3:11). That is one great title!

God's shekinah glory dwelt in the tabernacle of Moses, where the ark was usually located in the holy place. It represented the presence, power, and the glory of God. It was the symbol of God's manifest presence. In the days of the prophet Eli, Israel was not winning any battles. They kept losing every battle with the Philistines. It was the sin of the people and particularly the sin of the priesthood that was causing it. Eli had two sons, Hophni and Phinehas, and they were living very wicked lives. They were immoral and were thieves. Yet, they continued to function as the priests of God to the people.

Unfortunately, there are plenty of people in that role in the Body of Christ today. They have some official position in ministry or church, but they are immoral sexually, and they are thieves when it comes to finances. Yet, somehow, they still think they can manipulate God and His people to bless what they are doing. It is amazing how blind some people can be.

Israel kept losing every battle, so the people of Judah persuaded Hophni and Phinehas to take the ark, the symbol of God's physical presence, with them into battle to help them. It sounded like a fantastic plan, and God's people were very enthusiastic. We could make an allegory of this and compare it to an enthusiastic, unholy, charismatic group that has decided to go against the demonic principalities over their city while many of them are still living in sin. The group plans to have a special warring praise conference, and then they are going to attack these principalities and powers. However, if there is sin in the camp, they will not succeed just because they make a lot of noise.

AN UNHOLY SHOUT

You can read all about this in First Samuel 4:1-10. The warriors of Israel made a great shout, a very loud, charismatic shout, and it had its desired effect. The Philistines began to tremble at the sound. They said, "We haven't heard such a shout for decades. What is happening among God's people?"

It is good to shout, and it is good to come in warring praise against the powers of darkness, but you must do it in holiness and purity. If you make a lot of charismatic warring noises and your lives are compromised with sin, it will not give you victory but will lead to a worse defeat. Unholy shouting stirs up the opposition of the devil against you. Without the righteousness of God as your breastplate of protection, you will be heavily wounded, if not destroyed. It is not enthusiasm alone that wins; that enthusiasm must be coupled with real, biblical holiness. The shout of a holy people is a great weapon of warfare. The shout of an unholy people leads to defeat, disillusionment, and disaster.

So the shouting stirred up the Philistines and made them determined to fight even more strongly. Israel carried the ark into battle, but God did not come to fight for them. So the Ark of the

Covenant was taken captive by the Philistines, and Hophni and Phinehas were killed in battle (see 1 Sam. 4:11). The wife of Phinehas went into premature labor and gave birth to a baby boy. She died in childbirth, but not before naming the baby Ichabod, which means "the glory of the Lord has departed" (see 1 Sam. 4:19-22). Eli received the tragic news and was so shocked that he fell backwards, broke his neck, and he also died (see 1 Sam. 4:18).

It reminds me of the climax of a grand, tragic Italian opera when all the tenors and sopranos are lying around the stage dying in the final dramatic scene. Bodies are lying everywhere. Then with a great crash of symbols and a final crescendo of music, the opera comes to a dramatic conclusion. The lights come on, and the audience sits there in stunned silence.

Unfortunately, this was not a stage performance. This was real life. There was a terrible massacre of God's people, and the ark was captured and carried into the temple of Dagon, the god of the Philistines.

However, for the Philistines, this was when their problems began. They kept finding their god facedown before the ark of the covenant. They would put the god back up, but he would fall again on his face before the ark. All kinds of sicknesses and diseases broke out among the Philistines. Then, finally, they came in one morning and found their idol completely broken and lying in pieces before the ark (see 1 Sam. 5:1-5).

For seven months, the ark was among the Philistines, carted from Ashdod to Gath to Ekron, and the "hand of the Lord was heavy on the people...He ravaged them and struck them with tumors" (1 Sam. 5:6). The Philistines finally got the message, put the ark on an ox cart, and sent the ark away from them. Because they were Philistines and they did not know the protocol for moving the holy objects of God, God did not punish them for their ignorance and the wrong way in which they moved the ark (see 1 Sam. 6:7-9). The oxen went straight back into the land of God's people and came into the land of Beth Shemesh. At the time, the people of Beth Shemesh were out in the harvest field trying to reap a harvest.

THE MEN OF BETH SHEMESH

Now all of this has powerful allegorical meaning if you can see it. These men of Beth Shemesh were out working in the harvest field, and suddenly they saw the ark of the God of all the earth coming toward them. They were very excited for two reasons: First, they felt that God would now be with them to help them to make their harvesting activity more successful. Second, they would have the chance to see the ark at close quarters and even look inside to see what it contained. They had never had such an opportunity before (see 1 Sam. 6:13-15).

This presents two important allegorical pictures for us. The men of Beth Shemesh allegorically represent an evangelistic or harvesting ministry. In India and many parts of Africa right now, almost everyone trying to evangelize is successful. But in America and Europe, it's a different situation. Today in western society, most evangelistic activity is not very successful because we have to deal with the strong resistance to the Gospel that is now part of our society. We find ourselves much like the men of Beth Shemesh: we are trying hard to reap a harvest, feeling that it is such hard work and that nothing is happening. We are longing for God to show up and transform our experience of evangelism.

AT FIRST THEY REJOICED

When the ark arrived in the midst of the men of Beth Shemesh, they were absolutely delighted. They thought, *God has come! Great! This means we are going to see more success in our harvesting.* However, they also had an irreverent curiosity. As the ark came close, they must have thought, *I've always wondered what the ark looked like and what was in it. Here's our chance. Let's have a look.* They lifted up the lid, and, in spite of the burnt offerings and sacrifices the people of Beth Shemesh offered to the Lord that same day, 50,072 people dropped dead as judgment "because they had looked into the ark of the Lord" (1 Sam. 6:19). This great slaughter occurred just because they lifted up the lid of the ark.

LET'S HAVE A LOOK AT GOD

This is the second picture. In almost every theological institution in the Western world, we are *not* putting ourselves under the searching eyes of God and His Word so He can bring us to perfection. Instead, we are arrogantly using our intellect to examine God, as if He were some specimen under a microscope to be examined by us! It's as if we are saying, "Let's have a look at God, and see if He really exists. Let's find out what He is like and what makes Him tick."

Our so-called theologians have put God under their intellectual microscopes and with their puny, human intellects are having a look at God. "What do you think, Dr. Bardsley Smythe? Is God alive or dead? Is He relevant today? Is He big or small? Can He heal or not?" We have the audacity to look at God as if He were something to be examined with our human intellect instead of falling down before Him in awe, wonder, and worship.

It is no wonder that many people working or studying in a theological seminary end up "dead" like the men of Beth Shemesh lying around the ark. They may not die physically, but they experience a death that is much worse: they become dead in spirit. They become totally unresponsive to God, and in spite of the years spent studying Scripture, they do not know Him or understand Him.

WHERE SHALL HE GO FROM US?

The people of Beth Shemesh decided there was a problem. They discovered a deep incompatibility between themselves and God. God never changes, and the Bible says, "Can two walk together, unless they are agreed?" (Amos 3:3). If God is already perfect, then He cannot change; all the change must come from our side to line up with Him. He cannot meet us half way. So the people of Beth Shemesh discovered a terrible truth that much of the Christian world still needs to know. Many of God's people are unable to have fellowship with God or work together with Him because they have become totally incompatible with Him.

So the men of Beth Shemesh had a choice to make. There were only two possibilities open to them. Either they must radically change to become compatible with God, or they had to separate from God because of that incompatibility.

Now let's go to First Samuel 6:19-20: "The people mourned because of the heavy blow the Lord had dealt them, and the men of Beth Shemesh asked, 'Who can stand in the presence of the Lord, this Holy God? To whom will the ark go up from here?'" (1 Sam. 6:19-20 NIV).

288

They were saying, "We don't seem to be getting along too well with God. We are incompatible with Him, but we don't intend to change. So the only recourse is to send Him away. Where shall we send Him?"

Some organizations today are no different. "We have our ways of raising money and doing other things that may not be perfectly righteous," or "we have our denominational traditions and liturgy that may not be biblical, but we refuse to change them." In order to become compatible with God, it seems we would have to radically change all our ways and traditions. The only other option is to do our own thing separate from God. It seems much easier to get rid of God. So where shall we send Him from here?"

A few years ago, in the United States, there was a wonderful man of God who had great revelation regarding the Scriptures. I remember a group of us sitting with him one day while he told us this story.

A few years earlier, he had teamed up with a well-known, international, evangelistic ministry. On the outside, it was an effective, evangelistic ministry that was seeing a measure of success. However, they lacked a great, prophetic Bible teacher, which was exactly this man's gift. So he was invited by the leader of the organization to come and join them as their primary Bible teacher.

Many years earlier, he had been the main Bible teacher connected with a prominent faith healing ministry, and he had seen amazing miracles as he traveled together with the gifted leader of this ministry. When this leader began to go into biblical error, he tried desperately and lovingly to correct him, but the leader would not listen, and, in the end, he had to leave.

Since that time, he had always longed for another similar relationship, and this ministry seemed to offer such a relationship. But when he got inside the organization, he found that there were unrighteous things going on with the way money was handled. He confronted the leaders with their unrighteous behavior, saying, "If you don't change, then I cannot stay with you because I cannot cohabit with this unrighteousness."

Their reply was, "Look, we have been doing it this way for many years now. We cannot change. So, if you don't like our ways, then you will have to go, because we are not changing." So, regretfully, he had to leave.

Some organizations compromise righteousness and use manipulation for the sake of getting large amounts of money. You cannot do this in the Kingdom. If you do that, the presence of God will depart. The organization may continue for a while by the sheer drive of its human personality, but God will no longer be there.

ABINADAB—THE MAN WHO WAS WILLING

So, the people of Beth Shemesh sent the ark of God away to the house of a man named "Abinadab." It is interesting to note that this man's name means "father of a vow, or of willingness." This is such an allegory of where we have been in many of our Western church organizations for most of the 20th century. God has not been able to work with the church at large because of its unclean and unrighteous ways. He cannot work in that environment.

Nevertheless, here and there, God has found an individual who was willing. He found someone who would pay the price to live in face-to-face intimacy and fellowship with God when such a relationship was generally unknown in the Church. We could mention a number of names who were the exceptions, the ones who were willing. A.W. Tozer of Canada would be a good example in the Western world. He wrote books like *The Pursuit of God* and *The Root of Righteousness*. His books are absolute classics that everyone should read. One of his famous statements was this: "Many people long to be holy, but they are not prepared to go through the process of being made holy." They want the end product without the pain of the process. They will never become holy because they will not pay the price.

Pastor Blumhardt in Germany would be a good example in Europe during the late 19th and early 20th century. He is credited with restoring the healing gift to the church. He was a pioneer in the healing ministry. But what a price he paid! If you read the story of this man's life, you find yourself thinking, *Wow, I'm not sure I am prepared to pay that sort of price.* Other examples that come to mind are Smith Wigglesworth in Great Britain, often called "the apostle of faith"; Dr A.B. Simpson in the United States; Andrew Murray in South Africa; etc. They stood out from the Church at large and had a great impact upon many.

In the 1980s, I was privileged to meet a black Zulu pastor called Pastor Dumar who had lived in Durban, South Africa, during the worst days of apartheid, long before anything spiritual was stirring in that nation. This man was amazing. He had an incredible love for everybody. He was a black African, and there was not a single racist fiber in his body. He had a profound impact on my life when I was a new missionary just starting out.

Pastor Dumar had a multiracial church near Durban in the days when it was illegal for the races to mix, but the authorities never dared to touch him because the power of God was so upon him and his ministry. Mighty, powerful miracles flowed through him. However, in those days in South Africa, there was a sharp division of the material wealth between the whites and the blacks. There was nothing left over for the blacks, and they lived in poverty. This pastor had such a big vision from God that he needed greater financial resources. I remember him telling me how he prayed one day, "Lord, I need a lot more money to see the vision You have given me fulfilled. You gave me the vision, and I need the finances to fulfill it. I need a few millionaires in the church who would bring their tithes and offerings into this ministry. The only millionaires I know are white, so You will have to have to save some white millionaires and add them to my church."

In answer to his prayer he saw six white millionaires saved and added to the church in one year. All this money was used righteously for the Kingdom, and he himself continued to live a very simple, humble lifestyle. I could tell you story after story of this incredible man. I learned so much from him. He laid his hands on me when I was a young man, and he poured the power of God into my life. He was an Abinadab, "one who was willing."

But that was not happening across the whole church. Much of the church was in dead tradition. Only an unusual individual would pay the price.

IN DAVID'S DAY FEW PEOPLE KNEW GOD

That was the environment into which David, the shepherd boy, was born. The ark of the glory of God never went back to Moses' tabernacle. It stayed in the house of Abinadab for approximately 70 years (over 20 years before Saul came to the throne, plus the 40 years of Saul's reign, plus the first seven years of

David's reign in Hebron). All that time in the tabernacle of Moses, the Levites were conducting their regular services, and it was not bothering them at all that God was not there. Religion does not need God. In fact, God can get in the way, so it is better not to have God around at all.

This is tragically true of many of our Western Sunday services. You can't guarantee to start by 10:00 A.M. and finish by 11:30 A.M. if God is around, so many feel it is better if God is not there. If you finish late, someone else might get to the restaurant before you do! Many prefer a well-organized service where God does not interfere or spoil the routine. Sunday services are over quickly with predictable accuracy, and people can go back to living without God for the rest of the week.

I do not know how many times David went to Moses' tabernacle. I would imagine that this God-hungry boy went there eagerly from time to time, whenever his parents made the journey to Shiloh, but it was always a disappointing experience because God was not there.

David did not want religion; he wanted God. When he was back home looking after the sheep for his father on the hills near Bethlehem, he would get out his harp and begin to sing songs of his own composition that worshipped the God of creation he could see all around him. Then God would come and visit this young teenager. He thus developed a life of intimate relationship with God that became the foundation, source, and power of his life. It was this experience that made him yearn to raise up a tabernacle where this kind of intimacy could go on continually.

For at least half a century in the United States and almost a whole century in Europe, we've been in a period of largely dead, religious ceremony. The last major move of God in the U.S. and Europe was in the early years of the 20th century. The early days of the Pentecostal movement had a powerful effect in many countries on a small minority, but it quickly died down, became respectable, and never went through to full transformation. Some Pentecostal churches I have been to have a doctrine of the Holy Spirit but do not want the Holy Spirit as a person to come because He messes things up. They would rather have Him simply as a doctrine. It is one thing to believe in the Holy Spirit, but it's another thing to want His active, participating presence. Do you want the doctrine, or do you want the person? What price are you prepared to pay for Him to come and presence Himself among you?

DAVID'S CRY: "LET'S BRING BACK THE ARK OF HIS PRESENCE!"

So the ark of the covenant of the God of all the earth remained in the house of Abinadab for approximately 70 years. When David came to the throne, his passion was that God should come back to have the central role in the nation. David wanted God right at the center of the capital city of the Kingdom that he was being led to establish. God had shown him years earlier that Mount Zion was to be that place. But that ground was already occupied by the Jebusites.

This can be true of our lives individually. If you will pay the price for God to come to you unconditionally; if you will say, "Lord, I will do anything to have intimacy with You and to have You filling my life," then He will come. But He will want to destroy everything that is not of His Kingdom. You can either cheer with delight and joyfully receive His total takeover, or you can back off and say, "Lord, I didn't mean that. I don't really want you to take me over completely. I want to remain in control. Why can't you be my friend at a distance?"

In his book *The Pursuit of God*, A.W. Tozer says, "The main enemy which prevents God filling us is our own flesh." The biblical word *flesh* comes from the Greek word *sarx*, and is prominent in Paul's writings. In most English translations, it is translated "flesh." But the NIV uses the translation "sinful nature," which is an unsatisfactory translation of the Greek word.

The best concise definition of this word "flesh" that I have found is "the union [combination] of body and soul which acts independently of God," or, you could simply call it the "self-life." That is the biggest obstacle to God filling our lives and the platform upon which sin establishes its operation. If there is no flesh, then there is no place for sin to land. If you maintain fleshly habits, then sin can come, take opportunity through this flesh, and kill you.

If we seriously pursue God, we soon realize that the main enemy against God completely filling us is our flesh. Then we have to make a decision. That is why A.W. Tozer said, "There comes a day when we make a decision to take sides with God against ourselves." In other words, I join forces with God to put to death every manifestation of the flesh in my life. I come to hate flesh in me the way God hates it. When that decision is made, it is not hard for God to come and totally occupy our lives. *That stronghold of the Jebusite that we were talking about earlier is the place where God loves to come. He kills those Jebusites and then puts the tabernacle of His presence in their place. That is what is so wonderful about God. He takes the areas of greatest shame and failure in our lives and makes them the center of His victory, glory, and grace.*

That is what happens when the Jebusites are killed and the tabernacle of God's presence is erected in their place. This is what happened in the city of Jerusalem. For more than a hundred years, the Jebusites had occupied Mt. Zion. They had said, "David will never come in here!" That mocking voice was silenced, and it became the place where the ark of the covenant of the God of all the earth was triumphantly placed. What had once been a place of defeat occupied by the forces of the enemy became the center from which the power of the Kingdom went out to destroy all the enemies of God—such an incredible transformation! This is the power that God has to turn things around.

Chapter 18

RAISING THE TABERNACLE OF DAVID

HOW DO WE ACTUALLY DO IT?

David could not bring the ark to its God-designated resting place until he dealt with the Jebusites. Once the ground was cleared, it seemed there was nothing to stop him except a few logistical problems. However, there was still a major problem of which David was not aware. Over 70 years had gone by since God had actually been present in the tabernacle of Moses, and nobody in that present generation had ever experienced God's presence before. No one alive knew how to bring back the presence of God. No one knew what it was like, or how to dwell there.

A few years ago, that was the condition of our Western Christianity. There was almost no one among us who could say, "I have lived in God's unveiled presence for years, and I can tell you what it is like and how to live there permanently." No one that I knew in my generation had ever lived that way. So when God began to move again in the 1970s, there was no one around who knew how to respond correctly to God's returning presence.

David was absolutely sincere. With all his heart, he wanted God, and he wanted His presence, but the last time the Ark of the Covenant was moved, it was moved by Philistines. They used an ox cart to send it back to Beth Shemesh. There were probably a few old people in Beth Shemesh who remembered that ox cart coming back with the ark on it, and, therefore, they thought that was the way to do it.

In Numbers chapters 4–7, very precise instructions were given as to how the ark of the covenant and the holy vessels were to be moved. Some of the princes of Israel had given 12 oxen and six carts to Moses for the transport of all the furniture and material of the tabernacle of Moses. There was a very definite order set by God as to how it should be done. Only the direct descendants of Aaron were allowed to touch the holy objects. Each of the holy objects had long poles that were pushed through so that the priests could carry them on their shoulders. Only Aaron and his immediate family could cover up the holy objects and make them ready for transportation. God warned them that if anyone else did it they would die.

In the tribe of Levi, there were three separate divisions: the sons of Kohath, the sons of Gershon, and the sons of Merari. Each of them had definite duties they were to perform. The Kohathites had the responsibility of carrying the holy objects, but not on an ox cart. They were to carry them with poles on their shoulders (see Num. 4:4-15). The Gershonites were to carry the tent (see Num. 4:24-27). The Merarites were to carry the pillars and massive stuff that had to be moved each time (see Num. 4:29-33). Deliberately, Moses did not give one ox cart to the Kohathites (see Num. 7:9). He gave two to the Gershonites to carry the tent (see Num. 7:7), and four to the Merarites to carry the equipment (see Num. 7:8). God had made it clear that in order to move the holy objects, you had to do it exactly His way. It had to be carried by Kohathite Levites with poles on their shoulders. If they tried to do it any other way, they would die. That was written hundreds of years before. However, no one seemed to have read this in the Bible in David's day, and no one seemed to know about it.

In their ignorant enthusiasm to get the glory of God back, they did what the Philistines had done. With great enthusiasm, they put the ark on an ox cart and began to take it back to Israel to be established on Mount Zion. Then things began to go wrong. This is an example of that presumptuous familiarity I was talking about earlier. Uzzah was one of the sons of Abinadab. Perhaps he thought something like this: *Well, I've had the presence of God in my house for 70 years. I'm the expert. I know all about these things.* But it was a wrong familiarity. He was the one who was supervising the way the ark was to be moved. When they got to the threshing floor of Nachon, the oxen stumbled. What does Uzzah do? He puts his hand firmly on the ark: "Then the anger of the Lord was aroused against Uzzah, and God struck him there for his error; and he died there by the ark of God" (2 Sam. 6:7).

GOD IS NOT A BAPTIST

When we were crying out to God to come back to our church in Mumbai in 1965, I had never seen God's power, and I had never experienced God's presence. I had never seen Him come visibly and tangibly to a meeting because no such thing had ever happened in my life. I was the associate pastor of the Baptist church in Mumbai, which was founded by British people in the days of the British Empire. As a result, we were expecting God to come in a respectable British, Baptist way. A group of us had begun crying out to God because we so needed His power to evangelize our desperately needy city. I was also fed up with meetings where God was totally absent, because there was no life in them. However, my problems began when God answered our prayers, and He came. To my horror, I discovered that God was not respectably British. What's more, He was not a Baptist. Furthermore, He would not behave according to our Baptist church rules. He was just going to come and be God.

Everything fell apart. I almost said, "Dear God, I wish I never asked You to come." I got very close to the same sin as Uzzah. I almost tried to put my hand on what God was doing to steady it into a respectable, British, Baptist format with which I was familiar. I felt just like David, because when David tried to bring back the ark the first time, he did everything wrong, and it ended in disaster. Uzzah died for touching the ark, and they took the ark to the place of a man called Obed-Edom. For a period of three months, they would not come anywhere near the ark because it meant death, not life as far as they were concerned (see 2 Sam. 6:10-11).

Doing It God's Way

So David went to seek God. We are told that after Uzzah died, David was afraid and angry. That was exactly how I felt in Mumbai; I didn't like what was going on at all, but it was God. That was my problem. I was in absolute torment. I remember crying out one night in prayer, "God, I've cried out to You for more than a year for You to come, and when You came, You scared me terribly. Furthermore, I don't like a thing that You are doing. I'm in a terrible situation. I don't know what to do with myself in this situation. Lord, help me and show me what I need to do."

The thing that struck me with tremendous power at that time was the story in Second Samuel 6:1-23 where David finally brought back the ark successfully. This time he was doing it the right way with the Kohathites carrying the ark on poles on their shoulders as they walked on foot (see 1 Chron. 15:15).

Everything was going well, and David was abandoned in extravagant worship. His wife Michal looked out the window at him dancing before the ark with all his might, and she was offended. When she confronted him, saying he looked like a fool, David replied, "It wasn't before the people; it was before the Lord" (see 2 Sam. 6:21).

David had spent three months asking God what went wrong and what he had to do to make it right the next time. God showed him that he had not done it in the right order (see 1 Chron. 15:13). The Kohathite Levites first had to sanctify themselves, and then they had to carry the ark on their shoulders.

What does that mean today? It means that there is a burden in bringing back the glory of God that you cannot mechanize by multimedia presentations, computers, slick techniques, or learned methodology. It will cost you something. It will be hard work. You have to carry the burden yourself on your own shoulders, and you cannot pass it on to anyone else.

There is no simple, successful, modern technique that you can use. It is raw, on-your-face repentance and crying out to God. There is no other way. You cannot bypass this with some mechanized, charismatic technique. It won't work. If you yourself are not prepared to pay the price, and if you cannot find a group of people who will pay the price with you, it won't happen. Unless you are prepared first to be sanctified and then to become the burden bearers to carry the glory of God back into your dead church situations, you will never see God come. When that burden really comes upon you, then you don't really care what it looks like or what it sounds like. You just want God.

THE PROCESS OF BEING SET FREE

As we continued in God's presence, we set apart a week to seek God and prepare for Him to come to our church. During that week all sorts of things happened that I had not seen before, and many of them made me feel very uncomfortable. The first thing that happened was to my wife, Eileen. Because of her attitude of total abandonment to God, she was regarded by some as a bit over-the-top and extreme. But she didn't care. She was always free. I was more respectable, more bound, and more British. She was uninhibited, an unembarrassed extrovert, and desperate for God.

One of the first things that God did was to deal with me and my natural reservations. I am not an extrovert. I am an internal person, a reserved person, a shy person. The next time we came together, God's presence increased, and things were beginning to loosen up, especially with Eileen and a few other people really going after God.

God said to me, "Raise your hands!" I said, "Oh, I've never done that." God said, "Lift your hands." I said, "Why?" I felt His immediate rebuke, and I've never said, "Why?" again to God because it is too terrifying. So I raised my hands in obedience without really wanting to. I felt like the most conspicuous person in the whole world. My arms seemed to stick out like tree limbs. Nobody else probably noticed, but for me it was a real dying to something. He began to break all the hindrances of shyness and self-consciousness in my life. Just two days later, He had me dancing before the people. It was not particularly elegant, because I am not an elegant person, and I didn't particularly enjoy it. People were saying, "What has happened to our pastor? He's going crazy!" Believe me, inside, I was dying a thousand deaths.

At that same time, I was doing something that would have been really frowned upon by my legalistic Brethren friends. I was reading a book by Smith Wigglesworth. As I was reading this book, I said, "God, I want to be really filled with Your Holy Spirit." I was not clearly baptized in the Holy Spirit and had not yet spoken in tongues. I still did not know exactly if, when, or where I had been filled with the Spirit. It was a process that went on for several days as God broke down many barriers in me so that I became available for His unconditional use.

SHOUT IT!

I was still debating the theology of whether there had to be a definite experience of being baptized in the Holy Spirit, or, as I had been taught, whether the fullness of the Spirit was already within me, and it just needed to be released. Which was the true theological position? So, I was reading Smith Wigglesworth, who was a very uncultured, Bradford plumber from England. In *Ever Increasing Faith* he said, "If you have any doubts, the best way to deal with doubts is to take the Word of God and shout it with all your might. That will free you from your doubts and it will drive the devil right off your back. So if you have any doubts, just have a good shout!"

I read this and thought, "No way, I'd never do such a thing." Then God said to me, "That's exactly what I want you to do!" I said, "What do you mean?" He said, "When you go the Brethren Assembly meeting this morning, I want you to stand up in the meeting and shout at the top of your voice, 'I believe in the Baptism in the Holy Spirit, and I am seeking God to meet me in this way.'" I said, "Oh, Lord, I couldn't do that, I would die." He said, "Exactly! That's what I am after. I want you to die." So I went down to that meeting as a man under a sentence of death.

On that Friday morning, I arrived at the meeting we were having in the Brethren Assembly in Mumbai. A wonderful brother had come to preach the Word. He was an Irish Presbyterian who had been powerfully filled with the Holy Spirit. He was a great scholar and expositor of the Word, and because of this he had been accepted to be the preacher. But that morning he began to move in the Spirit.

We took out the Keswick hymnbook, we sang two respectable hymns, and nothing unusual was happening. Then the presiding brother said, "We will now ask the Reverend David McKey to share the Word of God." So David got up and said, "Just before I speak, God has just been speaking with me. Someone has come to this meeting, and God has told you to share something." He continued, "Before I preach you must share that word." So I stood up and said, "That's me, but God didn't tell me just to share it; He said I was to shout it." David said, "Brother, whatever God told you to do, you do it."

So I looked all around this room. Every respectable evangelical in the city was there. Everybody I didn't want to be there was there. I looked around and thought, "Well, this is certainly the death of my respectability, but I had better do it." So I opened my mouth, and I shouted, but because I was so nervous it came out all strange and squeaky. I shouted out, "I believe in the baptism in the Holy Spirit, and I'm seeking God to bless me in this way." It was terrible, and the respectable evangelical Alan Vincent instantly died of shame never to rise again. There is a great verse in a great hymn written by Charles Wesley that reads:

Long my imprisoned spirit lay,
Fast bound in sin and nature's night.
Thine eye diffused a quickening ray;
I woke, my dungeon flamed with light.
My chains fell off, my heart was free,
I rose, went forth, and followed Thee.[1]

These words exactly described my experience. I realized that up to that point, I was a prisoner to my respectability and to what people thought of me. Even when I taught the Word, I taught in such a way that people would say, "Good word, brother!" I needed people's approval. When I prayed, I wanted people to be pleased with the way I prayed. Now my reputation was so destroyed it didn't matter what I said or prayed. I couldn't make it any worse. In a strange way that freed me to proclaim the Word of God boldly, no longer caring what people thought, but very concerned about what God thought. My heart was free. I rose, went forth, and followed Him.

I received some immediate phone calls to cancel some speaking engagements. However, I had other phone calls asking me to come where I had never been before.

THE SPIRIT COMES

On the last Friday night of this week of meetings, we were singing, "Oh, for a thousand tongues to sing, my great Redeemer's praise…" And suddenly I heard this crash! Eileen was lying on the ground beside me, and I thought, "My Lord, Eileen has fainted!" She was flat on her back. Then I looked at her face, and she was glowing with the glory of God and worshiping Him quietly. I knew it wasn't a fainting fit; it was God. We all looked with amazement at this. When we closed the meeting, Eileen was laying right across the door so everyone had to step over her to get out of the church. She lay there for at least another 45 minutes.

At that time I rode a motorcycle. I didn't have a car. How was I going to get her home on a motorcycle? We had never had these problems before. After about one hour, she started to come around. I picked up this "drunken lady," strapped her on the back of my motorcycle, and rode home through the Mumbai traffic hoping she wouldn't fall off. I got her back home and put her into bed. She was still completely gone. I then came and lay on the bed beside her.

Somewhere in the middle of the night, I woke up. I hadn't slept well at all, and while I was lying on the bed, I said, "Lord, I don't know what you did to Eileen, but I want you to come to me. Please come!" Eileen and I have always done everything together. We were married together. We were saved together, baptized together. We've always done everything together. I said, "Lord, whatever you are doing with Eileen, please don't leave me out!" Then the room began to fill with the presence of God in a way I had never experienced before, but I knew it was God. He came toward me, and I felt His presence begin to envelop me. But there was something in me that was still frightened. I did not move physically at all, but in my inner man, I began to resist. I was not sure I wanted this complete takeover, and I put up a spiritual, internal barrier against God taking complete control of me. The moment I did that, He withdrew, and He was gone. The room became empty and desolate, and I felt so alone. I thought, "Lord, what is the matter with me? I desperately want You, yet when You come near, I push You away because I'm afraid of You."

So I said, "Lord, if You will come again, I won't push You away. I promise You." About 15 minutes later, He came again, and this time I was determined not to lose Him. Although I did not move physically, I was so desperate that in my inner man I tried to grab hold of Him possessively saying, "I will have You." When I did that, He was gone, and I was desolate and alone once again.

I was learning the first principles of living in the presence of God. If you put up a wall of resistance, He will not come to you. And if you go after Him in an aggressive, possessive activity of the flesh saying, "I'm going to get God," He will not come to you either. Again, the room emptied of His presence, and I began to cry in frustration. I said, "Lord, I don't know how to let You come to me. I've never done it before. I don't know what to do. Please, don't leave me. Teach me how to be the kind of man You can come to and dwell in. I so want that."

YIELD!

Suddenly, the word *yield* came to me. The Spirit was trying to teach me, "Don't take the controlling initiative; you can't own God and have control over Him at your demand. Yet don't run away from Him either when He comes to you because He will not force Himself upon you." So the third time I just lay there and said, "Lord, I've never done this before. I don't know how to do it. Please help me. Show me how to receive You." I made myself as wide open in my spirit as I knew how, but I made no active attempt to grab Him or possess Him. I just lay there, yielded, learning how to receive. I felt His presence come closer and closer until He was flooding me with His presence. I became aware that the bed on which I was lying was shaking under the power of God. Eileen woke up at this point and sensed immediately what was happening, and she began to pray. God just poured wave after wave of His incredible love into me.

Through this experience, I learned two important things. First, I learned how awesome, holy, and fearful God is. Second, I learned how much He really loved Alan Vincent. He loved me. He wrapped Himself around me, and I just lay there lost in His amazing love. This experience changed me; it changed everything.

My whole being cried out, "Daddy, Father." Just as Jesus had promised, the Spirit showed me the Father, and I have lived in His presence ever since. I never knew it was possible to know God like this. From that day, my favorite occupation has been to get alone, shut the door, and have intimate times with my Father.

I was desperate for God, but I didn't know how to let Him come. Many individuals are in this situation. We desperately want God, but we don't know how to let God come and just take us over and possess us. Maybe my testimony will help you to come to know Him as I know Him.

LEARNING TO LIVE IN GOD'S PRESENCE

The next thing we had to learn as leaders was how to let God come to the church, filling the church and the meetings with His presence. As leaders, we had a responsibility to lead others into this new environment of God's manifest presence in a way that was pleasing to Him. When we came together the next time, there was a small group of us who had experienced different, personal encounters with God. As a group, we were learning rapidly how to live in God's presence. We now had to learn corporately how to let God have the liberty to do what He wanted in our midst. At first, it was scary because we couldn't just follow a pre-planned, set program, but we gradually learned to work with God and just do whatever He said.

That was the beginning of the manifestation of the power of God. Once we were free, we were able to lead many others to freedom, and God visited our church. Miracles began to happen, and the power of God came.

THE GIFT OF TONGUES

I was free and began to speak in tongues, but I wasn't sure about it. You see, I was a typical product of Western intellectualism. I said, "Lord, I want to be able to speak in tongues." He said, "Go ahead." But I said, "How do you do it?" He said, "Just speak, and I will make it happen." I said, "Do I just make things up?" "No," He said, "Don't make things up. Just start, and I will make it come from Me." I asked, "How will I know?" He said, "Just trust Me." So I did my "practice" speaking in tongues. I tape-recorded it, and I listened to it to see if it had all the characteristics of language. I went on like this for weeks trying to decide whether this was real or whether I was making it up.

Then at the end of several weeks I said, "Lord, I'm still not sure." He said, "What does My word say? If you ask Me for a good gift what I am going to give you? I won't give you a serpent or a scorpion, but I will give you a good gift" (see Matt. 7:11; Luke 11:11-13). I said, "Oh, it's a matter of faith!" He said, "You've finally got it." So I said, "I'm going to do the same thing again and just believe that it is God." He said, "Right! You've got it now!" That's how I finally began to speak in tongues. As I decided to believe in what God had given me, it became more and more powerful and effective. It still does not make any sense to me. I never have been able to understand one word that I have said. But when I came to faith, it flowed out of me like a torrent.

I began to discover it was doing in me what the Bible said it would do. It says, "He who speaks in a tongue edifies himself" (1 Cor. 14:4). The Greek word for edify is *oikodomeo*. *Oikos* is a house, and *domeo* is to build. Something happens in your spirit. By speaking in tongues, you build a spiritual residence for God in your spirit that gets bigger and bigger the more you use this precious gift. This then provides a greater and greater residence for God to come and live within you. The more you speak in tongues, the bigger the house gets. As a result, there is a great reservoir of God within you that is available for any need or situation. That's why I like speaking in tongues because I want a lot of God in me. The more, the better. So I am getting larger and larger in spirit just by speaking in tongues. My capacity for God increases in me, and then He can dwell more powerfully in me and do more through me.

That is what happened to me and to our church. The glory of God came and we had to learn many lessons of how to live with Him. Because we have continued to walk in childlike obedience, He has continued to presence Himself among us.

THE NEW TABERNACLE ON MOUNT ZION

Once David learned how to bring back the ark successfully, they did not take the ark of the covenant back to the tabernacle of Moses, despite the fact that it was still standing. The tabernacle of Moses for a long time had been at a place called Shiloh (see Judg. 18:31; 1 Sam. 1:3,24; Ps. 78:60). It was about 30 miles from Jerusalem. At some point after David's tabernacle was raised, they moved it to a much closer location at Mount Gibeon or Mount Gibea. You can read about this in First Chronicles 16. Mount Gibeon was approximately six miles from Mount Zion.

This is another important allegorical picture. They brought the tabernacle of Moses closer to the tabernacle of David, but they did not merge them together. Throughout David's reign as king, David's tabernacle stood on Mount Zion and Moses' tabernacle stood on Mount Gibeon just six miles away. Literally, if you lived in Jerusalem, you could make a decision regarding which tabernacle you wanted to attend. God appointed Zadok the priest to super-vise the tabernacle of Moses so that the traditional meetings went on in just the same way. But the Ark of the Covenant never went back to the tabernacle of Moses. It was carried instead to this new tent of David on Mount Zion (see 2 Sam. 6:17). David's tabernacle was totally illegal according to the law of Moses, but God chose to presence Himself there.

Moses' tabernacle had three compartments. First, there was the outer court, then the holy place, and finally the Most Holy. The outer court contained the brazen altar to deal with the sacrifices for sin and the big laver for ceremonial washings. Then, inside the holy place were the table of showbread, the incense altar, and the seven branch candlestick. Only the priests went into the holy place, and no one at all went into the Most Holy, which was screened off by a second curtain. Normally, the only object in the Most Holy was the ark of the covenant. Once that was removed, it was just empty.

According to Moses' law, only the high priest went into the Most Holy, and he only went once a year. He went in on the Day of Atonement. Very complicated sacrifices were made, first of all, for himself, then on behalf of the people. He went inside in order to make atonement for the people's sin. It seems even the high priest was fearful of whether he would come out alive, and so were all the people. If he dropped dead before the ark, no one was going to go in to get him. The presence of God was far too terrifying for that. In fact, some traditions teach that before the high priest went in, they would tie a rope to his ankle so that if he dropped dead, they could pull him out without having to venture into God's presence.

GOD'S BENEFITS OR GOD'S PRESENCE?

Moses' tabernacle provided everything necessary for people who wanted the benefits of God without knowing Him. Moses' tabernacle provided forgiveness of sins. You could also bring your tithes and offerings, and then God could bless you financially. You could even go there to be healed, and the priests could testify that you had been healed. However, the priests were the ministers, and the people never saw God or had any contact with Him. You met with the priests, but that was all. All the benefits were available without meeting God, and that was the way most people wanted it.

No one ever went behind the curtain into the Most Holy. No one ever saw God or heard Him. For at least 70 years, the ark was not even there, but many people preferred it that way. So God kept the tabernacle of Moses open for those who wanted His benefits but were afraid of His presence. However, those who wanted His presence had to go to David's tabernacle. David's tabernacle was simply a resting place for the ark and the glory and presence of God. There was just a simple tent around it. You pulled back the flap of the tent and walked right into God's presence. You had to believe that the blood of the Lamb had made you holy.

David had received an amazing revelation of the cross, which he recorded in Psalm 22, and he was living in the joy of New Covenant faith, trusting in the blood of the perfect Lamb to make him righteous before God. Everybody who went with him had the same faith. Otherwise, they wouldn't have dared to go in. David was not a Levite. He was from the tribe of Judah. He had no priestly rights whatsoever according to the law of Moses. Instead, he was the king anointed by God. However, in addition to his kingly office, he also wore a linen ephod, which was the clothing of a priest (see 2 Sam. 6:14; 1 Chron. 15:27). David appeared before God as a priest and a king.

The priesthood of David's tabernacle was not the priesthood of Levi; instead, it was the priesthood of Melchizedek. Abraham had met Melchizedek in Genesis 14:18 after slaughtering the four kings. When you read Psalm 110, you realize that David also had met Melchizedek (see Ps. 110:4). They were living in the New Covenant with a New Covenant priesthood. Everything about David's tabernacle was New Covenant.

In David's tabernacle, you just stepped into the tent, and you were immediately in God's unveiled presence. This was impossible according to the law of Moses. You had face-to-face fellowship with the living God. You worshiped Him, you loved Him, and you adored Him. You didn't drop dead because the blood of the Lamb had already been eternally shed. In the tabernacle of David, not one sacrifice for sin was ever offered in all of its 33 years of existence. There was no need for any sin sacrifice because the blood of the Lamb of God had already done its perfect work.

This was the heart, power, and glory of the Kingdom. There could not be a Kingdom without a tabernacle of David at the center. The tabernacle was the powerhouse that brought the rule and government of God across the nations. David had amazing revelation to do these things. They were a type and shadow of Jesus and the Kingdom He would establish. The people who followed him were living as New Covenant believers in all the joy of that unveiled relationship.

Those who could not come to that level of faith went off to Moses' tabernacle, worshiped Him from a distance according to Moses' law, and received their benefits. But those who could come to the right kind of faith and abandoned worship went to David's tabernacle, worshiped as priests and kings to their God, and enjoyed God's intimate presence.

We are told in many Scriptures that from David's tabernacle a strong scepter of rule and government went out (see Ps. 45:6; 60:7; 108:8; 110:2; Isa. 16:5). The power of David's tabernacle was the power of the Kingdom. That was how David was able to establish and extend the Kingdom.

We are told very clearly in Scripture that this is the way the Kingdom will be restored (see Amos 9:11-12; Acts 15:15-16). The Kingdom will be restored when David's tabernacle is restored. In this book I want to focus on the Kingdom, so I will mark just four major things that characterized David's tabernacle.

1. It was a Center of Constant Praise and Worship

It was the place where David sought the face of God corporately with his leaders. As David came with his leaders before the presence of God, he was given wisdom and strategy for the conquering of all of his enemies. God also gave him the strategy for governing the city and ruling the nation. It was a place not simply of praise and worship, but where God gave revelation of how He wanted His Kingdom to be established and governed. David went there corporately with his leaders. They did not need business meetings and voting because they all simultaneously heard God speak.

You get an echo of the same thing in Acts chapter 6: "Then the twelve summoned the multitude of the disciples and said, 'It is not desirable that we should leave the word of God and serve tables'" (Acts 6:2). They said this not because they were too proud, but because they needed to have a right priority regarding their use of time. As apostles of God, this was their first responsibility. It was not a singular thing but a corporate thing. It says, "But *we* will give *ourselves* continually to prayer and to the ministry of the word" (Acts 6:4). That is the New Testament equivalent to David's tabernacle.

God has called certain locations to become regional center churches where His tabernacle will be raised up and His power will go out to bring the government of God over the whole region. In such places, there will be a gathering together of a plurality of apostles and other Ephesians 4:11 ministries. They won't do anything on their own, but together. Together they will seek the face of God, together they will hear God and get His strategy, and together they will obey what God tells them to do. That was the power of the administration of the Kingdom of God. It was not just a bunch of men and women getting together with good ideas and hoping God would bless them.

The tragedy is that those who have great responsibility usually feel they are too busy to spend much time in prayer. They want some ladies to pray for them because they are too busy to pray. Thank God for the ladies who pray, but according to Scripture the first mark of an apostle is that he or she, along with others, spends time first in prayer and then in the ministry of the Word.

One of the great things that Martin Luther once said was this: "I have a very busy day today. Therefore, I must spend at least three hours in prayer." As I mentioned previously, Eileen and I had some contact with Dr. David Yonggi Cho some years ago. I know what his daily practice was up until the end of the 1980s, and I'm confident it remains the same to this day. At that time, Eileen visited the church several times and was allowed some access to him. He would get to his office at 7:00 A.M. every morning. No one came into his office or was allowed to disturb him for any reason until 11:00 A.M. He spent his first four hours every day with God.

He was running a church at that time of hundreds of thousands of people. In his office, there was a desk at which he sat. Beside his desk, at an angle, was another desk that was bigger than his desk. It was empty and was kept there as a constant visible reminder to him that the Holy Spirit was the senior partner, and he was the junior partner. So right there in his office was a prophetic reminder that it was not he, but the Holy Spirit, who was in charge. His practice was not to do anything until he had the OK from the senior partner. That was the real practice of his life. I believe that many of us will have to alter the priorities of our life in order to get this right.

In David's tabernacle, certain men were given the privilege of living permanently in the tabernacle. The chief worshiper was Asaph (see 1 Chron. 16:4-5). He wrote some of the Psalms. Another man was the chief musician Chenaniah (see 1 Chron. 15:22). These men were there all the time, organizing, directing, and leading the changing order of different groups of musicians, worshipers, and intercessors in the tabernacle. They were permanently responsible for the organization of the tabernacle's activity. David and his mighty men went in and out, but they didn't stay there permanently. Their job was to run the city and the nation, and to destroy all the enemies of God. They had practical things to do as well.

When Jesus came to earth, we are told in John 1:14 that the Word became flesh and that He "tabernacled" among us. Jesus did not build a physical tent, but His human body became a spiritual tabernacle, which He retreated into all the time. He kept up the equivalent of David's tabernacle in the New Testament. We find Jesus was constantly in prayer (see Luke 5:16; 6:12; 9:28; 18:1). He would go to the mountain. He would go away all night and pray in the wilderness. Apart from His 40-day fast at the beginning of His ministry, we do not read of any more long fasts. His pattern was to go away frequently for a day or two of spiritual recharging, and then He would come back again into the fight. I believe that is the pattern that God is calling apostolic ministry to practice today.

To be like Jesus, the Great Apostle, it is necessary to know that the ability to do anything effectively is dependent on a vital relationship with the Father. Apart from one occasion, Jesus didn't stay in His personal tabernacle for long periods and leave the world to fend for itself. The most He ever stayed disengaged from the enemy was a day or two, and then he was back again into the fight. I believe that is the normal pattern for apostolic ministry. They cannot spend weeks and weeks at a time on long sabbaticals, away from their responsibilities.

Now certain key people who are called to this specialist "Asaph" or "Chenaniah" ministry may have that privileged ministry responsibility. But the majority of us have work to do. We have assignments from God to complete before He returns. We need to do those assignments in the power of David's tabernacle without permanently residing there.

In San Antonio, Texas, we have established a tabernacle of David. It will not belong to any individual church but will be for the whole city. We will pray for the whole Church of the city, the State of Texas, the whole of the United States of America, and all the nations of the world as God directs us. I believe it will have impact across the whole world. I frequently spend time there, but I will not be there permanently. The days are coming when people raised up by God will come, live there, and be the permanent staff. Intercessors and musicians will join us, and we will work closely with some great apostolic leaders and missionary strategists.

I can't wait for it all to drop into place and become fully functioning. We will be doing what we read concerning David's tabernacle: raising it up, repairing its walls, and restoring its ruins so that the Kingdom can be forcefully advanced.

2. *The Center of Government*

David's tabernacle was the center of government. From David's tabernacle on Mt. Zion the strong scepter of God's government, or rule, went out (see Isa. 16:5; Ps. 110:2, etc.). This is such an important subject that I am devoting much of the second book in the Kingdom series to this topic.

3. *The Priesthood Was After the Order of Melchizedek*

The tabernacle of David was totally free from Moses' tradition, from the Levitical priesthood, and from the law of Moses. That was the chief point of the great letter to the Hebrews, and it will profoundly change the effect and power of how we pray, once we comprehend it.

4. *It Was Developed Further by Jesus*

In Matthew 21:6-17, Jesus rode into Jerusalem in triumph on the tenth day of Nissan, four days before He was crucified, and seven days before He rose from the dead. The people went wild with joy and extravagant praise. God the Father had orchestrated a great coronation celebration to welcome His Son as the King of the whole earth, soon to be set on His glorious throne following His death and resurrection.

The children especially were touched and participated fully in this spontaneous outburst. This particularly made the chief priests and the scribes indignant. Jesus went to the temple and drove out the moneychangers, and for one day, these magnificent buildings, normally full of religious death, were used as God desired. They became a temporary manifestation of David's tabernacle.

The temple on that day was characterized by four things:

1. Extravagant praise and worship (see Matt. 21:8-9).

2. Full participation by children (see Matt. 21:15-16).

3. The lame and the sick came to Jesus and were healed once Jesus had cleansed the temple of the contaminating spirits of dead religion and love of money (see Matt. 21:14).

4. Jesus declared what had been written, *"My house shall be a house of prayer for all nations"* (see Matt. 21:13, quoting Isa. 56:7).

In addition to all the revelation that David had in his day, Jesus added these extra dimensions. As we raise up again the tabernacle of David, we need to see that all these things are part of its richer New Testament life and power.

ENDNOTE

1. Charles Wesley, "And Can It Be That I Should Gain" (1739).

Chapter 19

A CALL TO WAR

A KINGDOM AND A PRIESTHOOD THAT IS READY FOR WAR

In the third month after the children of Israel had gone out of the land of Egypt, on the same day, they came to the Wilderness of Sinai. For they had departed from Rephidim, had come to the Wilderness of Sinai, and camped in the wilderness. So Israel camped there before the mountain. And Moses went up to God, and the Lord called to him from the mountain, saying, "Thus you shall say to the house of Jacob, and tell the children of Israel: 'You have seen what I did to the Egyptians, and how I bore you on eagles' wings and brought you to Myself'" (Exodus 19:1-4).

This was not just a call to possess the promised land, but it was a call to possess the whole earth. This call came within three months of leaving Egypt. Ethnic Israel was the first group of people to be called, but they failed miserably to fulfill their call. Now listen to verse 6, *"And you shall be to Me a kingdom of priests and a holy nation"* (Exod. 19:6). The whole nation was called to be a kingdom, and it was also called to be a priesthood. This had nothing to do with the Levitical priesthood—that came much later. Here the whole nation was being called to priesthood.

> *"These are the words which you shall speak to the children of Israel." So Moses came and called for the elders of the people, and laid before them all these words which the Lord had commanded him. Then all the people answered together and said, "All that the Lord has spoken we will do!" So Moses brought back the words of the people to the Lord* (Exodus 19:6-8).

Now this sounds like fantastic, total, complete obedience. If only that generation had really meant what they said, then the whole earth would have become the Kingdom of God thousands of years ago. They were given this opportunity, but they blew it. There were some very simple conditions: "If you will indeed obey My voice and keep My covenant..." (Exod. 19:5).

You would think that these words came from the New Testament. Peter spoke almost identical words to God's new, multinational people, the Church, thousands of years later:

> *But you are a chosen generation, a royal priesthood, a holy nation, His own special people, that you may proclaim the praises of Him who called you out of darkness into His*

marvelous light; who once were not a people but are now the people of God... (1 Peter 2:9-10).

However, that generation of Israel failed completely because they did not put their words into action. I want you to see how important their example becomes to us. We will not catalogue all the examples of disobedience and the sins of the leaders and the people because there were so many of them. But there was one basic thing above everything else that caused them to turn back and miss their inheritance.

THEY REFUSED TO GO TO WAR

When they realized that in order to possess their inheritance, which God had so clearly promised to them, they had to go to war and fight, they would not do it. They were not prepared to become a warrior nation and go to war: "Then it came to pass, when Pharaoh had let the people go, that God did not lead them by way of the land of the Philistines, although that was near; for God said, *'Lest perhaps the people change their minds when they see war, and return to Egypt'*" (Exod. 13:17).

He couldn't take them by the straight, direct way, which would have only taken eleven days, because they would have seen war, and they would have immediately turned back. Therefore, God gave them a taste of the wilderness, hoping they would eventually say, "I would rather go to war than die here in this wilderness. Let's go to war and see what God will do on our behalf." When God tried again to get them to go into Canaan 18 months later, they still said, "It is too hard. We can't do that. The giants are too big, and the cities are too fortified." Ten of the spies brought a bad report, and only Caleb and Joshua brought a good report. Those two said, "Come on, men! We can eat these guys for breakfast. God is with us, and their demonic protection has been taken from them, so we can do it" (see Num. 13:26–14:10). However, the rest refused, and that whole generation died in the wilderness (see Num. 14:34-38).

Thirty-eight years later only Joshua and Caleb were alive, and they led the next generation to cross over the Jordan and miraculously enter the promised land. Nevertheless, they still had to fight for every inch of land, even though God said He had already given it to them.

A SECOND CHANCE WITH JOSHUA

After the death of Moses the servant of the Lord, it came to pass that the Lord spoke to Joshua the son of Nun, Moses' assistant, saying: "Moses My servant is dead. Now therefore, arise, go over this Jordan, you and all this people, to the land which I am giving to them—the children of Israel. Every place that the sole of your foot will tread upon I have given you, as I said to Moses" (Joshua 1:1-3).

The Hebrew word for *tread*, the place where you put your foot, is *darak*. This word is used in a variety of ways: to load and lock your weapons, to tread upon as an act of taking possession, to tread grapes in a wine press, or to use the foot to bend and string a bow in preparation to shoot arrows and fight. God is saying, "That which you tread upon, load and lock your weapons upon, or for which you string the bow for war, that is what I have given to you." In other words, you won't get a square inch of this land without being willing to fight for it. It has already been given to you, but you won't possess one inch of it without a fight.

So there they were, right back where they had been 40 years earlier with Moses.

Joshua began to exhort them. He told them not to be afraid, but to be strong and of good courage. He got them to a place where he was ready to command them to go into the land. He said that they would have to fight until the Lord God gave them rest. Now go to verse 16, "And they answered Joshua, saying, 'All that you have commanded us we will do, and wherever you send us we will go" (Josh. 1:16). Now listen very carefully to verse 17, "*Just as we heeded Moses in all things, so we will heed you...*" (Josh. 1:17). What? Was that a joke, or were they serious?

Can you see their incredible blindness? After 40 years of the most persistent disobedience by their parents, this new generation was saying, "We are going to obey you Joshua in just the same way that our parents obeyed Moses!" This new generation was being given a new opportunity, but they were speaking exactly the same language as their parents. What chance do you think they have of accomplishing anything with this new opportunity if they talk and think the same way as their parents did?

We need to recognize that the generation of Christians that I represent, who saw the great healing and evangelistic crusades of the 1940s and 1950s and were baptized in the Spirit between 1960 and 1990, by and large have been a failure as far as possessing their inheritance. If you belong to the new generation, take care that you do not repeat the sins of your parents and refuse to become the warriors that God is calling for at this time.

Finally, it's not a matter of age, but of spirit. Joshua and Caleb were of that failed generation who refused to fight and died in the wilderness. However, they were of a different spirit, and in spite of their age, they were far better warriors than even the new generation who they were about to lead over Jordan to possess the land. They were older, but they had the right spirit. You would have thought that this new generation would have acknowledged their parents' disobedience and said, "We are not going to behave like our parents! They made these quick promises but never kept one word of them. We are certainly not going to be like them. We are actually going to obey God and Joshua and go to war."

It is amazing that they seemed to be totally unaware of the sin of their parents' disobedience. They did not understand that the condition of their nation was a direct result of that disobedience. They did not seem to know that they were the children of a disobedient generation. They said to Joshua, "Just as our parents obeyed Moses in all that he said to them, we are going to do the same to you." If you had been Joshua, how would you have responded to that? The tragedy is they were speaking more truth than perhaps they realized: they did become just as disobedient as their parents. Therefore, they also failed to inherit as completely as they should have.

The Kingdom Imposed but Not Imparted

As long as Joshua and the elders who walked with him and carried the same spirit were still alive, they caused the people to come into a portion of their inheritance. The whole generation was being driven by the spirit of a few zealous leaders; they were not being motivated by God's fire and zeal within their own hearts. They had never really received the same spirit as Joshua and Caleb; it was just temporarily imposed upon them.

The moment these men who really knew God died, the true heart of the people was immediately revealed. They went into the worst period of gross sin, immorality, idolatry, and backsliding ever recorded in the history of God's people. It makes one almost sick just to read the record of it in the Book of Judges. The most incredible sins were committed by God's people. They quickly forgot what it was like to be led by holy men of God like Joshua, Caleb, and the elders who were with them.

There is a verse that appears several times in the Book of Judges as a summary of Israel's condition. The reason given for all of this terrible backsliding, sin, and failure to come into their inheritance is this: "There was no king in Israel; *everyone did what was right in his own eyes*" (Judg. 17:6; 21:25; etc.).

LET US FEAR LEST WE COME SHORT OF IT

I want us to hear and fear what we read. When the Pentecostal movement struck Europe and America in the early 1900s, some of the greatest revivals in the history of the Church hit these nations. Amazing things happened. But one thing the Christians did not do was go to war in the spirit of obedience, take possession of every pillar of our secular society, and change it for God and for His Kingdom. In fact, things politically, socially, and morally got much worse. As a result, every kind of sin that is described in the Book of Judges is now openly taking place today in our Western society, and it is even being condoned by many of our nominally Christian leaders and churches.

However, God is calling us again. He is raising up some godly Joshuas to lead a Joshua generation. He is giving us one more chance. The situation is much worse than it was 50 years ago, but it is not too late for God. We must be very careful that we don't make the same empty promises: "Oh, all that the Lord has said, we will do it! We are going to be as obedient as our fathers!" It doesn't matter who or what they were; they didn't go to war in the Spirit as they should have. They never pressed through in prayer and determined spiritual warfare to obtain the transforming victory that God was looking for in the Western world. He is giving us another chance, and we must make sure that we don't turn back.

Oh God, we cry out to You. Let the Spirit of Joshua, Caleb, and the apostle Paul empower us for these days of war! Let us be strong and very courageous! Powerfully enable us to exercise our authority on earth and in the heavens. Give us ears to hear Your orders and hearts to obey each command implicitly and immediately. Lord, we commit not to be those who shrink in fear or put our hands to the plow and look back. Prepare us, Lord, not only to withstand the attacks of the enemy, but also to stand in faith until You are righteously able to give us our legal rights and send us into battle. May we violently attack every demonic force that tries to usurp Your glory—and thereby forcefully advance the Kingdom of God. You said, "The zeal of the Lord will accomplish it" (see Isa. 9:7). Spirit of God, fall upon us. Find a generation through whom You can do all Your will. May Your Kingdom come, and Your will be done on earth as it is in Heaven.

Author Contact Information
and Ministry Resources

Outpouring Missions, Intl.
8308 Fredericksburg Rd.
San Antonio, TX 78229

Phone: 1-210-614-9330
Website: www.outpouringministries.org

Additional Teachings on CD by Alan Vincent:

A Warring Priesthood
Money Talks
The Melchizedek Priesthood
Buy A Sword
5 Steps to Powerful Praying

Longtime Best Selling Book
by Eileen Vincent

No Sacrifice too Great

The lives of pioneer missionaries CT Studd and
Priscilla confront us all today with the crying
need for zeal and sacrifice.

Extensive teaching collection available on-line.

Additional copies of this book and other
book titles from DESTINY IMAGE are
available at your local bookstore.

Call toll-free: 1-800-722-6774.

Send a request for a catalog to:

Destiny Image Publishers, Inc.

P.O. Box 310
Shippensburg, PA 17257-0310

*"Speaking to the Purposes of God for this
Generation and for the Generations to Come."*

For a complete list of our titles,
visit us at www.destinyimage.com